THE COSMOS IN THE
LIGHT OF THE CROSS

THE COSMOS IN THE
LIGHT OF THE CROSS

George L. Murphy

TRINITY PRESS INTERNATIONAL
A Continuum imprint
HARRISBURG • LONDON • NEW YORK

Trinity Press International, P.O. Box 1321, Harrisburg, PA 17105

Trinity Press International is a member of
the Continuum International Publishing Group.

Cover art: © Robert Huberman/Superstock

Cover design: Laurie Westhafer

Library of Congress Cataloging-in-Publication Data
Murphy, George L., 1942-
      The cosmos in the light of the cross / George L. Murphy.
      p. cm.
      Includes bibliographical references and index.
      ISBN 1-56338-417-5
      1. Religion and science.   2. Jesus Christ—Person and
offices.   I. Title.
BL240.3 .M87   2003
261.5'5—dc22
                                                                    2003014285

Printed in the United States of America

03 04 05 06 07 08   10 9 8 7 6 5 4 3 2 1

Contents

❧

ACKNOWLEDGMENTS

A number of people and organizations deserve my appreciation for their support of my work. I want first to thank my wife Dona for her invaluable encouragement and technical assistance in this project and in many others. Students in my classes at Trinity Lutheran Seminary and The Lutheran Theological Seminary at Philadelphia, as well as clergy at continuing education events, have helped with their questions and comments. The suggestions and criticisms of colleagues in the American Scientific Affiliation have helped in the development of some of the ideas set out here.

Special thanks are due to the Center for Theology and the Natural Sciences of the Graduate Theological Union in Berkeley and to the center's director, Professor Robert John Russell. I did much of the work on the book while I was a Visiting Scholar at the Graduate Theological Union, and I am grateful for the hospitality and helpful conversations that I enjoyed there. My former parish, St. Mark Lutheran Church in Tallmadge, Ohio, provided financial assistance for my study leave in Berkeley. Support from the John Templeton Foundation for several activities in the science-theology area has also been very helpful.

Some material from an earlier draft of this book was developed into a chapter entitled "Cosmology, Evolution, and Biotechnology," in *Bridging Science and Religion* (ed. Ted Peters and Gaymon Bennett; London: SCM-Canterbury Press, 2002), and in a book with the same title in simplified Chinese characters published by the China Social Sciences Press in Beijing.

Abbreviations

⚜

ANF   *The Ante-Nicene Fathers* (Grand Rapids, Mich.: Eerdmans, 1978–1979).

CD   Karl Barth, *Church Dogmatics* (Edinburgh: T&T Clark, 1936–1962). Volume and part numbers follow citations.

LW   *Luther's Works* (St. Louis: Concordia; Philadelphia: Fortress, 1955–1986).

NPNF   *The Nicene and Post-Nicene Fathers* (Grand Rapids, Mich.: Eerdmans, 1976–1980). Series and volume numbers follow citations.

WDCT   Alan Richardson and John Bowden, ed., *The Westminster Dictionary of Christian Theology* (Philadelphia: Westminster, 1983).

· 1 ·

AN INFORMAL ORIENTATION

Disturbing Topics in Science-Religion Conversations

The field of "science and religion" has grown tremendously during the past twenty years. Organizations devoted to various aspects of the field, conferences, publications, and media attention all attest to a general interest in this relationship. Colleges and seminaries offer courses in the field. Ethical issues raised by science-based technology have given practical dimensions to these conversations. Historians of science have come to see both positive and negative ways in which religion has influenced the development of the sciences. How different than a century ago when the relationship between science and theology was described as warfare![1]

Many scientists and religious believers continue to disagree over a number of matters, especially over biological evolution and creation. Some partisans still see themselves engaged in warfare,[2] and such attitudes continue to be influential in the public arena. But there is a growing body of informed people who are interested in a dialogue rather than combat.

Yet in this dialogue there are some disturbing themes. These do not simply involve matters that are difficult to understand. They are, rather, aspects of our knowledge whose implications tend to unsettle the ways in which we are used to thinking about the world, God, and ourselves.

The progress of science has resulted in an apparent absence of God from the natural world. What happens in our experience, from the scale of subatomic particles to that of clusters of galaxies, is being explained in terms of natural processes that obey rational laws. We don't need God to explain how grain grows or lightning strikes. We can still say that God is present in the world, but such a presence seems to have no connection with what goes on in nature.

This is an old problem for religion, which is illustrated by a story told of the great mathematical physicist Laplace. He had completed a treatise on celestial mechanics that had explained the detailed motions of the planets and satellites in the solar system on the basis of Newton's laws of motion and gravitation. When Napoleon heard that Laplace had not mentioned God in his work, he asked why. The scientist is supposed to have replied, "Sire, I have no need of that hypothesis."[3]

Such a reply is often attributed to scientific arrogance. Nevertheless, Laplace was right. Planetary orbits can be described and predicted with no reference to divine activity. In fact, such a reference would add nothing at all to the work. Today science has moved beyond limited domains like the solar system, and some scientists are trying to explain the universe itself. After sketching a provocative theory that attempts to do this, Steven Hawking asks, "What place, then, for a creator?"[4]

Theologians have developed models of divine action to address this issue, but many proposals do not provide an adequate theological answer to the question of *why* God can be ignored as far as a scientific understanding of the world is concerned. Is this just something that religious believers have to accept reluctantly, or can we gain a clearer rationale for it within a Christian understanding of God's relationship with the world?

Let us suppose, however, that we can see God involved in some way in the natural processes that science describes. We then encounter another disturbing reality when we study the development of living things through biological evolution. The general idea that species have evolved over long periods of time need not conflict with belief in a creator. It is often said simply that "evolution is God's way of creating." But the specific mechanism for evolution that was proposed by Darwin and Wallace separately in 1858, natural selection, is hard to reconcile with traditional religious ideas.

Natural selection proposes that not all organisms in a given environment will be able to survive and produce offspring. There are variations among members of a species, and those best able to survive and propagate will, on the average, do so. The environment will be more favorable for some than for others. Those who survive and reproduce will pass on to their descendants the characteristics that gave them a survival advantage, and over many generations this will lead to new species. Thus competition for resources and breeding, privation, and extinction play a central role in evolution. The natural question posed by this theory is, "How could a benevolent God work in that way?"

This challenge is sharper than the traditional one, "How can an all-powerful and all-good God allow evil?" Now we have to ask how God could *make use of evil* in order to create. How could any deity worthy of worship act through what Gould called the "messy, relentless slaughter"[5] of evolution? Admittedly such language is hyperbolic. The history of life has not been a monotonous bloodbath, and many extinctions have been due to slow declines in birthrates rather than literal slaughter. In addition, the ability of natural selection to explain all the facts of evolution has been the subject of debate among specialists in recent years. But as long as natural selection remains a significant aspect of the evolutionary process, there is a challenge to traditional religious beliefs: How could a loving God work in this way?

These issues raised by the successes of science in describing the world may seem purely theoretical and remote from daily life. Science has, however, given rise to many technologies whose impact on everyday experience cannot be ignored, and science-based technologies continually force upon us choices that our ancestors did not have to make.

These technologies have given numerous benefits to the world in recent centuries. The energies that have been made available to the human race, the possibilities for transportation, communication, information storage and retrieval, new materials, and abilities to treat and to prevent illness have all improved the quality of human life. But science-based technology has also damaged the environment and vastly increased the destruction that can be unleashed in war. The most ominous symbol of modern science is the nuclear mushroom cloud.

The goals of medicine are to preserve and improve life and to relieve suffering. Modern medical science has done these things in ways undreamed of a few centuries ago. But there is a price to be paid. Many people can now have their lives saved by receiving transplants of vital organs, but they and their families have had to wait for, and may have found themselves hoping for, the death of an appropriate donor. The renewal of life involves death.

Medical progress is not at an end. Research on embryonic stem cells or transplantation from other species may eliminate the need for human organ donors, but both possibilities raise theological and ethical questions of their own. We have had enough experience to know that there are often negative effects connected even with beneficial new technologies.

Different theological and ethical systems can deal with these aspects of science and technology with varying degrees of plausibility. But many of these systems find such issues disturbing to their basic assumptions about God, the world, and humanity. The picture of a God who is immune from suffering and death but who forces organisms through millions of generations of competition and extinction is disturbing to those who believe in a God of love. And a demand for correct moral choices in accord with divine law is difficult to live up to in situations in which new technologies require people to make choices that were not envisioned when the laws were written down.

VIEWING THE WORLD FROM THE CROSS

The types of difficulties sketched here provide one reason why I propose to deal with science and technology from the standpoint of a theology of the cross. Such a theology is an explication of belief in a God who becomes a participant in the history of the universe and thereby shares in the suffering, loss, and death that are part of worldly experience. God is willing to be condemned in the name of law, to be rejected and abandoned by humanity, to be abandoned somehow even by God (Mark 15:34). God seems to be completely absent here, for nothing seems less like the presence of an all-powerful and loving God than this scene in which a Jewish carpenter hangs as a dead criminal on a Roman cross. If this radical claim is true, if God is present in the cross of Christ and is acting there to save the world, some fundamental rethinking of conventional religious beliefs is necessary. But then we also are given new opportunities to understand the apparent absence of God in natural processes, the role of death in evolution, and the ethical ambiguities raised by science-based technologies.

The death of Christ is central to the Christian message, and any attempt to understand that message must involve some kind of "theology of the cross." But the technical sense of that phrase is more precise. For Martin Luther, *theologia crucis* was a theology that insists that the true God must be seen first of all "through suffering and the cross."[6] Dietrich Bonhoeffer was deeply imbued with that way of believing and thinking. In a letter from prison dated May 25, 1944, he wrote:

> Weizsäcker's book *The World-View of Physics* is still keeping me very busy. It has again brought home to me quite clearly how wrong it is to use God as a stop-gap for the incompleteness of our knowledge. If in fact the frontiers of knowledge are being pushed further and further back (and that is bound to be the case), then God is being pushed back with them, and is therefore continually in retreat. We are to find God in what we know, not in what we don't know; God wants us to realize his presence, not in unsolved problems but in those that are solved.[7]

A few weeks later, after commenting on the development of modern thought, he wrote:

And we cannot be honest unless we recognize that we have to live in the world *etsi deus non daretur*. And this is just what we do recognize—before God! God himself compels us to recognize it. So our coming of age leads us to a true recognition of our situation before God. God would have us know that we must live as men who manage our lives without him. The God who is with us is the God who forsakes us (Mark 15.34). The God who lets us live in the world without the working hypothesis of God is the God before whom we stand continually. Before God and with God we live without God. God lets himself be pushed out of the world on to the cross. He is weak and powerless in the world, and that is precisely the way, the only way, in which he is with us and helps us. Matt. 8.17 makes it quite clear that Christ helps us, not by virtue of his omnipotence, but by virtue of his weakness and suffering.[8]

It is tempting for religious people, faced with the ability of science to explain so many things without reference to God, to argue that God is needed for the things that science is *not* able to explain. Bonhoeffer's point is not just the commonly made one that such a "need" to use God as a "stop-gap" steadily diminishes with the progress of science. His theological insight is that such an idea of the divine is inconsistent with God's revelation in Christ.

Eberhard Jüngel has developed this theme in detail in his elaboration of a "theology of the Crucified One." In particular, he discusses the consequences of the "worldly nonnecessity of God" and of the idea that God is "more than necessary." Jüngel's insistence that we must be able to speak of perishability in connection with God will also suggest to us a fruitful theological way of thinking about the reality of suffering and death in the evolutionary process.[9]

Science fills us with amazement at the beauty and order of the world. We rejoice in the splendor of the galaxies spread across the universe, the precision of quantum fields that structure matter at its fundamental levels, the self-regulating capacities of ecosystems, and the beauty of flowers. In all of these we can see the creative love and power that raised Jesus from the dead. But if we start here, we may be baffled by the extinctions of splendid creatures, the growth of cancer in someone we love, or ethical choices that seem to have no right answer. We have to start at the bottom, not the top. Only the God who is really with us in death can be the God in whom we trust for life.

Both common sense theism and common sense atheism have greater prima facie plausibility than the claim that we are to know who God is by starting with the crucifixion of Jesus of Nazareth. But science has taught us to be wary of common sense. The development of modern science began with Copernicus's suggestion that instead of considering the earth to be at the center of the planetary system, as common sense held, it would be better to consider the sun to be at the center. This seemed to be a crazy idea, open to obvious objections. (If the earth were moving at thousands of miles an hour, the birds would be left behind!) Yet Copernicus was right, and his idea paved the way for all our present-day understanding of the physical sciences.

The parallel between science and religion is not exact because religious commitment is not just an intellectual matter of accepting postulates in the way in which one accepts the assumptions that underlie a mathematical system or scientific theory. Faith in the deepest sense involves trust, and is not the same thing as theology. On a superficial level theology may simply be an intellectual exercise, but in a more profound way it is an attempt to understand the implications of the commitment that is involved in faith. It is, as a classic phrase puts it, faith in search of understanding. There is some resemblance between that and the movement we have described in scientific theories, from assumptions to consequences. Unless one is open to the possibility of faith, there will be no way to judge whether or not that faith can lead to an adequate understanding of the significance of one's life or of the world. "If you do not stand firm in faith," the prophet Isaiah said, "You shall not stand at all" (Isa 7:9b).

Notes on Terminology

I have used the terms "religion" and "science" rather casually in these introductory remarks, and should specify more clearly what I mean by these and other important terms before going further. My concern will not be with religion in general, but specifically with Christianity. Other religious traditions are concerned with science and may have things to say about it that Christians need to hear. Discussion of the different ways in which we see science can be a useful part of interreligious dialogue. But my concern here is to develop a particular way in which the Christian tradition can interact with science. Since I will be working within that tradition, the word "theology" will generally be shorthand for "Christian theology."

The English word "science" encompasses a wide range of activities. In the following discussions it will be primarily the "natural sciences"—physics, astronomy, chemistry, biology, and geology—that will be in view. But this limitation of subject matter cannot be rigid. We cannot have an adequate understanding of the theological significance of biological evolution, for example, without taking into account some aspects of the human and social sciences. This book is intended as a contribution to theology-science discussions, and not as a definitive treatment of all the issues that arise in those discussions.

I will be dealing with "applied" as well as with "pure" science. Not only is there "science-based technology," but technology makes possible and often stimulates scientific development. Since technologies often give rise to significant questions about what use should or should not be made of them, ethics also needs to be involved. Christian ethics has close connections with theology, but is not simply reducible to the latter, and needs to take seriously ethical claims that arise from other religions or from essentially secular worldviews.

Thus I will be engaged in what might be called the theology-science-technology-ethics quadrilateral, a four-way conversation.[10] For brevity I will use the phrase that has now become fairly common, "science-theology dialogue," for this conversation.

NOTES

1. Andrew Dickson White, *A History of the Warfare of Science with Theology in Christendom* (repr.; New York: Dover, 1960).

2. For example, Henry M. Morris, *The Long War against God* (Grand Rapids, Mich.: Baker, 1989).

3. C. A. Coulson, *Science and Christian Belief* (London: Fontana, 1958), 41.

4. Steven Hawking, *A Brief History of Time* (New York: Bantam, New York, 1988), 141.

5. Stephen Jay Gould, "Darwin and Paley Meet the Invisible Hand," *Natural History* (November 1990): 8.

6. "Heidelberg Disputation," *LW* 31:40.

7. Dietrich Bonhoeffer, *Letters and Papers from Prison* (enl. ed.; New York: Macmillan, 1972), 311.

8. Ibid., 360–61.

9. Eberhard Jüngel, *God as the Mystery of the World: On the Foundation of the Theology of the Crucified One in the Dispute between Theism and Atheism.* (trans. Darrell L. Guder; Grand Rapids, Mich.: Eerdmans, 1983).

10. Robert John Russell, "Agenda for the Twenty-first Century," in *The New Faith-Science Debate* (ed. John M. Mangum; Minneapolis: Fortress, 1989), 91–105.

· 2 ·

THE QUESTION OF
NATURAL THEOLOGY

❧

KNOWLEDGE OF GOD

Science helps us to understand what happens in nature, but to what extent does that understanding enable us to speak about God? This question is part of a larger question that is older than the science-theology dialogue in its modern form and broader in scope than specific issues about the relationship between faith and science, the question of natural theology.

Do we have any reason to believe that there *is* a God? If so, what or who is God? What is God's relationship with the world, and what is God's relationship with me? While many different answers have been given to these questions over the centuries, we can divide the attempts at answering them into two broad categories.

The first way to respond to these questions is to try to answer them on the basis of generally available experience and reason. By observation of the world around us and/or our inner realm of thoughts and feelings, and by thinking clearly about these experiences, each person can conclude that there is a God. Perhaps further things can be known about God as well, such as that God is the creator of the world.

Such a response embodies the belief that there is a *natural knowledge of God* to which all people have access. The understanding of God that can be developed from this knowledge is then natural theology. Such knowledge and understanding is, in principle, available to all people throughout the world and at all historical epochs. In this regard, the natural knowledge of God is like scientific knowledge of nature. In principle, anybody in the world at any time could discover the circulation of the blood, or that water is composed of hydrogen and oxygen.

The other way of responding to questions about God is to appeal to revelation. God or a messenger from God must reveal something about God to particular people at particular times, and other people can have this knowledge only by recourse to the original recipients of revelation. Such knowledge will be called *revealed knowledge of God* and an understanding of God developed on this basis is thus theology based upon revelation. Theology itself is not revealed but is a human construction, the result of reflection in particular contexts upon what is thought to be the content of revelation.

Examples of claims to revelation abound. The words that came to Oppenheimer when he witnessed the first atomic bomb test are part of the account of Sri Krishna's revelation of his divinity in the Bhagavad Gita: "If the radiance of a thousand suns were to burst into the sky, that would be like the splendor of the Mighty One."[1] The revelation of God's will to Israel and Jesus of Nazareth as the revelation of God in the New Testament are crucial biblical examples.

The physicist and Episcopal priest William Pollard used Buber's distinction between "I-It" and "I-Thou" relations to distinguish between the two types of knowledge of God. Scientific knowledge of the world results from experiencing parts of the world as "it," and Pollard believed that the experience of the numinous as "it" also makes possible a natural knowledge of God. Revelation, however, he saw as something different, "a category of knowledge which belongs peculiarly to the world of *I and Thou*."[2]

I have already indicated another difference between these two putative knowledges of God. Natural knowledge is, in principle, accessible to everyone on the same terms, without appeal to anything beyond one's own experience and reason. It does not have to appeal to any other authority. In that way the natural knowledge of God is like scientific knowledge, and may be presented as a deduction from scientific knowledge.

Revealed knowledge is different. Careful observation and clear thinking do not necessarily make anyone the recipient of divine revelation. Ultimately the recipient is *chosen* to receive it, like Moses (Exod 3). This chosenness is offensive to many people and especially to scientists, for whom any claim for *scientific* knowledge from revelation would be anathema. A scientist may feel "inspired," may even (as with the chemist Kekulé's discovery of the Benzene ring) *dream* the answer to a scientific problem. But the scientific community will accept such "inspired" results only after they have been carefully tested.

If God is the creator of all things, then God is the source of both revealed and natural knowledge. The chemist C. A. Coulson stated his view as follows:

We must begin with Natural Theology—that which Francis Bacon defined as the 'spark of knowledge of God which may be had by the light of nature, and the consideration of created things: and thus can be fairly held to be divine in respect of its object, and natural in respect of its source of information'—because whatever we may find in our journey must inevitably be bound up with the measurements, the observations, the experiences which are the starting point of science.[3]

He then adds, "But the first thing to notice about these experiences is a sense of 'given-ness.'"

Belief in the givenness of natural knowledge suggests the use of terms like "general" or "primordial" revelation, but such terms tend to blur a necessary distinction so that a term such as "special revelation" would have to be used for something like the Sinai event. "Revelation" will refer here to something supposed to have been given originally to specific people, but whose content is indirectly available to, and intended for, all people, and in that sense is "public."

The two types of possible knowledge of God can be distinguished in theory without any decision about whether either one is real knowledge. For all that has been said so far, the set of all genuine natural knowledge of God, or the set of all genuine revealed knowledge, or both, might be vacuous. "Revelation" might refer to the claims of St. Paul or Muhammad.

Our concern here is with the Christian faith in interaction with science and technology. Revelation in this context refers to God's disclosure in the history of Israel, which culminates in Jesus of Nazareth, with the Bible as witness to this revelation. Because of this we can refer simply to "distinctively Christian theology" rather than the more general "theology based upon revelation." At the same time, "Christian theology" may include, in addition to distinctively Christian theology, aspects of natural theology that could be held in common with other faiths. Christianity also shares some understanding of the content of revelation with Judaism and Islam.

Possible Relationships between Natural Theology and Distinctively Christian Theology

What should be the relationship within Christian thought between the two types of theology? We may divide views about the proper relationship of natural and revealed knowledges of God into four general categories: the classic view; the Enlightenment view; the Barthian view; the dependent view. Lutheran theologian J. A. Quenstedt described the classic view.

The *natural knowledge of God* is that by which man, without any special revelation, may know of himself, though very imperfectly, by the light of Nature and from the Book of Nature, that there is some supreme Divinity, that He, by His own wisdom and power, controls this whole universe, and that He has brought all things into being. . . . The natural knowledge of God is not adequate to secure everlasting life, nor has any mortal ever been redeemed, nor can anyone ever be redeemed, by it alone.[4]

The idea of a valid natural knowledge of God was set out in detail by Aquinas with five ways of arguing for the existence of God.[5] His fifth way, an argument from design, has been especially important in later science-theology discussions. These arguments were developed further within the scholastic tradition and have continued to be emphasized in Roman Catholic theology. The First Vatican Council made the possibility of a valid natural knowledge of God *de fide* for that communion, and Stanley Jaki has been an advocate for this tradition in the modern science-theology dialogue.[6]

There are aspects of Luther's thought that go in a different direction, but he did think that all people are able to know that there is a God. Luther believed that Jonah 1:5 demonstrates that all people possess a knowledge of God: "Thus you also note that the people in the ship all know of God, but they have no definite God."[7]

With his famous analogy of a watch and the eye, William Paley gave prominence to design arguments in the nineteenth century.[8] Just as a person who came upon a watch lying on the ground would conclude from study of its mechanism that it was designed by someone for the purpose of keeping time, so examination of the eye can tell us that it was designed by someone for the purpose of seeing. It would make no more sense to think that the eye could have come about by chance than to think that the parts of the watch had just happened to assemble themselves. The ultimate designer to whom the argument points is, of course, God. Updated arguments of this sort provide the central thrust of today's claims that living things could not have come about by chance but must be due to "intelligent design."[9] Apologetic arguments frequently use some version of this classic view. Today the "anthropic coincidences" that suggest a "fine tuning" of the universe may be used for this purpose.

This view need not imply that obtaining a natural knowledge of God is entirely a human work in which God does nothing. However, a person who moves from atheism or agnosticism to belief in a creator can see the natural knowledge of God as given only after the fact, when there is belief in a giver.

Isaac Newton's statements about natural theology are especially significant, both because of his importance in the history of science and because his comments provide a transition to the second view that I will consider. Newton's *Principia* set out laws of motion and gravitation that provided a foundation for a system of mechanics that endured for more than two centuries and that, in spite of limits imposed by relativity and quantum theory, continues to be of great practical value. Newton added to the second edition a "General Scholium" in which he spoke about the religious significance of natural philosophy. After describing the distribution of bodies in the solar system and their motions, he wrote, "This most beautiful system of the sun, planets, and comets, could only proceed from the counsel and dominion of an intelligent and powerful Being."[10] After further statements about God he continued: "We know him only by his most wise and excellent contrivances of things, and final causes; . . . Blind metaphysical necessity, which is certainly the same always and everywhere, could produce no variety of things. All that diversity of natural things which we find suited to different times and places could arise from nothing but the ideas and will of a Being necessarily existing."[11]

Whatever Newton's own beliefs were, the successes of science led to a more robust idea of its religious possibilities than the classic view would allow. The Enlightenment view, that the natural knowledge of God and a natural theology are all we need, was a result.

The arguments now made for the existence of God and creation could be much the same as those that had been used in the Christian tradition as a preparation for the gospel. But the relationship between natural and distinctively Christian theology in the Enlightenment view differs by 180 degrees from that in the classic view. Natural theology is no longer merely a preparation for theology based upon revelation. Instead, revelation is at most a preparation for an understanding of God based upon natural knowledge. Gotthold Lessing's essay "The Education of the Human Race" is a good example of this approach.[12] Here revelation is not simply dismissed, but it is seen as part of an educational process to bring humanity from an immature state.

> Education is revelation coming to the individual man; and revelation is education which has come, and is still coming, to the human race. . . . Education gives man nothing which he could not also get from within himself; it gives him that which he could get from within himself, only quicker and more easily. In the same way too, revelation gives nothing to the human race which human reason could not arrive at on its own; only it has given, and still gives to it, the most important of these things sooner.[13]

When the human race has become sufficiently mature, it will know God purely from reason, and the need for revelation will fade.

Claims for the superiority or sufficiency of natural theology are often made in the context of discussions about science and religion today.

Physicist Paul Davies says, "It may seem bizarre, but in my opinion science offers a surer path to God than religion,"[14] and Thomas Berry speaks of "the natural world as primary revelation of the divine, as primary scripture, as the primary mode of numinous presence."[15]

The Enlightenment view makes revelation at most something of historical or pedagogical importance and may eliminate any need for it. The human subject and the human search for God take a central place. In reaction to such ideas, Karl Barth expressed a markedly different attitude toward natural theology, an attitude summarized in the title of a famous response to Emil Brunner on the subject: *"Nein!"*[16] It is a rejection of any valid natural knowledge of God and natural theology. We must depend upon revelation alone.

The negative character of the Barthian view was a result of Barth's objection to what he saw as an essential distortion of humanity's relationship with God.[17] This must, of course, be seen together with the claim that we do have a true and sufficient revelation of God in Christ: "God reveals Himself as the Lord."[18]

In this view science has nothing to contribute to theology. In the introduction to his treatment of the doctrine of creation in *Church Dogmatics*, Barth contended: "It will perhaps be asked in criticism why I have not tackled the obvious scientific question posed in this context. It was my original belief that this would be necessary, but I later saw that there can be no theological problems, objections or aids in relation to what Holy Scripture and the Christian Church understand by the divine work of creation."[19] But it is possible to argue that while Barth's negative view of natural theology is correct as far as it goes, it is incomplete, and that a positive dimension can be developed.

Thomas Torrance has argued for such a development and has devoted considerable attention to it in connection with relations between theology and science. He maintains that what Barth rejected was *independent* natural theology, which is supposed to have no need of revelation. It is a different matter to see a natural theology as part of a distinctively Christian theology.[20] In the latter case natural theology would depend upon revelation for its validity, though it might be able to give further insight into the significance of the revealed knowledge of God. We may thus speak of this fourth way of looking at the matter as the dependent view of natural theology.

Torrance argues that an appropriate way of knowing about God must be adapted to the real character of the God who is to be known, just as methods of scientific investigation must be adapted to the phenomena that they study. He points to the example of Einstein's general relativity theory as an example of the latter requirement.[21] The geometry of Euclid, in which the sum of the angles of a plane triangle is 180 degrees, was for a long time the only geometry known, and it was natural to assume that space must be Euclidean. But consistent non-Euclidean geometries were developed in the nineteenth century, and Einstein's successful theory of gravitation made the geometry of the world part of physics, something which had to be determined from appropriate observations instead of being imposed a priori. In the same way, Torrance suggests, we must try to understand God on the basis of who God really is, beginning with revelation, rather than by imposing a priori concepts of divinity upon God.

The world can be understood, "though God were not given."[22] But for that knowledge to tell us anything about God, it must be seen in the light of revelation. As Jüngel puts it, "In the book of revelation the human learns to read the book of creation and to recognize nature as creation."[23]

The categories set out here represent useful distinctions, but boundaries are blurred and people refuse to stay in one box. Those engaged in the science-theology dialogue today often do not make formal statements about their stances with regard to natural theology, and it is not always clear whether their ideas would come under the classic or the dependent heading.[24] It is important for those who work at the science-theology interface to state their positions on the relationship between revealed and natural knowledges of God.

TAKING STOCK

How do the approaches suggested by these different views function and what are their effects, especially with regard to the science-theology dialogue?

The classic view is traditional and widely accepted in the Christian church. Since it can appeal to the common experience and reason of human beings without having to refer to claims of revelation that may be debated, it provides a straightforward way of introducing the Christian message to people. But there are several problems. We have to ask first whether the arguments of natural theology actually are valid, and whether they are convincing to people in the modern world. Hume's *Dialogues Concerning Natural Religion*[25] dealt them a serious philosophical blow. Recently some philosophers have taken a more optimistic view of natural theology, recognizing that it is unreasonable to demand a strict logical "proof" for God's existence, and that feelings and beliefs can play a legitimate role in assessing arguments.[26] Such considerations suggest that natural theology may have some philosophical validity, but that it may also move in the direction of what I have called the dependent view.

What really struck at the heart of design arguments was the idea of Darwin and Wallace that the structures of living things had come about through the filtering of random variations by environments. Paley had said that complex structures with obvious functions such as the eye could not have happened by chance, but natural selection suggests a way in which they could have. Whether or not natural selection actually can explain the properties of living things in detail may be debated, but it does provide in general terms a plausible explanation for biological structures. Many people today will find that explanation more likely than design by a creator God.

This does not mean that natural selection has been shown to be the cause of organic features *instead of* design. The point is rather that natural selection and design are explanations that seem plausible to different people. If natural selection gives an adequate explanation of living things, a person may believe that that is how God has carried out the process of design. This is not an independent natural knowledge of God, but an understanding of the world from the standpoint of a faith in God. At the same time, such scientific advances allow those who wish to do so to echo Laplace and say that they have no need of the hypothesis of a creator.

But what can we say about the classic view from the standpoint of Christian theology? The most serious problem about starting with natural theology only becomes clear when we expand our subject to include the Enlightenment view as well.

The Enlightenment view does make contact with an aspect of biblical thought that is sometimes lost sight of: Christian understanding is to grow and become more mature, as Heb 5:11–6:3 and Eph 4:13–15 suggest. Some of this growth may take place through science. But the Enlightenment view removes from a central role, and may remove entirely, such distinctive Christian beliefs as the Trinity and justification of sinners for Christ's sake. It leads to a religion based on the common natural knowledge of God, and anything uniquely Christian can be at most of secondary importance. Doctrines such as the Trinity might be kept,[27] but they would not be based in an essential way on the belief that God is revealed in the death of Jesus on the cross. And it is ultimately the fact that the Enlightenment view cannot give the cross of Christ a central role that disqualifies it.

Complete dependence on science may even go all the way toward a natural anti-theology in which science is made to argue against the existence of God or creation. We should avoid a domino theory that suggests that such a development is inevitable, but it certainly can happen. Evolutionary biologist Richard Dawkins provides an example. The subtitle of his book *The Blind Watchmaker* is "Why the evidence of evolution reveals a universe without design."[28]

The danger to which the classic view is always subject is that it will gradually become the view of the Enlightenment. It is possible in theory to limit the role of natural theology, to allow it to be only the forecourt of Christian theology and to insist that one knows nothing about who the true God is, as distinguished from a mere knowledge that there is some God, without the revelation to which Scripture witnesses. But it is not easy to keep natural theology in that limited role. The fact that many church members think that "believing in God" is the heart of the Christian message, without giving much thought to the question of how "God" is to be identified, is the simplest illustration of this tendency.

The major strength of the Barthian view is that it eliminates such problems at their source by denying to any supposed natural knowledge of God a role in Christian theology. It focuses uncompromisingly upon a single revelation, as the Barmen Declaration of 1934 insists: "Jesus Christ, as he is attested for us in Holy Scripture, is the one Word of God which we have to hear and which we have to trust and obey in life and in death."[29]

There are good reasons to concentrate upon revelation. But in the Barthian view the scientific understanding of the world has no connection with belief that God is its creator, savior, and hallower.

While Barth envisioned some appropriate science-theology dialogue, he did not himself participate in it.[30] The limitations of the Barthian view are especially clear in connection with environmental issues. Paul Santmire, in his study of Christian attitudes toward nature, concludes that for Barth only human beings in their relationship with God have any eschatological significance.[31] The rest of creation has only a subsidiary role in support of this relationship.

Revelation does not merely convey abstract propositions, but speaks about God's involvement with the world of space, time, and matter. This does not mean that the world by itself conveys information about God, but our scientific information about humanity and the world is germane to theological discussion.

The incompleteness of the Barthian view needs to be removed and a positive dimension developed, and that is what the dependent view does. It insists that our knowledge of God must begin from God's self-revelation in the history of Israel, which culminates in Jesus. At the same time it holds that in the light of this revelation, scientific understanding of the world should be able to tell us something about this God and the way in which God interacts with the world, a world that faith sees not only as nature but as creation.

The science-theology dialogue is then approached with the presupposition that the world is created, sustained, and given a purpose by the God to whom the Bible bears witness. We rule out the possibility that the universe is merely the result of blind chance at the most fundamental level. In that sense we do not come to the dialogue with a totally open mind, but with trust that is in search of fuller insight into itself, faith in search of understanding.

At the same time, we are simply making our initial faith explicit. Arguments for the existence of God sometimes pretend to a neutral character that they do not really have. This does not mean that people who make these arguments are dishonest, but simply that we all are often unconscious of the ways in which our basic attitudes toward life and our beliefs influence our arguments. We can eliminate some misunderstanding if we set out our fundamental commitments at the beginning of the discussion.

The dependent view is open to a certain misunderstanding. The statement that scientific knowledge of the world can tell us about God and God's relationship with the universe only when viewed in the light of revelation might be confused with the idea that the scientific enterprise itself can be carried out properly only on the basis of Christian presuppositions. That would be a serious error. Science can be done successfully by people of many different religions or no religion at all. This nonreligious character of science is not only an empirical reality but also a theological requirement. Science qua science does not need religion. But science goes beyond its area of competence if it tries to make statements of *religious* significance without reference to revelation.

THE BIBLICAL WITNESS

If the Bible is the fundamental witness to revelation, then we need to consider what it may say about a natural knowledge of God. There are many passages that indicate that people who have not learned of God's revelation to Israel can know that there is a God. Barth made "an open concession" that "there are not only individual passages, but a whole strand running through Scripture" that suggest an approval of natural theology.[32] What role do these biblical statements play in the whole of Scripture? Can this natural knowledge in any way be seen as the subject of a separate "natural theology" within the theologies contained by Scripture?

We can separate the biblical material that praises aspects of nature as God's handiwork, celebrates God's wisdom in creation, and speaks of creation as involved in the praise of God. A number of the Psalms, such as 96, 104, and 148, are detailed proclamations of these themes. God's speeches to Job (38–41) and Wisdom's rejoicing in creation (Prov 8:22–31) present other aspects of these themes, as does Jesus' teaching about God's care for the birds and the flowers (Matt 6:25–33). These must be given adequate attention in the science-theology dialogue. The beauty and order of nature have often been appealed to as evidence for a creator. But these biblical passages in themselves do not present a natural theology. They are, rather, material for a theology of nature. The distinction between the two is not always sharp, but it should be made. A believer can celebrate the goodness of God that he or she sees in the world without thinking that nature would demonstrate the existence of God to a neutral observer.

To the extent that the biblical theology of nature can be used in a natural theology, the latter is of the dependent type, with the appreciation of the natural world placed within the context of faith. Psalm 148 is a good example. All things—angels, heavenly bodies, and nonliving and living things on earth—are to praise the Lord. The doxology takes in the human race, the part of creation that has words to voice God's praise. But it concludes:

> He has raised up a horn for his people,
> praise for all his faithful,
> for the people of Israel who are close to him.
> Praise the LORD! (Ps 148:14)

It is the people of Israel, the community that has received God's revelation, that knows the God praised by creation and is able to sing the creator's praise properly. This creator is not given the general title "God" throughout the psalm but the covenant name YHWH, "The LORD."

Two biblical passages speak most clearly of a natural knowledge of God: Ps 19 and Rom 1:18–32. Writers often appeal to these verses as a biblical basis for natural theology. Psalm 19 provides another example of a theology of nature in speaking of

> ... the sun,
> which comes out like a bridegroom from his wedding canopy, and
>   like a strong man runs its course with joy.
> Its rising is from the end of the heavens, and its circuit to the end
>   of them;
> and nothing is hid from its heat. (Ps 19:4b–6)

That almost sounds like solar worship, but its purpose is the praise of God:

> The heavens are telling the glory of God;
> and the firmament proclaims his handiwork. (Ps 19:1)

Verses 1–6 say that the heavenly bodies speak of God (vv. 2–4), and we might conclude that that speech could provide the basis for a natural theology. But it is not certain that human beings are able to *understand* this speech of the celestial bodies. The meaning of the relevant verses is unclear:

> There is no speech, nor are there words;
> their voice is not heard. (Ps 19:3)

More important, the first half of the psalm has to be read together with the second, which talks about the Lord's "law," the Lord's "decrees," in terms of praise that are not used of the speech of the heavenly bodies:

> The law of the LORD is perfect, reviving the soul;
> the decrees of the LORD are sure, making wise the simple. . . .
>   (Ps 19:7)

Thus the evidence for God in nature is placed in the context of revelation. Even if humanity is supposed to be able to understand and draw the right conclusions about God from nature, that knowledge is to be seen in the light of *torah*.

James Barr argues that the combination of the witness of nature and *torah* can be understood as a statement about a twofold revelation of God rather than as a subordination of the second to the first, and that "the law [*torah*] of the LORD" need not refer to the Mosaic covenant but to a more general type of instruction. Evaluation of the first suggestion depends on the assumptions about natural theology with which one approaches the text. It is persuasive if one requires only that negative statements not be made about natural theology in order to legitimate it, and is not if one requires explicit statements in its favor. Barr's second suggestion is unconvincing because the second part of Ps 19 repeatedly uses the divine name YHWH, while the first uses the general title 'El. This gives the impression that in going from the first to the second part we have moved into the area of the distinctive faith of Israel.

In Rom 1:18–32, probably influenced by Wis 14, Paul begins to describe the seriousness and universal scope of the problem of sin. He argues that there is evidence for God in the created world:

> For what can be known about God is plain to them, because God has shown it to them. Ever since the creation of the world his eternal power and divine nature, invisible though they are, have been understood and seen through the things he has made. So they are without excuse. (Rom 1:19–20)

Thus the material exists for the development of a natural theology. There is evidence but it does not result in true knowledge and true theology, a distinction similar to that which Brunner emphasized.[34] The problem is that people "suppress the truth" (v. 18) and misuse the evidence to construct *bad* natural theologies and become idolaters, being led to worship the products of their supposed natural knowledge of the divine:

Claiming to be wise, they became fools; and they exchanged the glory of
the immortal God for images resembling a mortal human being or birds
or four-footed animals or reptiles. Therefore God gave them up in the
lusts of their hearts to impurity, to the degrading of their bodies among
themselves, because they exchanged the truth about God for a lie and
worshiped and served the creature rather than the Creator, who is
blessed forever! Amen. (Rom 1:22–25)

Paul does not say that people are atheists because they reject evidence for
God, but that they become idolaters because they distort it.

After stating the root problem of sin, Paul sketches the individual sins
that proceed from it. He then discusses how sin affects both Jews and
Gentiles, concluding with the statement that "all, both Jews and Greeks,
are under the power of sin" (Rom 3:9). In 3:19–20 he points out that the
Law, whose Decalogue begins with the command that we are to have no
other gods before the God of Israel, always functions to identify sin.

We might expect that Paul would say that since we are now aware of the
distortions that sin can introduce into natural theology, we need to go back
to the beginning, consider the evidence for God's power and deity in the
world, and develop a *correct* natural theology. But he does nothing of the
sort. Instead, he immediately moves to God's revelation in Christ in 3:21–31.

Paul is not arguing in these opening chapters of Romans for a use of
natural theology.[35] Instead, he points out why natural theology is a problem. Though there is evidence in nature that should lead people to
acknowledge the true God, the radical and universal problem of sin keeps
that possibility from ever being actualized.[36]

Did the apostles ever use arguments of natural theology? The speeches
in Lystra and Athens attributed to Paul in Acts (14:15–17 and 17:22–31)
indicate that he did. But arguments that may be used for apologetic effect
are not necessarily good systematic theology. We might compare them
with Pascal's "wager," in which he argued that the eternal "payoff" for
believing in God is vastly greater than any temporal good that might be
lost because of that belief.[37] Such an argument may get the attention of an
unbeliever and be the first step on that person's journey to faith, but it
could hardly be made part of a mature Christian theology.

We should also remember the example of Sherlock Holmes, who
found a critical clue in "the curious incident of the dog in the night-
time"—the curious incident being that "the dog did nothing in the night-
time."[38] One of the crucial stories of the Bible is the call of Abraham, and
we may wonder why God chose him. An old extrabiblical legend told of
how Abraham came to the knowledge that there is only one God by con-
templating the heavens.

When Abraham came forth from the cave, his mind was inquiring into the creation of the world, and he was intent upon all the luminaries of the world, to bow down to them and serve them, in order that he might know which of them was God. He saw the moon, whose light shone in the night from one end of the world to the other, and whose retinue [of shining stars] was so numerous. Said he: "This is God!" (and) he worshiped her all the night. But when at day-break he saw the sun-rise, and at its rising the moon become dark and her strength wane, he said: "The light of the moon only proceeds from the light of the sun, and the world is only sustained by the light of the sun," and so he worshipped the sun all day. At evening the sun set, and its power waned, and the moon and the stars and the constellations emerged (once more). Said [Abraham]: "Verily there is a Lord and a God over these."[39]

The "curious incident" is that the Bible has nothing of the kind. Genesis 11:26–32 introduces Abraham to identify and locate him, and Josh 24:2 says that he "served other gods." Then, in Gen 12:1–3, God simply calls Abraham to obey, and gives him promises. We may speculate about ways in which this might have happened, but the Bible says nothing about Abraham's astronomical observations or any other way in which proponents of independent natural theology might feel that the ancestor of the faithful must have begun to come to faith.

THE REVELATION OF THE CROSS

We cannot simply rule out the classic approach, but there are significant dangers connected with its use. The Enlightenment view, while expressing a theme that needs to be heard, eliminates the distinctive features of the Christian faith. Barth's view of natural theology is a valuable warning about the risks of that enterprise; it cannot, however, stand on its own as a complete view. The route I will take in the following contribution to the science-theology dialogue will be in the dependent category, with science and technology viewed in the context of revelation.

But what is the revelation with which we are concerned? The general Christian answer would be that it is the history of God's relationship with the people of Israel that culminates in Jesus of Nazareth, the subject matter of the Bible. This answer allows considerable latitude for understanding the religious significance of scientific knowledge. Christians who insist on the scientific accuracy of Genesis are taking a dependent view when they reject evolution because it does not agree with their reading of the Bible. The difference between that approach and the present one lies in the fundamental principles we bring to the interpretation of

Scripture—a particular view of biblical inerrancy or the cross of Christ and its implications.

My intention here is to choose a specific center of Scripture and way of reading the biblical story, and to let them inform our understanding of the significance of science and our uses of technology. That center is Christ crucified, as Paul claims in 1 Cor 1:18–31, and we read Scripture with reference to Christ. Scientific knowledge of the world and technological capabilities will be able to contribute to our understanding of God and God's relationship with the world when they are placed in the context of a theology of the cross.

Viewing things from the standpoint of the cross is not simply a statement about our starting point, or about theological method. It is also a statement about the content of theology, and in a sense describes an important *goal* of the science-theology dialogue. The God who is revealed to the universe is the crucified.

In Plato's account of creation in the *Timaeus*, the creator shaped the World Soul into two bands and placed it like the letter chi (X) in the universe. The idea behind that is the intersection of the equator and the ecliptic on the celestial sphere. The second-century apologist Justin Martyr saw the statement that the creator "placed him crosswise in the universe" as a prophecy of the cross of Christ.[40] That is unlikely but it gives a good picture of our goal, which is to discern the presence and activity in the universe of the God revealed in the cross. This approach to the science-theology dialogue may therefore be called "chiasmic cosmology."

Chiasmic cosmology is not supposed to replace scientific cosmologies such as the big bang theory. The vantage point of the cross provides us with a worldview, a way of understanding reality, of which the subject matters of science and technology form a part. Chiasmic cosmology is intended to be Cosmology with a capital C.

Although Blaise Pascal did not contribute as much to mathematics or physics as Newton, he was a considerably better theologian. His *Pensées* are a collection of notes for an apology for Christianity, at a time when the wars of religion, the rise of science, and other factors had led many people to doubt traditional Christianity.

> It is a remarkable thing that no canonical writer ever used nature as a proof of God's existence. All set out to convince us of it. But David, Solomon, and the rest never said: "There is no void; therefore there is a God." They must have been cleverer than the cleverest of their successors, every one of whom has used this argument. The fact is worth pondering on.

> If it is a sign of weakness to use nature as a proof of God, do not despise Scripture for it; if it is a sign of strength to have recognized these contradictions, give Scripture the credit for it.[42]

(Pascal's barometric experiments demonstrating the existence of a vacuum explain his reference to the "void.") But Pascal did not think that God was absent from the world. With Isa 45:15, "Truly, you are a God who hides himself, O God of Israel, the Savior," in mind, he says, "What meets our eyes denotes neither a total absence nor a manifest presence of the divine, but the presence of a God who conceals Himself. Everything bears this stamp."[43]

NOTES

1. Robert Jungk, *Brighter than a Thousand Suns* (New York: Harcourt, Brace & Co., 1958), 201.

2. William G. Pollard, *Physicist and Christian* (Greenwich, Conn.: Seabury, 1961), chapters 5 and 6. The quotation is on p. 151.

3. C. A. Coulson, *Science and Christian Belief* (London: Fontana, 1958), 122–23.

4. Heinrich Schmid, *The Doctrinal Theology of the Evangelical Lutheran Church*, (3d ed.; Minneapolis: Augsburg, 1961), 105 and 110.

5. Thomas Aquinas, *The "Summa Theologica" of St. Thomas Aquinas* (Chicago: Encyclopedia Britannica, 1952), Q.2, Art.3, pp. 12–14 of vol. 1.

6. Stanley L. Jaki, *The Road of Science and the Ways to God* (Chicago: University of Chicago Press, 1978), and *Cosmos and Creator* (Edinburgh: Scottish Academic, 1980). The statement of Vatican I is discussed on pp. 84–86 of the latter book.

7. *LW* 19:56.

8. William Paley, *Natural Theology (Selections)* (Indianapolis: Bobbs-Merrill, 1963).

9. For example, William A. Dembski, *Intelligent Design* (Downers Grove, Ill.: InterVarsity, 1999).

10. Isaac Newton, *Principia* (Berkeley: University of California Press, 1962), 544.

11. Ibid., 546.

12. Gotthold Ephraim Lessing, "The Education of the Human Race" in *Lessing's Theological Writings* (Stanford, Calif.: Stanford University Press, 1957), 87–98.

13. Ibid., 83.

14. Paul Davies, *God and the New Physics* (New York: Simon & Schuster, 1983), ix.

15. Thomas Berry, *The Dream of the Earth* (San Francisco: Sierra Club, 1988), 105.

16. *Natural Theology: Comprising "Nature and Grace" by Emil Brunner and "No!" by Karl Barth* (London: G. Bles, 1946).

17. For Barth's treatment of the knowability of God and natural theology, see *CD* 2:1:63–178.

18. *CD* 1:1:339 ff.

19. *CD* 3:1:ix.

20. Thomas F. Torrance, *Reality and Scientific Theology* (Edinburgh: Scottish Academic, 1985).

21. Thomas F. Torrance, *Transformation and Convergence in the Frame of Knowledge: Explorations in the Interrelations of the Scientific and Theological Enterprise* (Grand Rapids, Mich.: Eerdmans, 1984), 263–83.

22. The phrase *etsi deus non daretur* originated with Grotius in the seventeenth century. Torrance (*Reality and Scientific Theology*, 61.1) would prefer *acsi deus non daretur*, "as if God were not given."

23. Eberhard Jüngel, *Entsprechungen: Gott—Wahrheit—Mensch* (Munich: Chr. Kaiser Verlag, 1980), 197 (my translation).

24. In a response to an essay in which Owen Gingerich presented a modest claim for natural theology, Nancey Murphy gives an endorsement of the dependent view:

> Gingerich uses the metaphor of the two books, the Book of Scripture and the Book of Nature, both pointing to God. However, it seems clear to me, based on the considerations I have raised here, that these books ought not be read independently of one another. In fact, the Book of Nature ought to be read as a sequel to the Bible. As with the sequel to a novel, it is important to read the first volume to find out about the characters.
>
> Or, to drop the metaphor, we get our hypothesis of design from revelation. Discoveries like the fine tuning come along later, and their strength as evidence lies in confirming an already-existing hypothesis that already has other confirmation from other realms of experience. Without revelation, we would be at a loss to know what we mean by "designer" in such arguments.

Murray Rae, Hilary Regan, and John Stenhouse, eds., *Science and Theology* (Grand Rapids, Mich.: Eerdmans, 1994), 69–70. The essay by Owen Gingerich is on pp. 29–48.

25. David Hume, *Dialogues Concerning Natural Religion* (New York: Hafner, 1948).

26. For example, Eugene Thomas Long, ed., *Prospects for Natural Theology* (Washington, D.C.: Catholic University of America, 1992).

27. For example, Lessing, "The Education of the Human Race," 94–95.

28. Richard Dawkins, *The Blind Watchmaker: Why the Evidence of Evolution Reveals a Universe without Design* (New York: W.W. Norton, 1987).

29. "The Theological Declaration of Barmen," in *The Reformed Confessions of the Sixteenth Century* (ed. Arthur C. Cochrane; Philadelphia: Westminster, 1966), 334.

30. See, for example, Harold Nebelsick, "Karl Barth's Understanding of Science," in *Theology beyond Christendom* (ed. John Thompson; Allison Park, Pa.: Pickwick, 1986), 165–214.

31. H. Paul Santmire, *The Travail of Nature: The Ambiguous Ecological Promise of Christian Theology* (Philadelphia: Fortress, 1985), chapter 8, and *Nature Reborn: The Ecological and Cosmic Promise of Christian Theology* (Minneapolis: Fortress, 2000), 117–18.

32. *CD* 2:1:99. The discussion of the biblical material here is on pp. 97–126.

33. James Barr, *Biblical Faith and Natural Theology* (Oxford: Clarendon, 1993), 85–89.

34. Emil Brunner, *The Christian Doctrine of God* (Philadelphia: Westminster, 1950), 132–36.

35. It is also worth noting that in Rom 10:18 Paul cites "Their voice has gone out to all the earth, and their words to the ends of the world" from Ps 19. But he interprets this as a reference to the proclamation of Christ, not a natural knowledge of God given by the heavens.

36. Compare the arguments of Käsemann summarized by Barr, *Biblical Faith and Natural Theology*, 46–47.

37. Blaise Pascal, *The Pensées* (trans. J. M. Cohen; Baltimore: Penguin, 1961), no. 451, 155–59.

38. Sir Arthur Conan Doyle, "Silver Blaze," in *The Complete Sherlock Holmes* (Garden City, N.Y.: Doubleday, 1930), 347.

39. G. H. Box, *The Apocalypse of Abraham* (London: Society for Propagation of Christian Knowledge, 1919), appendix I, p. 92.

40. Plato, "Timaeus," in *Collected Dialogues of Plato* (ed. Edith Hamilton and Huntington Cairns; Princeton, N.J.: Princeton University Press, 1961), 1166. Justin Martyr, "The First Apology of Justin," *ANF* 1:183. Justin is not a representative of the dependent view, but he thought that Plato got his idea by reading Moses, specifically Num 21:8, and thus from revelation.

41. George L. Murphy, "Chiasmic Cosmology: A Response to Fred Van Dyke," *Journal of the American Scientific Affiliation* 38 (1986): 124–26.

42. Pascal, *The Pensées,* nos. 6 and 7, p. 32.

43. Ibid., no. 602, p. 222.

· 3 ·

THEOLOGY OF THE CRUCIFIED GOD

Crucifixion as Event and Pattern

"The cross" refers first to a single historical event, the death by crucifixion of Jesus of Nazareth near Jerusalem under the Roman governor Pontius Pilate in approximately A.D. 30. As Christian faith developed from belief that the crucified Jesus had been raised from the dead, the church interpreted the cross in various ways and connected the history of Israel in the Hebrew Scriptures with it. The cross plays an important role in every serious reflection on the Christian faith, and Luther in particular insisted that "the CROSS alone is our theology."[1] My purpose is to consider the scientific picture of the world in the context of such a theology. I begin by setting out the cruciform pattern of Scripture in order to be able to discern that pattern in the universe. I will then clarify the method and the content of a theology of the cross.

Golgotha

The canonical Gospels all deal at length with the crucifixion of Jesus, and there are many references and allusions to it in the rest of the New Testament. There is no serious doubt about the historical reality of this event. Scholars debate about whether or not many of the things described in the Gospels really happened and about which of the sayings attributed to Jesus actually were uttered by him. The accounts of the empty tomb and the appearances of the risen Christ are especially controversial. But there is little scholarly debate about the claim that Jesus died on a cross. There is, of course, far less agreement on the significance of the cross.

As a historical event the crucifixion of Jesus was by no means unique. Two thieves were crucified with him. Crucifixion was a common method of execution in the Mediterranean world of the time.[2] The Romans reserved this penalty for slaves and foreigners; the form of sentencing was "Lay the cross on the slave." The condemned person would carry the heavy crosspiece to the place of execution, where the upright was already fixed in the ground.

Crucifixion was an especially painful, prolonged, and humiliating death. The naked victim was completely helpless, with wrists nailed or tied to the cross, and had no defense against the insults or thrown stones of onlookers, or against insects, birds, or even wild animals. Death was certain but could be very slow: A victim could linger for days before the torment ended. A previous scourging might so weaken the condemned person that the time on the cross would be shortened. This may have contributed to Jesus' death after only a few hours. The crucified one was exposed to the world as totally powerless and contemptible, an object of ridicule and abuse to enemies and of horror to sympathizers. Such horror was one of the purposes of crucifixion. Rome needed to control a huge slave population and rebellious inhabitants of occupied territories, of which Palestine was one of the most troublesome. Crucifixion was intended to strike terror into the hearts of potential troublemakers.

Crucifixion was seen by all people as a disgusting form of death— "the utterly vile death of the cross," as Origen put it.[3] For the Jews it was an especially unclean death: according to the Mishnah, "None is hanged save the blasphemer and the idolater."[4] In Gal 3:13 Paul sees the statement of Deut 21:23 that "anyone hung on a tree is under God's curse" as having special reference to Jesus.

Against this background, in a society in which public crucifixions took place, Christians began to proclaim that Jesus was the Messiah and Son of God. It would have been absurd to try to persuade people to listen to a teacher or follow a political leader who had died on a cross. How much more grotesque to claim that a crucified man was Savior and Lord! Paul was hardly exaggerating when he said that this message was "a stumbling block to Jews and foolishness to Gentiles" (1 Cor 1:23). Though the cross was central to the life of the Christian community, it is not pictured in the early Christian art of the catacombs. The earliest known "crucifix" is an anti-Christian caricature showing a crucified figure with an ass's head and the inscription "Alexamenos worships god."[5] Not until the empire stopped the practice of crucifixion and people no longer saw it in use did the cross become a visual object of devotion.

There is general archaeological agreement that the site identified by tradition, the location now enclosed within the Church of the Resurrection in Jerusalem, has the best claim to be Golgotha.[6] This church also encloses the traditional site of the tomb of Jesus. There is little left of the tomb, since much of the stone was hacked away by the pagan Persians during their occupation of Jerusalem in A.D. 614. But if the Christian claim about an empty tomb is true, then there is a sense in which the tomb cannot be desecrated.

Jesus' resurrection does not receive the assent that his crucifixion does. Christianity looks for a general resurrection, as does Pharisaic Judaism and Islam, but sees the resurrection of Jesus as unique. It is not supposed to be simply a resuscitation but a passage to a new kind of life: "Christ, being raised from the dead, will never die again; death no longer has dominion over him" (Rom 6:9). A person may reasonably ask for stronger evidence for such a claim than for events of a more familiar type. This does not mean that one is justified in discounting all testimony to such an occurrence, as Hume thought.[7] A case can be made for the essential historical truth of the resurrection appearances and of the accounts of the empty tomb.[8] But whether or not a person believes will depend to a great extent on how well the claim that the crucified one has been raised helps to illumine that person's experience of his or her life and of the world.

THE CROSS IN THE BIBLE

The suffering and death of Jesus is the primary element in the Gospels.[9] Mark sets out the synoptic framework, which has been described as "a passion narrative with an extended introduction."[10] Two chapters out of sixteen, 18 percent of the verses, are devoted to the passion narrative proper. But already in the third chapter (3:6) the death of Jesus is being planned, and from the middle of the gospel on, the three predictions of the passion (8:31–9:1, 9:30–32, 10:32–34) make the direction of the story unmistakable. Some ancient lectionaries include chapter 13, the eschatological trials of Jesus' disciples and the world, in the passion narrative.[11] Such a connection between the cross of Jesus and the lives of Christians is made explicit in the statement about the need for disciples to take up their crosses and follow Jesus (Mark 8:31–38).

The Gospels do not end with the death of Jesus but with his resurrection. This does not make the cross simply an event of the past that can now be forgotten. The messengers at the empty tomb identify the risen one as "Jesus of Nazareth, who was crucified" (Mark 16:6), and in two of the gospels (Luke 24:39–40, John 20:24–29) he is identified by the wounds of the cross.

The Book of Acts connects the beginning of the church with proclamation of the lordship of the one who had died: "God has made him both

Lord and Messiah, this Jesus whom you crucified" (Acts 2:36). The New Testament writers deal with the death and resurrection of Jesus in different ways. It is especially Paul who insists upon the central place of the cross in the Christian message.[12] He reminded the Galatians of his preaching to them in which "Jesus Christ was publicly exhibited as crucified" (Gal 3:1) and in 1 Corinthians (1:18–2:16) insisted upon the message of the cross in contrast to what the world considers wise and impressive.

A great deal of modern discussion about the death of Jesus has had to do with the motives for his condemnation and execution and the roles of Jewish religious leaders and the Roman authority, but those were not vital concerns for Paul. His emphasis was on *God's* involvement.[13] Through Jesus' blood God justifies sinners (Rom 3:21–26). God shows his love for sinners by Christ's death (Rom 5:8), and it is through Christ crucified that God is revealed in a way that confounds human expectations (1 Cor 1:18–31). The folly of the cross is God's wisdom and the weakness of the crucified (cf. 2 Cor 13:4) is the power of God (1 Cor 1:25). The one who dies as a sinner reveals God's righteousness and God shows his love for those who are unlovely.

The cross and resurrection must be seen together: God has highly exalted the one who humbled himself to death (Phil 2:5–11). The resurrection does not erase Jesus' identity as the crucified or remove the scandal of the cross. In an important sense it becomes even *more* scandalous. "[W]hat makes the message of the crucified Christ offensive is not simply the manner of his death once, but that through the resurrection Christ is still known to the church as the crucified one."[14] I will return to this theme, for my central thesis is that Christ is to be known to the entire universe as the crucified one.

The argument in the fourth chapter of Romans is interesting here. Having said that God's righteousness is given to faith without works of the law, Paul wants to show that Abraham also received righteousness as a gift. God is characterized as the one "who justifies the ungodly" (4:5) and "who gives life to the dead and calls into existence the things that do not exist" (4:17). Giving life to the dead is impossible by human standards, but happened in a sense to Abraham with the birth of a son when his body "was already as good as dead" (4:19), and was shown definitively by God's action when he "raised Jesus our Lord from the dead, who was handed over to death for our trespasses and was raised for our justification" (4:24–25). That returns us to the initial statement that God "justifies the ungodly," which is again an apparent impossibility. The pervasive belief in works righteousness in all religions shows how contrary to natural ways of thinking is the idea that God justifies those who cannot justify themselves. But this follows the pattern of cross and resurrection, God doing what seems impossible.

The claim that God "calls into existence the things that do not exist" (4:17) suggests that *creatio ex nihilo* is part of this pattern. It contradicts the conventional belief expressed by Lucretius that "nothing can ever be created by divine power out of nothing."[15] Paul's language opens up the possibility of seeing the creation of the universe as a divine work that bears the mark of the cross. And because God is not bound by assumptions that the dead are not raised, that the ungodly cannot be justified, and that nothing comes from nothing, it is possible for people also to look beyond those assumptions and, like Abraham, to be "hoping against hope" (4:18).

The cross shows not just how God works but what kind of a deity God is. Philippians 2:3–11 will be emphasized in several places in the following chapters. Particularly relevant here are verses 5–8: "Let the same mind be in you that was in Christ Jesus, who, though he was in the form of God, did not regard equality with God as something to be exploited *[harpagmon]*, but emptied himself *[heauton ekenōsen]*, taking the form of a slave, being born in human likeness. And being found in human form, he humbled himself and became obedient to the point of death— even death on a cross."

There has been recent debate about whether Christ being "in the form of God" refers to preexistence.[16] James Dunn begins his treatment by saying, "*Phil. 2:6–11* certainly seems on the face of it to be a straightforward statement contrasting Christ's pre-existent glory and post-crucifixion exaltation with his earthly humiliation," but then challenges this view.[17] He argues that the reference is to Christ as a new Adam who did not cling to the image of God like the first Adam. But that view is problematic. The sin of the first humans in Gen 3 is not clinging to equality with God but disobeying God's command so as to achieve knowledge and be like God.

The natural interpretation of the text is indeed that it begins with the preexistent Christ, as Gordon Fee argues, with the above verses describing the descent of Christ: "As God he Emptied Himself" (vv. 5–7) and "As Man he Humbled Himself" (v. 8).[18] "Taking the form of a slave" refers to the incarnation. (This does not mean that Paul had in mind the full Christology of the later church.) *Harpagmos* can be understood either as "an abstract noun, emphasizing the concept of 'grasping' or 'seizing'" or as "a matter to be seized upon."[19] With either meaning Christ did not cling to the privileges of deity. This gives a picture of God quite different from conventional ideas of divinity. "For in 'pouring himself out' and 'humbling himself to death on the cross' Christ Jesus has revealed the character of God himself."[20]

The New Testament sees the cross-resurrection complex in the Old. It is part of the early tradition that Paul received "that Christ died for our sins in accordance with the scriptures, and that he was buried, and that he was raised on the third day in accordance with the scriptures" (1 Cor 15:3–4). To the Emmaus disciples Jesus shows from "Moses and all the prophets" that it was "necessary that the Messiah should suffer these things and then enter into his glory" (Luke 24:26–27). Jesus' cry of abandonment from the cross in the words of Ps 22:1 (Matt 27:46, Mark 15:34) is just the most obvious aspect of the use of that psalm on which the whole passion narrative can be seen as patterned.[21] The evangelists state that several events of the passion happened in fulfillment of the Scriptures (e.g., Zech 12:10 and John 19:37), and Acts 8:26–40 sees Jesus as the suffering servant of Isa 52:13–53:12.

Events in Israel's history, and especially the Passover and Exodus, were connected with Jesus' death and resurrection. This is not surprising in view of the fact that the Exodus is the fundamental event of salvation and liberation in which God created Israel as a people (Exod 19:4–6). References and allusions to it fill the Old Testament, as the death and resurrection of Christ permeate the New. The passion narratives are related to Passover first because the death and resurrection of Jesus took place at Passover time. The fact that the Last Supper is a Passover meal in the Synoptics while in John the festival seems to begin the next evening[22] (so that the Passover lambs are being slaughtered in the temple while Jesus is dying on the cross) shows that the evangelists could express in different ways the idea that "our paschal lamb, Christ, has been sacrificed" (1 Cor 5:7). Luke's description of the transfiguration, where Moses and Elijah speak with Jesus "of his departure *[exodon],* which he was about to accomplish at Jerusalem" (Luke 9:31), may be intended to relate what will happen with Jesus to the *exodos* of Israel through the waters of death to freedom.

Thus there are several ways in which the Exodus tradition can be used to describe the passion. But we can also look at the relationship in the other direction and see the Exodus as having a cross-resurrection pattern. By bringing a group of oppressed and dispirited slaves (Exod 6:9) out of Egypt through the sea, God gave life to a dead people.[23] This theme has frequently been emphasized by Latin American liberation theologians.[24]

Centuries later Israel had to experience death again. The destruction of the nation of Judah and the cult of YHWH by the Babylonians seemed total, with the Davidic monarchy ended, the Temple burned, and political and religious leaders killed or taken into exile. By the religious standards of the time the God of Israel had been defeated. He had not been able to defend his people and cult. The disaster had cosmic scope: As it approached, Jeremiah (4:23–26) saw the return of the "waste and void" *(thohu wabhohu)* of primordial earth (cf. Gen 1:2).

It was not just the Babylonian armies that had destroyed Jerusalem but, the writer of Lamentations said, *God* who had done that:

> The Lord has destroyed without mercy all the dwellings
>   of Jacob;
> in his wrath he has broken down the strongholds of
>   daughter Judah;
> he has brought down to the ground in dishonor the
>   kingdom and its rulers. (Lam 2:2)

James Sanders has provocatively described the radical message proclaimed by prophets such as Jeremiah and Ezekiel, and the contrast between that message and the words of their contemporaries, the ones we now call false prophets.

> For the prophets were true monotheists, and nothing they said so stressed their monotheism as the idea that God was free enough of his chosen people to transform them in the crucible of destitution into a community whose members could themselves be free of every institution which in his providence he might give them. Their real hope, according to these prophets, lay in the God who had given them their existence in the first place, in his giving it to them again. Normal folk, in their right minds, know that hope is in having things turn out the way they think they should—by maintaining their view of life without let, threat, or hindrance. And normal folk believe in a god who will simply make things turn out that way. For them it is not a question of what God ought to do, that is clear: he will do what we know is right for him to do, if we simply trust and obey. Nobody in his right mind could possibly believe that God would want us to die in order to give us life again, or to take away the old institutions he first gave us in order to give us new ones.[25]

But the story of the exile did not end simply with death. As Ezekiel's vision of the dry bones foreshadows, it is also a story of resurrection (Ezek 37:1–14). Here again is the pattern of the cross in the promise that the Spirit of God will give life to a community from whom all signs of life had departed. The God who brought Israel out of Egypt will bring them home again in a new Exodus even greater than the escape from Pharaoh's armies (Isa 43:16–21). YHWH's power is not limited to a particular land or to specific religious or political conditions. Now the universal scope of Israel's faith becomes clear. The God who promises restoration to the exiles is the God who created the entire universe (Isa 40:25–26, 44:24).

Israel experienced God's work as salvation and as its own creation in the Exodus,[26] and the first creation account of Genesis (1:1–2:4a) was probably written against this background of the Babylonian exile. In the context of the New Testament, this account of the creation of the universe is also illumined by Christ's cross and resurrection. As Dietrich Bonhoeffer put it:

[T]he God of creation, of the utter beginning, is the God of the resurrection. The world exists from the beginning in the sign of the resurrection of Christ from the dead. Indeed it is because we know of the resurrection that we know of God's creation in the beginning, of God's creating out of nothing. The dead Jesus Christ of Good Friday and the resurrected κύριος of Easter Sunday—that is creation out of nothing, creation from the beginning. The fact that Christ was dead did not provide the possibility of his resurrection but its impossibility; it was nothing itself, it was the nihil negativum. There is absolutely no transition, no continuum between the dead Christ and the resurrected Christ, but the freedom of God that in the beginning created God's work out of nothing. Were it possible to intensify the nihil negativum even more, we would have to say here, in connection with the resurrection, that with the death of Christ on the Cross the nihil negativum broke its way into God's own being.— O great desolation! God, yes God, is dead.—Yet the one who is the beginning lives, destroys the nothing, and in his resurrection creates the new creation. By his resurrection we know about the creation.[27]

Second Maccabees 7:28 is the first explicit statement in the biblical tradition of the idea of creation out of nothing. It is not a philosophical thesis but part of an exhortation to martyrdom put in the mouth of a Jewish mother, who will herself be put to death, encouraging her last son to follow his brothers in undergoing torture and death rather than apostatize: "I beg you, my child, to look at the heaven and the earth and see everything that is in them, and recognize that God did not make them out of things that existed. And in the same way the human race came into being. Do not fear this butcher, but prove worthy of your brothers. Accept death, so that in God's mercy I may get you back again along with your brothers" (2 Macc 7:28–29). The God who gives the hope of resurrection is the one who created the universe out of nothing.

The New Testament's understanding of Jesus' death and resurrection was influenced by ideas about God's final vindication of the righteous, which developed in connection with the Maccabean martyrs. (Compare, for example, Matt 27:43 with Wis 2:17–20.) But the passion of Christ goes deeper. On the one hand, there is a sense in which Jesus did not die as a righteous sufferer but as a lawbreaker, one made to be sin (2 Cor 5:21). On the other hand, he is not simply a human martyr. It is one who had "the form of God" who accepted "death on a cross" (Phil 2:6, 8), and those who handed him over to death "killed the Author of life" (Acts 3:15).

The crosslike pattern of creation means that Christ crucified has cosmic significance. This comes to full expression in the Christ hymn of Col 1:15–20. The one in, and through, and for whom "all things have been created" (v. 16), "in [whom] all things hold together" (v. 17), is the crucified. "For in him all the fullness of God was pleased to dwell, and through him God was pleased to reconcile to himself all things, whether on earth or in heaven, by making peace through the blood of his cross" (Col 1:19–20).

This hymn has been the subject of considerable analysis and debate.[28] It seems that the phrases "through the blood of his cross," as well as "the church" and "from the dead" in verse 18, were added to an earlier hymn to make it more explicitly christological. This shows that the author of Colossians thought it important to emphasize that the reconciliation of "all things" to God does not happen through some mythic process but by the cross of Jesus of Nazareth. The object of this reconciliation is "all things *(ta panta)*." It is not limited to human beings but has universal scope, the same scope that is given in Eph 1:10 to God's plan for creation, "to gather up all things in him [Christ], things in heaven and things on earth."

This survey of the biblical story discloses a common pattern. Creation, the birth of Isaac, the Exodus, exile and return, the deaths of the martyrs, the justification of the ungodly, the Christian life, the hope of resurrection, and the fulfillment of God's ultimate purpose for creation all have a cruciform character. They carry the mark of power hidden in weakness, of death out of life, which is seen in the cross and resurrection of Jesus Christ. The cross is the sign of all God's work, what may be called "the trademark of God."[29]

LUTHER'S *THEOLOGIA CRUCIS*

For Luther, "theology of the cross" was more than an important theological locus or even a theme that runs throughout his theology. For him the whole of theology is to be judged in terms of the cross, and any "theology of glory" that tries to reach a knowledge of God apart from the cross is bad theology or even not real theology at all. Simply speaking, we can equate "theology of the cross" with "true theology" and "theology of glory" with "false theology."[30]

A theology must be centered on Christ crucified in order to be a theology of the cross in Luther's sense, but more is required than that. For example, an "imitation of Christ" understood as a meritorious human work that could earn salvation would be simply the expression of a self-righteous theology of glory in spite of all the "cross" language that it might use.

Luther's clearest single presentation of the theology of the cross is in theses prepared for a disputation at Heidelberg in 1518.[31] There are twenty-eight theological theses with proofs and twelve philosophical theses that are not expounded further. The theological theses contrast provocatively with conventional religion. Luther offers them as *Theologica paradoxa*,[32] and the paradoxical pairing of theses clarifies their significance. He was concerned here with the issues that were central to the Reformation—sin and salvation, law and gospel, human incapacity and God's grace. Gerhard Forde has recently given a helpful exposition of the Heidelberg theses from this standpoint.[33] Luther's focus is made clear in the first two theses: "The law of God, the most salutary doctrine of life, cannot advance man on his way to righteousness, but rather hinders him"; and "Much less can human works which are done over and over again with the aid of natural precepts, so to speak, lead to that end." The latter statement, which is explained on the basis of Rom 3:10–12, has to do with the question of how human beings can be righteous in God's sight. The corresponding positive statements are theses 25 and 26: "He is not righteous who does much, but he who, without work, believes much in Christ"; and "The law says, 'do this,' and it is never done. Grace says, 'believe in this,' and everything is already done."

Questions about the relationship between human understanding of the natural world and God's presence and activity were not Luther's concern here. The science-theology dialogue has often concentrated on matters closely related to the doctrine of creation. That is understandable, but it runs the danger of separating the dialogue from the message of salvation. At the same time, many theologians have focused almost exclusively on sin and redemption, treating creation as a mere prologue to those issues and regarding science-theology dialogue as peripheral. Both attitudes are unfortunate and hinder the fruitful interaction of theology and science. Grounding the discussion on the theology of the cross is one way of avoiding those separations. It is a central claim of the Christian faith that the one true God is both creator and redeemer, and since the Heidelberg theses address the question of knowledge of the redeeming God, they are relevant to the question of God's presence and activity in creation. But we need to remember Luther's soteriological focus and should not expect his theses to deal explicitly with questions about creation.

Theses 19 through 21 set out most clearly an understanding of how God is to be known.

19. That person does not deserve to be called a theologian who looks upon the invisible things of God as though they were clearly perceptible in those things which have actually happened [Rom. 1:20].
20. He deserves to be called a theologian, however, who comprehends the visible and manifest things of God seen through suffering and the cross.
21. A theology of glory calls evil good and good evil. A theology of the cross calls the thing what it actually is.

In thesis 19, the Latin rendered above as "those things which have actually happened" could also be translated as "what is made."[34] The wording is related to the Vulgate of Rom 1:20, "[God's] invisible nature, namely, his eternal power and deity, has been clearly perceived in the things that have been made" (RSV). Luther believed that Rom 1 taught the possibility of a natural knowledge of God. But the person who wants to understand who God is on that basis "does not deserve to be called a theologian." The proof cited for this thesis is based on the same passage from Romans: "This is apparent in the example of those who were 'theologians' and still were called fools by the Apostle in Rom. 1[:22]."[35]

We can see now why the problem of sin has to be faced in connection with science-theology issues, and why theses 19 through 21, which speak directly about the knowledge of God, need to be seen as part of Luther's whole argument.[36] The basic sin, according to Paul's argument in Romans, is the refusal to acknowledge God as the creator, and the distortion of any knowledge of God into a worship of the creature. Thus genuine knowledge of God is not possible on the basis of understanding of the natural world alone. Thesis 20 then tells us how we *can* have such genuine knowledge of God. As Luther says in his proof of this thesis, "True theology and recognition of God are in the crucified Christ."[37]

Again there is a question of translation here. The phrase "the visible and manifest things of God" is the translation of *visibilia et posteriora Dei,* which more literally means "what is visible of God, God's 'backside.'"[38] The allusion is to Exod 33:23 where, after Moses asks to see God's glory, God tells him that he will cover him with his hand while the divine glory passes by, "then I will take away my hand, and you shall see my back *[posteriora mea]*; but my face shall not be seen."

What of God is "manifest" is God's "backside." The expression sounds crude and unspiritual, and that is appropriate because it refers first of all to a man dying on a cross. As Luther explains it, "The invisible things of God are virtue, godliness, wisdom, justice, goodness, and so forth. . . . The 'back' and visible things of God are placed in opposition to the invisible, namely, his human nature, weakness, foolishness."[39] They are "weak" and "foolish" in the sense in which Paul uses the terms in 1 Cor 1. The real theologian does not avoid the cross but in and through it comprehends the *posteriora Dei* as the true revelation of God.

The twenty-first thesis distinguishes the theology of the cross from a theology of glory. The latter says that human works done without faith are good and that the cross is evil, while Luther insists that the cross is the "true theology and recognition of God" and that works done without faith are sinful. A theology of glory is deceiving and self-deceptive. The theology of the cross sees things as they are in relation to God. The weakness and suffering of the crucified reveal God to the theologian of the cross and hide God from the theologian of glory.

But Golgotha is not the only place where God is hidden. In discussing creation we will emphasize that God is continually active but unobserved in the world.[40] Natural processes can also be considered as *posteriora Dei* and are recognized as the work of the true God when viewed "through suffering and the cross." The connection is especially clear when we think of the processes involved in evolution through natural selection.

Luther saw the sufferings of the cross manifested in the lives of believers in what he called *Anfechtung,* which he experienced at different times in his life.[41] The German is difficult to translate satisfactorily in a single English word. *Anfechtungen* are temptations in the strong sense of assaults upon a person that produce doubt and anxiety. The cry of dereliction from the cross shows God's participation in this experience. People today are subject to the same temptations and assaults as those of the Bible or the sixteenth century. But there are new causes of doubt and potential despair for those who are aware of scientific and technological realities. American children during the cold war sometimes had nightmares about nuclear war. Today what they learn about threats to the environment may fill them with dread.

We might try to avoid these doubts either by refusing to accept scientific developments that challenge our beliefs or by imagining that science and technology will be able to solve all our problems. Neither response is possible if we face these issues as theologians of the cross, who call things what they actually are. Nor do we need to respond in self-delusive ways if we believe God to be present in those situations that bring us doubt and anxiety in order to destroy our idols and bring salvation.

Luther saw attempts to minimize the problem of human sin and to gain for human beings some ability to contribute to their own salvation as the primary threats to a true theology of the cross. Many examples of popular theologies of glory can be identified on the religious scene today.[42] In religion as in economics, bad money drives out good.

An important question for us is how the distinction between theologies of glory and the theology of the cross is related to our earlier discussion of natural theology. One might ask how, in particular, scholastic arguments for the existence of God such as those given by Aquinas are to be seen in the light of this distinction.

That question is not addressed directly in the Heidelberg theses. In fact, there seems to be no recorded statement of Luther that relates directly to Aquinas's doctrine of God or to his arguments for God's existence. Luther did have a good deal to say about Aquinas and his influence on the church, much of it negative, but left no comment on this particular issue.[43] He did not think that arguing for a natural knowledge of the existence of God would in itself make one a theologian of glory. (Recall his statement on Jonah 1.) But he was wary of all claims that unaided human abilities can achieve anything in relation to God, so that a claim to know *who* God is or to develop a genuine theology on the basis of a natural knowledge of God would be rejected. We do not know whether or not Luther thought that any of Aquinas's five ways were within the acceptable limits, but it is certain that attempts to know "the mind of God"[44] through science alone would have been unacceptable to him. "'For who has known the mind of the Lord so as to instruct him?' But we have the mind of Christ" (1 Cor 2:16).

Luther was especially critical of the use of Aristotelian philosophy in theology and of the scholastics for giving so much weight to Aristotle.[45] The first of the philosophical theses for the Heidelberg Disputation is, "He who wishes to philosophize by using Aristotle without danger to his soul must first become thoroughly foolish in Christ."[46] Again it is theological method that is at issue. It is probably safe to infer that Luther would not view favorably arguments for God that are based upon Aristotelian concepts, such as that of the Unmoved Mover.

The primary task set to us by the theology of the cross, however, is not deciding what the verdict of Luther might be on one or another argument. Nor is it the purely negative one of detecting theologies of glory, necessary though that is. If "true theology and recognition of God are in the crucified Christ," then the principal task of theologians in dialogue with scientists is to participate *as* theologians of the cross. We are called to discern in matters of science and technology the presence of the God who is revealed in the cross. A theology of the cross has a distinctive content as well as a distinctive method, and we now turn to that content and to theological developments that in some ways go beyond Luther.

THE CRUCIFIED GOD

The statement that Christ crucified is God's revelation could be understood in various ways. The cross might be a symbol of God's wrath or of God's love. It could mean God's judgment upon sin and the possibility of forgiveness because the crucified one has borne this judgment. Each of these ideas has elements of truth but by themselves they do not get at the full depth of the cross as revelation. It is necessary to ask who the crucified one is.

Christians very quickly began to use language about Jesus that sharpened the paradox of proclaiming "Christ crucified." The one who had died on the cross was not only the Messiah of Israel but Lord and Son of God and divine Logos. This process, which began within a few years of the crucifixion, culminated in the fourth century in the statement of the First

Council of Nicaea that Jesus Christ is "true God from true God, begotten not made, of one Being with the Father." The Jewish carpenter who was scourged by Pilate's soldiers, who had hung on the cross and cried out "My God, my God, why have you forsaken me?" (Mark 15:34), who had died and was buried, was God Incarnate. "The One who lives forever has fallen a prey to death."[47]

The Greek philosophical heritage that influenced Christianity held that the supreme being is beyond change, for what is perfect could change only for the worse and then would no longer be perfect. This makes it difficult to identify the one who died on the cross with God, and the Council of Nicaea did not state explicitly that he *did* die. Its creed says simply that he "suffered."[48] The later Nicaeo-Constantinopolitan Creed expands this to "was crucified for us under Pontius Pilate, and suffered and was buried"[49] but still does not state the fact of death unambiguously. Many English-speaking Christians today use the text of the International Consultation on Liturgical Texts, which says, "he suffered death and was buried."[50] This is better theologically and one can argue that "suffered and was buried" implies death, but the bishops at Nicaea and Constantinople did not say this clearly.

In the twentieth century voices began to be raised against the concept of a God who cannot suffer and who is immune from perishability. This has not been a purely theoretical concern, but has been motivated in part by the massive evils and suffering that came upon the world during that period. An oft-quoted passage in Elie Wiesel's *Night* tells of the hanging of a young boy at Auschwitz:

> For more than half an hour he stayed there, struggling between life and death, dying in slow agony under our eyes. And we had to look him full in the face. He was still alive when I passed in front of him. His tongue was still red, his eyes were not yet glazed.
> Behind me, I heard the same man asking:
> "Where is God now?"
> And I heard a voice within me answer him:
> "Where is He? Here He is—He is hanging here on this gallows. . . ."[51]

Somehow we are forced to think of death and God together.

Such ideas are not exclusively modern, for an unprejudiced study of the Bible and later Jewish and Christian thought makes it clear that attributing immutability and imperishability to God is not as straightforward a matter as the philosophical tradition has held.[52] There are Bible verses that speak of God as unchanging (Mal 3:6, Jas 1:17), but when the people of Nineveh turn from their sins, "God changed his mind about the calamity that he had said he would bring upon them; and he did not do it" (Jon 3:10). God is represented as saying, "My heart recoils within me; my compassion grows warm and tender" (Hos 11:8). It is only because of presuppositions that the divine nature cannot *really* change its mind or be compassionate that theologians have thought that the latter verses had to be interpreted figuratively while the former had to be understood as unqualified literal truths.

In spite of these common assumptions about divine immutability, impassibility, and imperishability, Christians have said that in some real sense God suffered and died on the cross. Early in the second century Ignatius of Antioch spoke of this as "the passion of my God,"[53] and about a hundred years later Tertullian wrote, "It is a part of the creed of Christians even to believe that God did die, and yet that He is alive for evermore."[54]

The theological tradition interpreted the claim that God is truly present in the human Jesus with the idea that two natures, divine and human, are united in the one person of the divine Word. The accompanying doctrine of communication of attributes in the personal union then allowed properties of either of the two natures to be spoken of in connection with the person of Christ. Mary could be said to be *theotokos,* "God-bearer," even though the divine nature did not have its beginning in Mary's womb. In a similar way it could be said that the crucified was "one of the Holy Trinity," even though the divine nature was not nailed to the cross.[55]

Luther used the communication of attributes in speaking about God's relationship with humanity. With a typically down-to-earth image he says:

> We Christians should know that if God is not in the scale to give it weight, we, on our side, sink to the ground. I mean it this way: if it cannot be said that God died for us, but only a man, we are lost; but if God's death and a dead God lie in the balance, his side goes down and ours goes up like a light and empty scale. Yet he can also readily go up again, or leap out of the scale! But he could not sit on the scale unless he had become a man like us, so that it could be called God's dying, God's martyrdom, God's blood, and God's death. For God in his own nature cannot die; but now that God and man are united in one person, it is called God's death when the man dies who is one substance or one person with God.[56]

"God in his own nature cannot die," but in speaking bluntly of "a dead God" Luther pushes the classical doctrine to its limits. He and the later Lutheran tradition would go beyond those limits in one way. In arguing for the omnipresence of the humanity of Christ in connection with debates about the Lord's Supper, the properties of the divine nature were said to be communicated not only to the person but also to the human nature, so that Christ's humanity was endowed with the divine majesty.[57] The presupposition of the immutability of God has often kept Lutheran theologians from saying that this communication could go in the other direction, and that the humiliation of the human nature could be conveyed to the divine. That Luther himself did not observe this limitation is noted by Marc Lienhard, who speaks of the "Dei-passianism" of some of Luther's statements.[58]

The Japanese theologian Kazoh Kitamori's *Theology of the Pain of God* was written in a nation that experienced destruction and defeat at the same time that Dietrich Bonhoeffer in a Gestapo prison was writing the reflections that I cited in the first chapter.[59] Referring especially to God's words in Jer 31:20 ("therefore my bowels are troubled for him" [KJV][60]), Kitamori argued that it is not only possible but *necessary* to speak of the pain of God. Aware that he is challenging traditional ideas, he suggests that we should speak of "pain as the Essence of God"[61] and asserts that "the cross is in no sense an external act of God, but an act within himself."[62]

Jürgen Moltmann's book *The Crucified God* argued for the need to speak of God's involvement in the cross and against the limitations that traditional theological concepts had imposed upon such speech.[63] For our purposes Jüngel's *God as the Mystery of the World* is of greater significance, for it can be considered as a detailed treatment of the basis and implications of the fragmentary comments of Bonhoeffer, which I sampled in the first chapter.[64] Jüngel's reflection on the fact that the world can be understood "though God were not given," and thus that God is in important senses not necessary, leads him to a detailed study of the concept of the death of God as a means of understanding how it is possible to speak of God in the modern world. "[W]hen we attempt to think of God as the one who communicates and expresses himself in the person Jesus, then we must always remember that this man was *crucified*, that he was killed in the name of God's law. For responsible Christian usage of the word 'God,' the Crucified One is virtually the real definition of what is meant with the word 'God.' Christian theology is therefore fundamentally the theology of the Crucified One."[65]

Language about a "death of God" is often connected with Nietzsche and seen as an attack upon Christianity from the outside. Jüngel's analysis of the philosophical development from Descartes to Nietzsche shows that this language should be understood in connection with the specifically Christian claim of the death of Christ on the cross. God did not simply cease to exist, but we can and must speak of God's unity with perishability[66] or of "death *in* God."[67] This can be elucidated only through belief in the resurrection and a trinitarian concept of God. The worldly nonnecessity of God means that God is not based on anything outside God, and thus cannot be shown to be "necessary" by any arguments that do not already begin with God. Conversely, the existence of everything else is dependent upon God, so Jüngel can conclude that "as groundless being, God is not necessary and yet more than necessary."[68]

God is not only a passive victim on the cross, nor does the Son suffer while the Father remains aloof. The Father also suffers in the separation consequent upon the "giving up" of the Son (Rom 8:32), and the being of God is maintained in the unity of the Holy Spirit.[69] In that light we must try to understand God's activity as creator in the sufferings of the world and the *Anfechtungen* of believers. The cross does not provide a straightforward logical solution to the problem of evil in the world, but it identifies the God whose actions a theodicy is supposed to "justify" as one who is struck by the evil in the world and suffers with it.

This has important implications for chiasmic cosmology, which speaks about the God "placed crosswise" in the universe, which science explores and technology controls. As Jüngel puts it:

> Based on the word of the cross, which emphatically proclaims that the one *who was raised from the dead is the Crucified One,* we answer that the being of God is first revealed as creative being in the struggle with the annihilating nothingness of nothing. This means hermeneutically that we are not to expound the word of the cross on the basis of the biblical statements about the imperishability of God, which are directed toward God the Creator. Rather, conversely, we learn how to understand who God the Creator is on the basis of the biblical statements directed toward the Crucified One, which statements force us to think God in unity with perishability. A theology of the Crucified One does not abstract itself from creation—precisely the opposite, it establishes *proper* theological talk about God the Creator. But such a theology is not to be designed on the basis of a theology of creation.[70]

We begin with the cross and then move to the creation of the universe. I will consider the significance of the theology of the crucified one for our understanding of science and technology in later chapters. One example of this is the way in which Ronald Cole-Turner and Brent Waters have given the suffering of God and death in God a place in their discussion of pastoral care for persons involved with issues of science and technology at the beginning of life.[71]

The God we seek in creation is the one whose activities bear the mark of the cross. If we keep that in mind we will be able to resist the temptation to force God into the mold of our preconceptions of the divine. God rules, gives life, and is the source of the world's rationality, but we are not to look for the work of a cosmic dictator, a fertility deity, or the ultimate philosopher. We are to seek instead the God who "is reigning from the tree,"[72] who brings life from death, and whose wisdom is the foolishness of the cross.

THE SPECIFICITY AND GENERALITY OF THE CROSS

A good deal of modern theology could be discussed under the rubric of Lessing's statement that "accidental truths of history can never become the proof of necessary truths of reason."[73] Lessing was concerned about the problem of getting general religious truths from the historical events described in the Gospels, but it is interesting that he was writing at about the same time that Hume was criticizing inductive arguments, which are common in the sciences.[74] And Hume was right that there is no strictly logical way in which we can conclude from the fact that something has happened N times that it will occur the N+1st time. We cannot with certainty derive general truths about the world from any finite set of observations.

Lessing's statement should be seen in connection with his attitude toward revelation and natural theology, which I discussed in chapter 2. Revelation that takes place in specific historical events cannot establish necessary truths of reason, and if we want religion to be an expression of necessary truths of reason, we must find them in some other way.

The cross of Christ is a historical event for which Christianity has claimed quite general significance, though not as a necessary truth of reason. It has led us to ideas about the suffering of God. But it is possible now to take those ideas as general religious truths, and to see the cross of Christ as a specific example or symbol of such suffering. The passion and death of Christ may then be considered as an important event that has given insight into general religious truth, but the suffering of God could actually be discussed without reference to that event.

Process theologies based on Alfred North Whitehead's philosophy are important examples of such a movement. They are relevant to our present concerns because they have often been used in the modern science-theology dialogue. Whitehead worked in pure and applied mathematics before turning to philosophy, and process philosophy has to be seen against the background of modern science. Biological evolution and ecology are areas in which the idea that God is in process along with the world has been seen as especially useful.[75]

Whitehead's idea that God draws the world forward by call and persuasion provides a distinctive concept of divine power. He described traditional options for conceptualizing God as the images of the divine ruler, the personification of moral energy, and an ultimate philosophical principle. His own proposal has more than a hint of a theology of the cross.

There is, however, in the Galilean origin of Christianity yet another suggestion which does not fit very well with any of the three main strands of thought. It does not emphasize the ruling Caesar, or the ruthless moralist, or the unmoved mover. It dwells upon the tender elements in the world, which slowly and in quietness operate by love; and it finds purpose in the present immediacy of a kingdom not of this world. Love neither rules, nor is it unmoved; also it is a little oblivious as to morals. It does not look to the future; for it finds its own reward in the immediate present.[76]

The importance of "the Galilean origin of Christianity" must be kept in mind in connection with Whitehead's statement a little later that "God is the great companion—the fellow-sufferer who understands."[77] These ideas become in Whitehead's hands part of a general philosophical system. A natural theology may be developed that makes use of process thought rather than traditional theistic philosophy, so that ideas suggested by the cross will play a role.[78] But this is not the same thing as giving the cross the role of a unique revelation that determines the method and content of theology. In particular, it is difficult for the trinitarian picture of God, which the cross and resurrection seem to require, to be expressed in a way that is coherent with process understandings of God.[79]

This is an instance of a general difficulty with natural theology. It is not that natural theology says something that is simply false, but that it tries to develop a general truth of which the specific truth of revelation can be seen as a special case. In doing that it distorts truth by severing it from its basis in revelation.[80] We will be speaking of the presence, activity, and suffering of the one revealed in the cross-resurrection event, but we are not free to make any statements we wish about the suffering of God in the world. They have to be evaluated in the light of the "once for all" (Heb 9:12, 26, 28) event that happened "under Pontius Pilate."

At this point we need to consider the scientific picture of the world, which we want to view in the light of the cross. Then we will turn to the question of how we are to understand the God revealed in the cross as active in the phenomena that science describes.

NOTES

1. "CRUX Sola Est Nostra Theologia," in *D. Martin Luthers Werke, Kritische Gesammtausgabe* (Weimar: Hermann Böhlau, 1892), 5:172. The capitalization is in the original.

2. Martin Hengel, *Crucifixion in the Ancient World and the Folly of the Cross.* (trans. John Bowden; Philadelphia: Fortress, 1977).

3. Ibid., xi.

4. Herbert Danby, ed., "Tractate Sanhedrin 6.1," in *The Mishnah* (Oxford: Oxford University Press, 1933), 390.

5. Hengel, *Crucifixion,* 19.

6. Bruce Schein, *Following the Way* (Minneapolis: Augsburg, 1980), appendix 11.

7. David Hume, *An Inquiry Concerning Human Understanding* (New York: C. W. Hengel, 1955), 138.

8. N. T. Wright, *The Resurrection of the Son of God* (Minneapolis: Fortress, 2003).

9. Raymond E. Brown, *The Death of the Messiah: From Gethsemane to the Grave* (2 vols.; New York: Doubleday, 1994).

10. Martin Kähler, cited in Paul J. Achtenmeier, *Mark* (Philadelphia: Fortress, 1975), 82.

11. Roy Harrisville, *The Miracle of Mark* (Minneapolis: Augsburg, 1967), 16–17.

12. Charles B. Cousar, *A Theology of the Cross: The Death of Jesus in the Pauline Letters* (Minneapolis: Fortress, 1990).

13. Ibid., chapter 1.

14. Ibid., 104.

15. Lucretius, *The Nature of the Universe* (Baltimore: Penguin, 1951), 31.

16. References are given in Gordon D. Fee, *Paul's Letter to the Philippians* (Grand Rapids, Mich.: Eerdmans, 1995), 191–229.

17. James D. G. Dunn, *Christology in the Making* (2d ed.; Grand Rapids, Mich.: Eerdmans, 1996), 114–21.

18. Fee, *Paul's Letter to the Philippians,* 197–218.

19. Ibid., 205–7.

20. Ibid., 196.

21. John H. Reumann, "Psalm 22 at the Cross,"*Interpretation* 28 (1974): 39.

22. Brown, *The Death of the Messiah,* 1350–1378.

23 The cruciform character of Israel's origins is not changed by the likelihood that the historical process was more complex than escape from Egypt and invasion of Canaan by a unified nation. Theories that the settlement was due in part to slave revolts in the Canaanite city states get support from Josh 6:22–25 and 9:3–27. But these have the same general character as the escape of a band of slaves. If Israel had arisen as the result of actions of those in positions of power, there would be discord with the biblical picture and the pattern of the passion.

24. For example, J. Severino Croatto, *Exodus* (Maryknoll, N.Y.: Orbis, 1981).

25. James A. Sanders, *Torah and Canon* (Philadelphia: Fortress, 1972), 87.

26. Gerhard von Rad, *Old Testament Theology,* (New York: Harper & Row, 1962), 1:136–39 and 175–79.

27. Dietrich Bonhoeffer, *Creation and Fall* (vol. 1 of *Dietrich Bonhoeffer Works;* trans. Douglas Stephen Bax; Minneapolis: Fortress, 1997), 34–35.

28. Eduard Lohse, *Colossians and Philemon* (Philadelphia: Fortress, 1971), 41–61.

29. George L. Murphy, *The Trademark of God: A Christian Course in Creation, Evolution, and Salvation* (Wilton, Conn.: Morehouse-Barlow, 1986).

30. Walter von Loewenich, *Luther's Theology of the Cross* (trans. Herbert J. A. Bouman; Minneapolis: Augsburg, 1976). Alister E. McGrath, *Luther's Theology of the Cross* (Cambridge, Mass.: Basil Blackwell, 1985).

31. "Heidelberg Disputation," *LW* 31:35–70. The original Latin is in *D. Martin Luthers Werke, Kritische Gesammtausgabe* (Weimar: Hermann Böhlau, 1883), 1:353–74.

32. *LW* 39:39.

33. Gerhard O. Forde, *On Being a Theologian of the Cross: Reflections on Luther's Heidelberg Disputation, 1518* (Grand Rapids, Mich.: Eerdmans, 1997).

34. John Dillenberger, ed., *Martin Luther: Selections from His Writings* (Garden City, N.Y.: Doubleday, 1961), 502. Forde, *On Being a Theologian of the Cross*, 72.

35. *LW* 31:52.

36. Forde, *On Being a Theologian of the Cross*, 69–70.

37. *LW* 31:53.

38. Dillenberger, *Martin Luther*, 502.

39. *LW* 31:52.

40. In his argument for thesis 20, Luther cites Isa 45:15, which Pascal had in mind in the statement that was quoted in the last chapter.

41. McGrath, *Luther's Theology of the Cross*, 169–75.

42. Daniel Erlander, *Baptized We Live* (Chelan, Wash.: Holden Village, 1981), 24.

43. Denis R. Janz, *Luther on Thomas Aquinas* (Stuttgart: Franz Steiner Verlag Wiesbaden GMBH, 1989).

44. For example, Paul Davies, *The Mind of God* (New York: Simon & Schuster, 1992).

45. Janz, *Luther on Thomas Aquinas*, 17–24.

46. *LW* 31:41–42.

47. *CD* 4:1:176.

48. J. N. D. Kelly, *Early Christian Creeds* (3d ed.; London: Longman, 1972), 216.

49. Ibid., 297.

50. The quoted passages from the Nicene Creed are from the *Lutheran Book of Worship* (Minneapolis: Augsburg, 1978), 64.

51. Elie Wiesel, *Night* (New York: Bantam, 1982), 62.

52. See, for example, Joseph M. Hallman, *The Descent of God* (Minneapolis: Fortress, 1991).

53. "The Epistle of Ignatius to the Romans," *ANF* 1:76.

54. Tertullian, "The Five Books against Marcion," *ANF* 3:309.

55. "The Fifth Ecumenical Council," *NPNF* 2:14:314.

56. "On the Councils and the Church," *LW* 41:103–4.

57. Martin Chemnitz, *The Two Natures in Christ* (St. Louis: Concordia, 1971).

58. Marc Lienhard, *Luther: Witness to Jesus Christ* (Minneapolis: Augsburg, 1982), 171. He says here that Lutheran theologians "recoil before the idea of the *genus tapeinoticum,* which envisages the communication of the sufferings of the humanity to the divinity— an idea which was, however, already there in Luther. . . ."

59. Kazoh Kitamori, *Theology of the Pain of God* (Richmond, Va.: John Knox, 1965).

60. Ibid., 151–67.

61. Ibid., 44–57.

62. Ibid., 45.

63. Jürgen Moltmann, *The Crucified God: The Cross of Christ as the Foundation and Criticism of Christian Theology* (trans. R. A. Wilson and John Bowden; New York: Harper & Row, 1974).

64. Eberhard Jüngel, *God as the Mystery of the World: On the Foundation of the Theology of the Crucified One in the Dispute between Theism and Atheism* (trans. Darrell L. Guder; Grand Rapids, Mich.: Eerdmans, 1983).

65. Ibid., 13.

66. Ibid., 184–225.

67. Moltmann, *The Crucified God*, 207.

68. Jüngel, *God as the Mystery of the World*, 33.

69. Moltmann, *The Crucified God*, 235–49.

70. Jüngel, *God as the Mystery of the World*, 218.

71. Ronald Cole-Turner and Brent Waters, *Pastoral Genetics: Theology and Care at the Beginning of Life* (Cleveland, Ohio: Pilgrim, 1996), especially chapter 6.

72. Hymn #162, verse 2, in *The Hymnal 1982* (New York: The Church Hymnal Corporation, 1985). This is a translation of Venantius Fortunatus's *Vexilla Regis Prodeunt.*

73. Gotthold Ephraim Lessing, "On the Proof of the Spirit and of Power," in *Lessing's Theological Writings* (Stanford, Calif.: Stanford University, 1957), 53.

74. David Hume, "An Enquiry Concerning Human Understanding," in *Enquiries Concerning Human Understanding and Concerning the Principles of Morals* (3d ed.; Oxford: Clarendon, 1975), 32–39.

75. For example, Ian G. Barbour, *Religion and Science: Historical and Contemporary Issues* (San Francisco: HarperCollins, 1993), chapters 11 and 12.

76. Alfred North Whitehead, *Process and Reality* (New York: Free Press, 1978), 343.

77. Ibid., 351.

78. For example, John B. Cobb Jr., *A Christian Natural Theology* (Philadelphia: Westminster, 1965). Cobb recognizes the need for theology to be formulated in connection with a community of faith so that his natural theology has elements of what I have called the dependent type.

79. Ted Peters, *God as Trinity: Relationality and Temporality in the Divine Life* (Louisville, Ky.: Westminster/John Knox, 1993), 114–22.

80. Cf. Eberhard Jüngel, "Gott—um seiner selbst willen interessant: Plädoyer für eine natürlichere Theologie," in *Entsprechungen: Gott—Wahrheit—Mensch* (Munich: Chr. Kaiser Verlag, 1980), 194.

$\cdot\,4\,\cdot$

THE SCIENTIFIC PICTURE
OF THE WORLD

A MECHANICAL UNIVERSE

If we are to view the natural world in the light of the cross, we need to know about the picture of the world that science has developed. This chapter will sketch a few important aspects of the way scientists understand the universe.

The motions of the heavenly bodies gave humanity some of its first clues toward an orderly understanding of the world. But science did not succeed by first speculating about the entire universe. Attempts to understand the cosmos began in our local neighborhood of space and time, and the knowledge gained there has gradually been extrapolated to larger regions.[1]

Copernicus and Kepler provided a model of the solar system in which the planets travel around the sun in elliptical orbits. Telescopic astronomy, which began with Galileo, made possible a great deal of new knowledge of the solar system and the stars. Stellar distances were first measured in the nineteenth century by using the earth's orbit as a baseline to triangulate positions of nearby stars. The vastness of interstellar space is shown by the use of the light-year, the distance light travels in one year, to describe it. Sirius, one of the nearest stars, is about nine light-years away, while it takes only eight minutes for light to reach us from the sun.

In the 1660s Newton was able to explain the motions of the planets and many other phenomena with mathematical laws of motion and gravitation. These laws are expressed in terms of the position and momentum (mass multiplied by velocity) of each body in a system. If we know these quantities at a given instant and the forces that are acting, the laws make it possible in principle to calculate how the state of the system will change with time. The implications of this were put in classic form by Laplace:

> Given for one instant an intelligence which could comprehend all the forces by which nature is animated and the respective situation of the beings who compose it—an intelligence sufficiently vast to submit these data to analysis—it would embrace in the same formula the movements of the greatest bodies of the universe and those of the lightest atom; for it, nothing would be uncertain and the future, as the past, would be present to its eyes.[2]

"Laplacian determinism" looked at the whole universe as a vast machine. Chaos theory has now shown that that picture of the world is oversimplified, for we can never know the initial positions and motions of all the bodies in a system with complete accuracy.[3] In many systems a tiny uncertainty in knowledge of the initial conditions grows rapidly to a large uncertainty in the future state of the system. The earth's weather systems are of this type. We will never be able to forecast their behavior with the accuracy of eclipse predictions because it is not possible to have sufficiently detailed knowledge of initial weather conditions.

The laws of motion can be stated in terms of energy. A moving body can make things happen (for example, move another body when the two collide), and this ability is quantified by associating "kinetic energy" with it. There is also energy of interaction between bodies. If it is known how the total energy depends on the positions and momenta of the bodies in the system, and if the initial conditions are known, the future state of the system can be calculated.

All mechanical systems on Earth slow down if left to themselves, and thus seem to lose energy. But this loss is associated with the generation of heat through friction, and the amount of heat produced from a given amount of mechanical energy is always the same. This information led to the idea that heat is a form of energy, and to the law of conservation of energy, or the first law of thermodynamics: The total energy in a closed system always remains the same.

The amount of energy that comes out of an engine must be the same as the amount that went in, but the fraction of input converted to useful work is never 100 percent because some heat is exhausted or dissipated by friction. The total energy of any closed system is constant, but the amount available for useful work never increases and generally decreases. This is the second law of thermodynamics. It means that there is an "arrow of time," for we can identify the direction from past to future as the direction in which things run down.

The second law is sometimes described as the law of increasing disorder, or entropy, because it expresses a tendency of the molecules in a system to move from highly ordered states to less orderly ones. But "disorderly" is not synonymous with "lawless." When a system contains huge numbers of molecules, we can apply the laws of mechanics in a statistical fashion and calculate the behavior of the whole system by processes of averaging.

FIELDS, WAVES, AND RELATIVITY

Attempts to explain electricity and magnetism in mechanical terms were unconvincing, but Michael Faraday had an intuitive way of describing these phenomena. He thought of "lines of force" or a *field,* which filled space and exerted forces on electric charges and currents. James Clerk Maxwell then wrote equations describing the behavior of electric and magnetic fields as parts of a single entity, the electromagnetic field. Maxwell's equations have solutions that describe waves traveling through empty space at a speed of approximately 300,000 kilometers per second (denoted by the symbol c). And that is just the measured speed of light in vacuum!

Nineteenth-century physicists thought of these electromagnetic waves as oscillations in a material medium, the "aether." Light would have speed c relative to the aether, but someone moving through the aether would measure a different speed. This is a result of the commonsense way of combining velocities, but careful optical tests to detect the earth's motion through the aether were unsuccessful. There was a contradiction between Maxwell's theory and the concepts of space and time that underlie Newton's mechanics.

Albert Einstein realized that commonsense ideas of time and space had to be changed.[4] In 1905 he accomplished this with two postulates. First, all the laws of physics are the same for all observers in uniform motion with respect to one another. And second, the speed of light in a vacuum is the same for all such observers.

The second postulate seems absurd: If one observer sees a beam of light moving at speed c, how could another observer, moving relative to the first in the same direction, see it moving with the same speed? Einstein suggested that traditional ideas about space and time be given up and new ones adopted. Like all theories, Einstein's must be evaluated by its consequences, not by whether or not it is in accord with our preconceptions.

And Einstein's theory has many consequences that agree with experiment. Moving clocks run slow, mass and energy are equivalent ($E = mc^2$), and Newton's laws of motion must be modified. These effects are imperceptible when speeds are much less than c, but differences between Einstein's physics and Newton's become marked at high velocities. Hermann Minkowski introduced, in place of Newton's absolute three-dimensional space and absolute time, a unified four-dimensional space-time that is the natural setting for Einstein's theory.

This theory is called "special relativity" because it applies only to observers moving with uniform velocity and does not incorporate gravitation. Einstein overcame both limitations in his *general* theory by using non-Euclidean geometry. Massive bodies curve space-time, changing the geometry of space and rates of clocks. Particles do not travel along straight lines because there are generally no straight lines in curved space. General relativity suggests possibilities for the structure and evolution of the universe, which I will consider in later chapters.

QUANTUM THEORY AND THE NATURE OF MATTER

A description of matter on the atomic scale required a new type of mechanics, which began with the study of radiation emitted by heated objects.[5] Attempts to understand this behavior gave the ridiculous result that the energy radiated every second by a heated object should be infinite! In 1900, Max Planck removed this absurdity by suggesting that atoms could emit or absorb energy only in discrete amounts, or *quanta*. Einstein's proposal that light is actually *composed* of particle-like quanta, or photons, was confirmed by the observation that interactions between x-rays and subatomic particles are in some ways similar to collisions between two objects like billiard balls. Light thus has a twofold character, behaving like a stream of particles in some situations and like a wave in others. This duality was extended by de Broglie's suggestion that particles such as electrons also displayed wavelike properties.

The introduction of quanta challenged the belief that "nature does not make jumps." Niels Bohr invoked discontinuous changes to explain the interaction of radiation with atoms and the term "quantum jump" entered the popular vocabulary. Because these jumps are very small, the "jerkiness" of quantum processes is imperceptible at the level of everyday phenomena.

Two equivalent mathematical versions of quantum mechanics were developed in the 1920s. Schrödinger developed an equation for the waves associated with physical systems, and Heisenberg found rules that look like Newton's laws but in which quantities such as energy are represented by "q numbers," which do not obey all the familiar rules of algebra. Heisenberg's analysis of the process of observation revealed basic limitations on what we can know. In order to observe an electron's position, photons must interact with it, and a collision with a photon will change the electron's momentum so that we won't know how it is moving. If we avoid this problem by using "soft" photons with negligible momentum, the image of the electron will be blurred and its position will be uncertain. The uncertainties of momentum and position cannot both be reduced to zero. This uncertainty principle cuts down Laplacian determinism at the roots. We can't predict the future state of a system precisely because we can't know its present state precisely.

What then can we know? The wave that is the solution of Schrödinger's equation gives probabilities for various positions or motions. Where the wave's intensity is large, there is a high probability of finding a particle, and where the intensity is zero, there is no chance of observing it. Quantum mechanics is a fundamentally statistical theory.

Atomic theories, associated in antiquity with materialism and atheism, were revived by chemists in the nineteenth century, and the chemical elements were correlated with different atoms, those of each element having the same properties. Similarities among the groups of elements that are enshrined in Mendeleev's periodic table imply similarities between their atoms. This table originally had some blank spaces where elements had not yet been discovered, and the filling of these spaces indicated that the table represented real regularities in nature.

But atoms are not literally *atomos,* "uncuttable," and are not the ultimate building blocks of matter. The electron, much smaller in mass than the lightest atom, hydrogen, was discovered at about the same time that it was found that heavy atoms such as uranium undergo radioactive decay and pass through a series of changes. Quantum mechanics yields a model of the atom in which negatively charged electrons are pictured as a cloud of probability around a nucleus composed of more massive positively charged protons and electrically neutral neutrons.

New insights were gained when Dirac combined relativity and quantum theory. All particles have antiparticles and the two can annihilate one another if they collide. The energy they had by virtue of Einstein's mass-energy relation is converted into radiation. The reverse of this process, pair production, also occurs. Even if there is not enough energy to create real pairs, the uncertainty principle allows them to come into being for very short times. Calculations must take into account the probability of "virtual pairs" at any point of space. This sounds like the field concept, and phenomena arising because of these particles are best dealt with by quantum field theory, in which particles are described as excitations of fields.

The use of energetic particles as probes led to ever-deeper penetration into the structure of matter. Energy is released if heavy atomic nuclei are split into smaller fragments (fission) or light nuclei come together to form a heavier one (fusion). Generation of energy and formation of elements such as carbon and oxygen by stars, and thus the existence of life, depend on fusion processes in which nuclei combine at high temperatures.

Protons, neutrons, and other massive particles are composed of quarks, which never appear in isolation but only in combination with other quarks. Forces between particles are due to the exchange of other particles. Electromagnetic forces between charges are transmitted by photons, while the weak interaction, responsible for some radioactive decays, and the strong force holding quarks together are carried by massive particles. The electromagnetic and weak forces are now understood as aspects of an "electroweak" interaction. There are attempts to develop a "grand unified theory" that includes the strong force, and even to include gravity with the other interactions in a single description. But physicists are still some distance from a successful "theory of everything."[6]

THE PHENOMENA OF LIFE

In some complex systems life arises not because of the addition of a new substance but because of the system's organization.[7] Though a great deal can be learned about living things by studying the chemicals of which they are made, biology is not just chemistry. "Organic chemistry" is the study of the compounds of carbon, which is essential for life as we know it because of its ability to form complex molecules. It used to be thought that organic substances could be made only by living things, but in 1828 Wöhler showed that urea, an organic compound found in urine, could be formed from an inorganic one, ammonium cyanate, simply by heating it.

The simplest way to define "life" is to list some properties of living things. First, living systems are complex, with parts in relationship with one another. Cells contain many types of molecules and multicellular organisms are made up of cells with differing structures and functions.

Second, living systems involve flows of energy and matter. Green plants get energy from the sun and store it in the chemical bonds of glucose, which is formed from water and carbon dioxide with the release of oxygen by the process of photosynthesis. This energy is then available for the functions of the plant, and if it is eaten by an animal it becomes available to that organism. Any organism must get rid of waste materials and heat, and will run down and eventually die. But dissipation of energy does not always lead immediately to decay. Recent work in thermodynamics has found "dissipative structures" in fluids whose order is *maintained* by such dissipation,[8] and living systems may be complex dissipative structures.

A third feature of life is reproduction, the ability to give rise to offspring similar to, but not identical to, the original organism. Offspring are not identical to their parents, and there has been a long history of evolutionary development of life forms in which variations have been as important as the transmission of features.

Proteins are important organic structural elements as well as catalysts that make many of the chemical processes of life possible. They are constructed by connecting together amino acids, of which there are about twenty varieties, in long chains. A vast number of such chains is possible, and many different proteins play roles in biological processes. Proteins may be folded into three-dimensional shapes, which play a critical role in their abilities to attach to other molecules and catalyze chemical reactions.

For our cells to store energy in the chemical bonds of organic compounds and then use it for the things the organism needs to do, there must be metabolic processes that get the energy from other molecules.[9] Nutrients undergo a complex series of chemical reactions that release energy, with proteins acting as catalysts. By-products are water and carbon dioxide, which plants need in turn for photosynthesis to make glucose and oxygen and continue the cycle.

Energy must be made available for processes such as muscular contraction and cell division, but energy is also needed to combine amino acids to make the proteins that are needed in order for the metabolic cycle itself to run. The cellular factory has to keep rebuilding its own machinery! These processes are so intricate that there must be directions for them. Cells have information that tells them how to construct various proteins so that all these processes can take place, and organisms must be able to pass this information on to their offspring at a molecular level. This brings us to the topic of genetics.

Critical steps toward understanding heredity were made in the nineteenth century by the monk Gregor Mendel. He studied properties of the pea plant, such as seed color and shape, and found that the inheritance of these properties could be explained with a simple model in which there is a gene for each trait. Bodies called chromosomes in the nuclei of cells become visible under the microscope during cell division, and their behavior during cell division suggests that they are associated with the theoretical genes.

Chromosomes contain deoxyribose nucleic acid, DNA, whose double helix structure was elucidated by James Watson and Francis Crick.[10] Each strand of the double helix contains many molecules of the four bases, adenine, guanine, cytosine, and thymine, which bond to one another in specific ways. Thus the sequence of bases on one strand uniquely specifies the sequence on the other. When the strands separate, each can be matched with a new partner identical to its original one. The base sequence carries information for the construction of proteins. Each "codon" of three bases specifies an amino acid or an instruction such as "start" or "stop." There is also machinery using single-stranded RNA (ribonucleic acid) to read the instructions and carry them out.

Genes do not code directly for properties such as intelligence, but tell cells what proteins to manufacture. In some cases it is easy to see how this results in large-scale properties. Eye color is due to pigment, and DNA can code for production of specific pigments. But other situations are not so simple.

The transfer of genetic information is a one-way process from DNA to protein, genes to body, and not the other way. This is important for the mechanism of evolution because it means that to change the information that will be passed on to the offspring of an organism it is necessary to modify the genetic material and not merely the body of the parent.

There is a tremendous variety of living things. Viruses, on the borderline between life and nonlife, are simply nucleic acid cores surrounded by protein coats. They have no metabolic machinery of their own, but invade cells and take over their machinery to make new viruses according to their genetic blueprints, generally destroying the cell in the process.

Cells are collections of molecules needed for metabolism and heredity surrounded by a membrane that allows material to pass back and forth. The simplest ones, such as blue-green algae, are prokaryotes, little bags of relatively undifferentiated material. Fossil remains of prokaryotic cells 3.5 billion years old have been found. Eukaryotes, in contrast, have nuclei in which genetic material is contained. Their earliest traces date back about 1 billion years. More complex multicellular organisms are built up of eukaryotic cells.

The classification scheme for living things that is used today originated with Linnaeus in the eighteenth century. Organisms are grouped into kingdoms and then into phyla, classes, orders, families, genera, and species. The scientific name of an organism is the Latin name of the genus with an adjective denoting the species. *Homo sapiens,* "wise human," is the only surviving species of the genus *Homo.*

For our purposes the most important category is the species, a set of organisms that can breed among themselves, but not with those outside the set, to produce fertile offspring. New species develop from old, often by some process of divergence produced, for example, by geographic isolation. It may be impossible to pinpoint the precise generation when two species have come into being in place of one, but there is no doubt that in the overall picture new species *have* arisen.

THE HISTORY OF THE EARTH AND LIFE

Vertical sections cut into the earth show that rocks are often in distinctive layers, or strata. We expect that, other things being equal, the upper strata will contain newer fossils and that we will find older remains as we dig deeper. But the earth's surface is always being eroded, and parts of it move with respect to one another. There is no place on Earth where a complete sequence of strata from the formation of the planet to the present exists. But the sequence can be reconstructed by seeing where parts of it overlap and correlating those in different places. Strata at different locations can be matched to construct a theoretical "geologic column."

When people believed that the Bible mandated an age for the earth on the order of six thousand years, it could be thought that the world was created essentially as we find it. Some of its features might be the result of the Noachian flood or of a series of such worldwide disasters. But while catastrophic events like volcanoes and asteroid impacts have played roles in the history of the earth, the general features of strata are the result of relatively slow processes such as erosion, the building up of sediments on sea bottoms, and slow motions in the earth's crust. The existence of fossils, many of organisms no longer alive today, shows that life-forms inhabiting the planet have changed over time. Both the earth and living things have evolved.

The first precise values for the age of the earth came with the discovery of radioactivity, which changes the composition of minerals over time. If we make reasonable assumptions about the initial makeup of a sample and know its present composition and the rates at which the radioactive elements decay, we can find the sample's age. This method, used with many different samples, gives an age of about 4.5 billion years for the earth.

Evidence was emerging in Linnaeus's time that many species that used to live on Earth are now extinct. I will discuss the theological impact of this discovery later, but for now I will consider what happens to our scientific picture when we extend it to include the organisms of the past.[11]

The bodies of most plants and animals are dispersed or decay soon after death, but sometimes they leave molds in the rock that forms around them or parts are replaced by minerals. These fossils then provide a record of the organism. Some species have left no traces and some fossils have been destroyed or are never found. The fossil record is like a chance selection of sentences from a novel, and paleontologists have to reconstruct the story.

Strata older than about 600 million years contain remains of unicellular life-forms and a few other simple organisms. The Cambrian period, from about 600 to 500 million years ago, is rich in invertebrates. Life appeared on land some 440 million years ago, and extensive forests of around 300 million years ago left today's coal deposits. Dinosaurs appeared about 220 million years ago and dominated the land for more than 150 million years. Mammals spread and diversified rapidly after the extinction of the dinosaurs. The first members of the genus *Homo* came on the scene perhaps 3 million years ago. This suggests that a radical process of evolution has been taking place. The same type of thing can be seen on smaller time scales in situations in which an abundant and undisturbed sequence of fossils can be found.[12]

There is other evidence to support evolution. The geographic distributions of *living* plants and animals are significant. Similarities in organisms, such as the bones in a human arm, a whale's flipper, and the wing of a bird, suggest that an ancestral structure has developed in different ways. Even more impressive relationships are seen on the molecular level. Human hemoglobin is very similar to that of the great apes, and virtually all organisms use the same genetic code that relates DNA to amino acids. This suggests common ancestry.

Evolution had been discussed before Charles Darwin and Alfred Russel Wallace, but it was with their independently developed theories of evolution through natural selection that the idea took hold. The full title of Darwin's 1859 book describes his theory: *On the Origin of Species by Means of Natural Selection, or the Preservation of Favored Races in the Struggle for Life.*[13] Major changes have taken place in evolutionary theory since then, but the basic idea continues to be properly defined natural selection, which I sketched in chapter 1.

Natural selection should not be thought of as involving any kind of absolute fitness or superiority of surviving organisms. It favors populations that are well suited for survival and reproduction in a particular environment, but they may be poorly suited if the environment changes. The catastrophic environmental effects of an asteroid impact some 65 million years ago apparently led to the demise of the dinosaurs.

Evolutionary theory itself continues to change. It has been suggested that evolution occurs in brief bursts followed by longer periods of relative constancy of species, rather than by slow continuous change.[14] It will not be surprising if some challenges are substantiated, for the complexity of life is such that there may be no single explanation that describes its development adequately throughout the whole biosphere and all of earth's history.

The most serious difficulty with evolutionary theory is the lack of understanding of how life began—the process of chemical evolution. I will consider this problem in chapter 8.

ECOLOGY

The whole biosphere, the network of living things that inhabit the narrow zone of water, land, and air near the earth's surface and their supporting media, is the subject of ecology. We can distinguish different types of large-scale environments, such as tropical rainforests or the oceans, with their typical life-forms. On a smaller scale we study individual ecosystems, such as a forest region in the Temperate Zone with distinctive types of plants and animals. Each species, such as a woodpecker, which eats insect grubs from certain trees, has an ecological niche within the system, and what happens to one species affects the whole.

Two species suited for the same niche will be in competition, and this competition gives a major thrust to evolution through natural selection. The available niches and the sizes of populations they can support provide the filter for evolution. Conversely, empty niches or the development of new ones through environmental change provide opportunities for species whose variations may move them toward those niches.

Ecosystems as well as individuals change over time. A forest does not come into being instantaneously. Small plants first move into an area of sparse or poor soil and their growth and death builds up soil and slowly creates niches that larger plants can occupy. With these plants come insects and other animal life to fill niches made available for them. Eventually a steady state may be reached. But there may be slow changes in global climate or sudden changes, such as a forest fire, that alter the whole environment, closing some niches and opening others.

Or *Homo sapiens* may come on the scene, clearing the forest or putting out fires to preserve it. The evolution of this intelligent species with its technology has given it the ability to inhabit the entire earth and even space beyond it, far past the bounds of other species' ecological niches. With that ability goes the capacity for profound impacts on other species, ecosystems, and the whole biosphere. The related ethical issues will be discussed in chapter 11.

This seems an appropriate point at which to conclude my sketch of the natural sciences and to broaden the view to a wider intellectual and spiritual ecology. In the next chapter, I will be reflecting on scientific and theological methods, and I will then move on to look at the scientific understanding of the world in the context of a theology of the crucified.

NOTES

1. Albert Einstein and Leopold Infeld, *The Evolution of Physics* (New York: Simon & Schuster, 1966).

2. Shmuel Sambursky, ed., *Physical Thought from the Presocratics to the Quantum Physicists* (New York: Pica, 1975), 356.

3. James Gleick, *Chaos* (New York: Penguin, 1988).

4. Albert Einstein, *Relativity* (New York: Crown, 1971).

5. J. C. Polkinghorne, *The Quantum World* (Princeton, N.J.: Princeton University Press, 1989).

6. John D. Barrow, *Theories of Everything* (Oxford: Clarendon, 1989).

7. Mahlon Hoagland, Bert Dodson, and Judith Hauck, *Exploring the Way Life Works* (Sudbury, Mass.: Jones and Barlett, 2001).

8. Ilya Prigogine, *From Being to Becoming* (New York: W. H. Freeman, 1980).

9. Isaac Asimov, *Life and Energy* (New York: Bantam, 1962).

10. James D. Watson, *The Double Helix* (New York: Atheneum, 1968).

11. N. Gary Lane, *Life of the Past* (2d ed.; Columbus, Ohio: Charles E. Merrill, 1986).

12. For example, P. C. Williamson, "Palaeontological Documentation of Speciation in Cenozoic Molluscs from Turkana Basin," *Nature* 293 (October 8, 1981): 437.

13. Charles Darwin, *On the Origin of Species by Natural Selection* (London: J. W. Dent & Sons, 1972). For Wallace's contribution see, for example, Michael Shermer, *In Darwin's Shadow: The Life and Science of Alfred Russel Wallace* (New York: Oxford University Press, 2002).

14. N. Eldredge and S. J. Gould, "Puncuated Equilibria: The Tempo and Mode of Evolution Reconsidered," in T. J. M. Schopf, ed., *Models in Paleobiology* (San Francisco: Freeman, Cooper & Co., 1972), 82–115.

· 5 ·

WHAT CAN WE KNOW
ABOUT THE WORLD?

❧

PHILOSOPHY, SCIENCE, AND THEOLOGY

In the previous chapter scientific knowledge of the world was sketched from the standpoint of a rather naive realism. Fields, quarks, genes, and other entities were described as if they were objects like stones or cats whose existence and properties are obvious to anyone who cares to look at them carefully. It might seem better to have begun with discussions of the philosophy of science and scientific method in order to present a more sophisticated view, but the choice to begin with the current state and content of science was deliberate.

Scientists do not follow a single recipe-like "scientific method." Einstein, for example, described the two basic components of natural science, observation and reason. On the one hand, "Pure logical thinking cannot yield us any knowledge of the empirical world; all knowledge of reality starts from experience and ends in it. Propositions arrived at by purely logical means are completely empty as regards reality." On the other hand, "Experience may suggest the appropriate mathematical concepts, but they most certainly cannot be deduced from it. Experience remains, of course, the sole criterion of the physical utility of a mathematical construction. But the creative principle resides in mathematics. In a certain sense, therefore, I hold it true that pure thought can grasp reality, as the ancients dreamed."[1] Some sciences are not as mathematical as Einstein's but "experience" and "pure thought" are necessary components of all science. The order in which they come into play will vary, depending on the phenomena and the inclinations of the scientists studying them.

In chapter 2, I mentioned Kekulé's discovery of the benzene ring: After pondering on the data about this substance and trying to solve the problem of its structure, the answer came to him in a dream. The discovery began with observation and, as the chemist himself emphasized in an account of his discovery, had to be tested by experience: "Let us learn to dream, gentlemen . . . then perhaps we shall find the truth . . . but let us beware of publishing our dreams before they have been put to the proof by the waking understanding."[2]

Few scientists operate in accord with some explicitly formulated philosophy of science. The comments of Claude Bernard, originally published in 1865, are worth noting:

> In a word, if men of science are useful to philosophers, and philosophers to men of science, men of science remain free, none the less, and masters in their own house; as for myself, I think that men of science achieve their discoveries, their theories and their science apart from philosophers. . . . As for Bacon and other more modern philosophers who try a general systematization of precepts for scientific research, they may seem alluring to people who look at science only from a distance; but works like theirs are of no use to experienced scientists; and by false simplification of things, they mislead men who wish to devote themselves to cultivating science.[3]

Other scientists might speak more diplomatically, but the attitude is not uncommon.

The history of science is replete with examples of the baneful effects of a priori philosophizing. The roadblocks that an overly high estimate of Aristotelian thought presented to the development of science are well known. Closer to the present is Comte's declaration in 1835 that it was meaningless to speak about the composition of the stars since there could be no way of finding out what they were made of. Within a few years, however, spectroscopy was being used to obtain information about the chemical elements in stellar atmospheres.[4]

If most scientists would agree that philosophy must play a subsidiary role in the conduct of science, an even greater number would say that theology should play no role at all in it. No scientist, whatever her or his faith, would be content to explain a puzzling experimental result by saying, "God did it." The theological approach that I am taking here also argues that God's activity in the world is hidden, and encourages a methodological naturalism in which scientists rule out explanations in terms of divine causation. Conversely, any attempt to prove the truth of Christianity from scientific results about natural phenomena is part of a theology of glory that we are committed to reject.

But it would go too far to say that theology can make no contribution at all to the scientific enterprise. Modern science developed in a culture that was strongly influenced by the Judeo-Christian tradition.[5] Individuals may be motivated to work in science or technology because they believe that such work glorifies the creator or because it can contribute toward helping their neighbors. Theology should also challenge a constrictive reductionism that defines out of existence anything that science cannot deal with. Science can, without reference to God, discover the patterns of natural phenomena, but it cannot explain why some patterns rather than others are found. It cannot answer the fundamental question of why anything exists at all, nor can it tell us the ultimate meaning or purpose of life.

One can refuse to ask such questions and say with Bertrand Russell, "The world as a whole just is, that's all. We start there."[6] Then there is no ground for discussion of anything outside the domain of science. But if such questions are asked, Christians should be prepared to respond. That is the essence of Paul Tillich's method of correlation, that theology should speak to the existential questions that concern people. It should not only respond to questions but help to direct questioners to what may be more fundamental issues. "We seek to answer *their* questions," says Tillich, "and in doing so we, at the same time, slowly transform their existence so that they come to ask the questions to which the Christian message gives the answer."[7]

Philosophy and science become problematic for Christian faith only when they are allowed to control theology and by imposing their presuppositions distort the basic themes of Christian thought. We saw earlier how assumptions about divine impassibility and immutability have made it difficult for the message of the cross and its implications to be communicated fully. Philosophy and the natural sciences are necessary for the theologian but they must play ministerial, not magisterial, roles.[8]

An important aspect of a scientific approach in any field has been emphasized repeatedly by Thomas Torrance: The method we use to enquire about anything must be suited to what that thing is. "[The] scientific way of acting and thinking which is to be pursued in every field of learning and discovery . . . is no more and no less than the rigorous extension of our basic rationality, as we seek to act toward things in ways appropriate to their natures, to understand them through letting them shine in their own light, and to reduce our thinking of them into orderly forms on the presumption of their inherent intelligibility."[9]

We don't learn about the psychology of rats by rolling them down inclined planes or study gravity by putting balls through mazes. This seems obvious but in other cases it is difficult to rid ourselves of preconceived ideas about things. If we bring mistaken ideas about some phenomenon to a study of it, we are treating it as if it were something that it is not and we will not really be able to understand it.

Torrance's example of the way in which Einstein's theory of general relativity overcame belief in the necessary character of Euclidean geometry and its relevance to the question of natural theology has already been noted in chapter 2. The properties of space and time have to be learned by studying the space-time world. Similarly, a priori ideas about God have to be overcome, and God's character has to be learned from God's self-revelation.

Imre Lakatos's view of science has been of interest to theologians since Nancey Murphy used it to explicate a way of speaking about theology as an enterprise that proceeds in a scientific manner.[10] Lakatos described science in terms of research programs, which consist of sets of theories and collections of data. The theories do not all have the same status. One, the "hard core" of the program, is to remain constant, while other theories that surround it as a "protective belt" are susceptible to changes that may be needed to accommodate new data. The development of science involves competition between such research programs.

To be progressive rather than degenerating, a research program must meet three conditions. Each new stage of its theory must preserve the successes of its predecessors. It must predict some "novel facts," thus having greater scope than its predecessors. And some of the novel predictions must be verified by observations. A program is degenerating if changes that must be made in the theories of the protective belt serve only to explain some new piece of data, but do not predict anything beyond that.

This description treats science as an ongoing activity rather than a static body of knowledge. A mature science will be active in two ways, pursuing plans to defend its hard core and developing theories to encompass more phenomena.[11] We may call a discipline a science in Lakatos's sense when it involves a generally progressive series of theories. One research program is superior to another if the first has a more progressive record than the second.

This view of science is in general accord with the way many scientists see their work. It does not attempt to prescribe precisely what course a scientist should take at a given point in experimental or theoretical work, and not many scientists would pay attention to it if it did. Such an analysis may be helpful in suggesting in broad terms how a research program may be pursued, but is likely to be more useful in systematizing understanding of what science has already accomplished.

THE LIMITS OF NAIVE REALISM

What do our observations and theories tell us about? A simple answer is that there is a real world, external to us and existing independently of whether anyone observes it or not. The task of science is to discover the kinds of things that exist in the world and the ways in which they behave. There are two significant problems with this naive realism. The first is connected with our limitations as observers. The second has to do with the fact that modern physics will not let us make a sharp separation between observers and the world that they observe.

Human observers cannot be totally objective. We have biological, cultural, and historical prejudices as well as physical limitations. Each of us has been brought up with a certain set of beliefs and views the world as a member of a certain gender, race, economic class, and nation. The recognition of such prejudices has been pushed to extremes by those who think that the scientific understanding of the world is simply a construct that helps certain groups to control society, and that it is no more "true" than any other construct.[12] This might be called "the sociologist's revenge": Sociology, sometimes looked down upon by those in the "hard sciences," can reply that *all* sciences have to be interpreted sociologically. The logical end of this argument is a solipsism in which everyone constructs his or her fantasy world. Those who take such a position finally have to be left to themselves because any challenge to it can be "suspected" away.

There is some validity in the sociological critique, but it overshoots the mark considerably to argue that social forces are conclusive for science.[13] Science does accurately correlate known phenomena and is quite successful in predicting new ones. Prejudices and tendencies to cling to familiar ways of looking at the world must be recognized, but they can be countered by training in intellectual integrity, free communication, and rewards for innovation. Prejudices cannot be eliminated entirely, but their effects can be reduced to a point where they do not determine the direction that scientific investigation takes.

Physical and cultural limitations can, in principle, be overcome or corrected for. But there are more serious challenges to naive realism from quantum theory, which suggests that what happens in the world depends to some extent on what observations we choose and carry out. The uncertainty principle says that the position and momentum of a particle cannot both be known with complete precision. We can in principle know either one as precisely as we wish, but only at the expense of increasing uncertainty in the other. What we know with precision will depend on what we choose to measure. This is also the case with certain other pairs of variables, such as energy and time.

We may argue that an electron really has a precise position and momentum even if we cannot know them, but do we have good reasons to think that this is so? To insist that these things exist is to impose our everyday understanding of the world upon phenomena at the microscopic level, and thus refuse to take seriously the way the world is actually disclosed to us.

Before any measurement is made on a system, its wave function represents a state in which there are probabilities for physical quantities to have many different values. When a measurement is made, the wave apparently "collapses" to one in which the quantity that is measured has just one value. But it is in part up to the observer to decide whether it collapses to a state with a definite position or to one with a definite momentum. Einstein could not accept what he saw as this denial of an objective real world, and in a classic paper with coworkers Boris Podolsky and Nathan Rosen he argued as follows that quantum theory was incomplete.[14]

Consider a physical system made up of two parts, 1 and 2, which interact and then separate. Initially we do not know the position or momentum of either subsystem, but only probabilities for their possible values. After 1 and 2 are well separated, we have a choice of whether to measure position or momentum for either 1 or 2. If we measure the momentum of 1 precisely, the uncertainty principle says that we can know nothing about its position. We now also have no choice about whether to measure position or momentum for 2 because the law of conservation of momentum requires that the sum of the momenta of 1 and 2 remain constant. If we knew the initial momentum for the total system, then the momenta for 1 and 2 must always add up to that value, and a knowledge of the momentum of 1 allows us to calculate that of 2.

Thus our measurement of the momentum of subsystem 1 forces the momentum, rather than the position, of 2 to have a definite value, even though 1 and 2 are now widely separated. We cannot simultaneously measure the momentum of 1 and the position of 2, for then we would be able to know both momentum and position for 2, which the uncertainty principle forbids. This is so even if 1 and 2 have become so far apart that not even a signal with the speed of light could connect them in the time between the two measurements. It seems that there would have to be some sort of mysterious action at a distance in order for such a connection to be possible.

Einstein and his coworkers thought that this was impossible, and that they had shown the limitations of quantum mechanics. But in recent years experiments of the required type have been carried out. These use photons as 1 and 2 and measure not position and momentum but polarizations. The prediction of quantum theory is correct: The decision that is made about which measurement to make on 1, and the carrying out of that decision, affects 2.[15] Not only is reality somehow connected with the observer, but this connection is nonlocal, extended over space and time.

It is the total process of choosing to make a measurement and carrying it out that affects the rest of the world. Simply choosing what to measure doesn't change anything until that choice is put into effect: The acts of observation of which quantum theory speaks involve real physical measurements with Geiger counters, film, and so forth. Thought alone does not create the physical world. Quantum mechanics does not say that there is no external reality at all, but that that reality is not strictly separated from our consciousness.

Gravitational theories provide an example of a different type. Newton explained gravity as a force acting between any two bodies and causing them to deviate from uniform motion in a straight line. Einstein spoke about the curvature of space-time caused by masses, and attributed the fact that bodies don't move in straight lines to this curvature. Einstein's is the better theory because it explains the same phenomena as Newton's and also predicts novel facts, which have been observed. Newton's theory is accurate enough for many purposes and is not simply "wrong." But if Einstein's theory is better as a fundamental description of the world, how can it be correct to speak even in an approximate way about gravitation as a force? "Force" and "curvature of space-time" are two qualitatively different concepts.

The predictive capacity of scientific theories, their ability to be extrapolated beyond known phenomena to grasp things that have never been observed before, shows that they are more than simply ways of organizing observational data. In light of successful predictions such as those of general relativity, it is hard to deny that science deals with something real. But what?

"GOD IS ALWAYS DOING GEOMETRY"

The existence of some reality beyond ourselves shows itself in the existence of a basic mathematical pattern of the world. In the quantum realm only the probabilities of events can be predicted and the consciousness of the observer seems to play some role in determining which probabilities are actualized. But the relative probabilities for different occurrences, the ways in which they change with time, and the properties of different states in which systems can exist are governed by Schrödinger's equation, which has objective validity. There is a rational pattern in the world, which we discover rather than make. Our mathematical laws are attempts to approximate parts of the pattern that underlie the phenomena we observe.

The mathematical pattern that characterizes the world is not necessary, for there are other possible patterns to which our world might conform. Mathematicians early in the nineteenth century realized that the traditional geometry of Euclid was not the only possible one, and developed self-consistent non-Euclidean systems. The actual geometry of the world has to be decided on the basis of observations of the world. The successes of Einstein's theory, which made use of the more general geometries, show that it gives a better approximation of the world's pattern than does Euclid's.

This begins to give us some insight into the nature of the reality that we discover in the world. Einstein's gravitational theory describes gravity in terms of curved space-time, and Newton's does it in terms of a quite different idea of force. But Einstein's equations reduce to Newton's when gravitation is weak and bodies move slowly.[16] In this sense Newton's theory is an approximation of Einstein's. Similar results can be found in other areas of physics.

This section is headed by a statement attributed to Plato, and what has been said here has some similarity with his view of reality.[17] For Plato, the eternal forms or ideas are what is most real, and the world of our experience is a changeable representation of the unchangeable realm of forms. His "likely story" of the creation of the visible universe after the model of the ideal "living creature" is told in the *Timaeus*.[18] It is not hard to see the mathematical pattern of the world as something akin to Platonic forms.

A number of prominent twentieth-century physicists expressed views with a strongly Platonic ring. We have already heard Einstein's belief that "in a certain sense . . . pure thought can grasp reality, as the ancients dreamed." The most sustained statement is that of Heisenberg, who tells of the puzzling but strong and lasting impression that his reading of the *Timaeus* made on him in his student days, and how Plato's account of a world constructed in accord with mathematical symmetry came to dominate his scientific thinking.[19]

Mendel's discovery of the basic laws of genetics demonstrates the crucial role that mathematics can play in biology. Others before him had carried out plant-breeding experiments. Mendel, however, concentrated on a few clear-cut traits such as seed shape and color, and analyzed the frequencies of their occurrence in a quantitative way.[20] A statistical study of his results for several thousand seeds suggested a simple model for heredity that has been elaborated into the vast discipline of modern genetics. Mendel's statistical analysis of data was essential. If he had been content to observe only qualitative tendencies of inheritance, nothing significant would have come from his work. Mathematics was needed for the breakthrough.

A case then can be made for some aspects of Platonism in the scientific understanding of the world, and we will see how this may be helpful in expressing the Christian doctrine of creation. But there are crucial scientific and theological qualifications. In the first place there is not, as Plato thought, a single mathematical pattern according to which the world must operate. We must imagine a variety of sets of forms, only one of which is represented by our universe.

This contingency of the universe means that observation and experiment are needed to discover how things are. Pure thought by itself cannot know reality. A pure mathematician need not care whether the theorems he or she proves have anything to do with the visible world, but those who want to understand that world have to look at it. Scientists who observe the world are not like students looking in the back of the book for solutions to problems that they aren't able to think through on their own. The world is the problem they are trying to solve!

The material world is not inferior to some realm of pure thought. The development of Greek science was hampered by the unwillingness of most philosophers to get their hands dirty. In contrast, the medieval craft tradition was an important factor in the development of modern science. The Judeo-Christian belief in the goodness of the material creation allows us to see the world as "embodied mathematics"[21] and to hold that the material realm of "clothed" mathematical pattern is superior to that of pure form. Thus we might speak of an "inverted Platonism" in which mathematics finds its fulfillment in the material world.[22]

We must also reject the Greek belief that true knowledge is of being, not becoming,[23] and that for both scientific and theological reasons. At a fundamental level the mathematical pattern of the world describes change, for quantum field theory gives us a dynamic picture of matter. The second law of thermodynamics describes a tendency for change that cannot be undone, and recent work in thermodynamics emphasizes not just change but *irreversible* change.[24]

The biblical picture of creation is one in which God makes the world for a purpose that is accomplished through the processes of history, so that change is part of God's plan for creation. In the incarnation God becomes a participant in change, and the world's history becomes part of God's history. In many religions and philosophies, what Mircea Eliade called "the terror of history" is fended off by a cyclic worldview in which the universe returns to its primordial state.[25] There are traces of this motif in the Bible, but they are subordinated to the theme of God's purpose being worked out in history.[26] The conclusion of the Book of Revelation has paradisal features, but there is more in its holy city than there was in the garden of Genesis.

The pattern underlying the world must be dynamic. We can catch a bit of the necessary flavor by paraphrasing Plato: "God is always doing calculus."

So science and Christian theology suggest similar modifications of a purely Platonic view. There is, however, another distinctively theological point. The biblical picture of divine sovereignty will not allow us to say that mathematical patterns or any other forms have the same ontological status as God. They cannot be pictured as existing "alongside" the creator, as Plato seems to have seen the relationship between the demiurge and the model after which the universe is fashioned.[27] The patterns of possible worlds will have to be thought of as freely "thought" by God. I will consider this further in chapter 7 when I speak about the biblical concept of creation through the divine Word.

The section of the *Timaeus* that we have been considering is where Justin Martyr believed that he had found a prophecy of the cross, as I noted in chapter 2. He was wrong in thinking that Plato's description of the demiurge arranging the intersecting bands of the World Soul in the universe was a recollection of the biblical story of Moses and the brazen serpent! Nevertheless, Justin's image is a powerful one. Our theological goal in considering scientific knowledge of the world is neither to see beyond the sensible world to an unchanging realm of ideas nor to demonstrate the existence of a divine mathematician. It is to discern the presence and activity of the God "placed crosswise in the universe."

THE WISDOM OF GOD

The mathematical order of the world is only hinted at in Scripture, as when God "drew a circle on the face of the deep" (Prov 8:27). This will not surprise us if we recognize that the biblical writers were not intent on giving a scientific understanding of the world. At the same time, the Bible reminds us that there are other types of order. The harmonies displayed in poetry or a just society cannot be captured by geometry or algebra.

While the Bible does not present us with natural science in the modern sense, the biblical wisdom tradition does have some features in common with the scientific approach to the world, as well as some interesting differences.[28] This tradition is an important intersection between the thought of Israel and the cultures of its neighbors.[29] "Wisdom" has many connotations, including human skill, cleverness, ethical conduct, piety, cosmic wisdom, and divine wisdom.[30] Solomon is the "patron saint" of wisdom in Israel, and it is significant that in the story of his dream in 1 Kgs 3 wisdom is pictured as a gift of God and not simply as a human achievement.

Gerhard von Rad, in a chapter titled "The Self-Revelation of Creation," argues that Wisdom's role as "the primeval world order" is the central element in Prov 8, Job 28, and Sir 24.[31] Through Wisdom, creation speaks of God to the wise person, so that we have a kind of natural theology. But the phrase "the fear of the LORD is the beginning of wisdom" is repeated a number of times with variations, and might almost be regarded as the motto of the mature biblical wisdom tradition (Prov 9:10, Ps 111:10; cf. Prov 1:7 and 15:33, Job 28:28, and Sir 19:20). A human being cannot through some knowledge achieved entirely by her or his own efforts know God or God's purposes for the world. In particular, only the person who is grounded in the fear of the Lord can use knowledge of the world in proper ways.

Wisdom has an objective existence outside humanity and is pictured in some passages as a personal being, "Lady Wisdom." (The Hebrew *ḥokhmah* and Greek *sophia* are both grammatically feminine.) This personification is especially vivid in Prov 8, where the origin and role of Wisdom are treated, and is developed further in Wis 7 and Sir 24. In the New Testament, Luke 7:35, Matt 11:2–19, Luke 11:49, Matt 23:34, and 1 Cor 1:24 and 30 suggest that Jesus is a representative of divine wisdom, or even Wisdom incarnate.[32] This identification was widely assumed in the early church and has received a good deal of attention in modern christologies, especially those of feminist theologians.[33] It is found liturgically in the first of the Advent "O Antiphons" for the week before Christmas, *O Sapientia:* "O Wisdom, proceeding from the mouth of the Most High, pervading and permeating all creation, mightily ordering all things: Come and teach us the way of prudence."[34]

In Prov 8:22–31, Wisdom is present at the world's creation. The rare but critical word *'amon* in verse 30 might mean "master workman," "little child," "confidante," or "coordinator." Wisdom is pictured either as God's coworker or "as a child playing in its father's workshop."[35]

Von Rad's characterization of Wisdom as the primeval world order is similar to the concept of a pattern that is approximated by scientific laws. Scientific investigation itself neither compels nor forbids connection of the primeval world order with a creator, a connection that the biblical tradition assumes from the outset. A christological connection is made in Col 1:15–20. Though the term "wisdom" is not used here, Christ is described precisely as the primeval world order in whom "all things hold together" (v. 17; cf. Sir 43:26).

The Bible gives us no "scientific method," but the frame of mind that the wisdom tradition encourages is instructive for a person who wants to understand the world. Many of the objects of today's natural science are placed within the realm of Wisdom:

> For it is he [God] who gave me unerring knowledge of what exists,
> to know the structure of the world and the activity of the elements;
> the beginning and end and middle of times,
> the alternations of the solstices and the changes of the seasons,
> the cycles of the year and the constellations of the stars,
> the natures of animals and the tempers of wild animals,
> the powers of spirits [or winds] and the thoughts of human beings,
> the varieties of plants and the virtues of roots;
> I learned both what is secret and what is manifest,
> for wisdom, the fashioner of all things, taught me.
>   (Wis 7:17–22a)

Wisdom is the fashioner of things and the one through whom humanity can understand them.

Just a few verses before this the writer says of Wisdom,

> I loved her more than health and beauty,
> and I chose to have her rather than light,
> because her radiance never ceases. (Wis 7:10)

In the light of the cross we can see why the pursuit of knowledge may have something deathlike about it: "Abaddon and Death say, 'We have heard a rumor of it with our ears'" (Job 28:22). The history of science gives us examples like that of the *Challenger* astronauts, who gave their lives in this pursuit.[36]

The Old Testament has the obvious antithesis of "the wise" and "the fool." In 1 Cor 1, however, Paul contrasts the wisdom of God, which the world considers foolish, with the world's wisdom, which God *makes* foolish. First Corinthians 1:18–31 is the clearest biblical exposition of the difference between what Luther would call "theology of glory" and "theology of the cross," proclaiming Christ crucified as the genuine Wisdom of God (vv. 24 and 30).

The message of the cross is not some "Christian science" that gives new data about the physical world, but is the framework without which all the understanding of the world that science may gain is finally "pointless."[37] Knowledge of the world that is cut off from the wisdom of God leads to destruction, for science cannot of itself provide ethical guidance for the use of its technological fruits. The Bible tells us that "when Solomon was old, his wives turned away his heart after other gods; and his heart was not true to the LORD his God" (1 Kgs 11:4). Careful reading of the account of his reign in 1 Kings reveals that his vaunted wealth and building programs were parts of a push toward absolutism that was disastrous for the people of Israel. It is appropriate that in Friedrich Dürrenmatt's play *The Physicists* it is King Solomon who represents the scientists whose discoveries have unleashed devastation upon the world.[38]

The split between facts and values that has been common since the Enlightenment has freed science from restrictions in its study of the world, but has also set the world up for despair when there seems finally to be no meaning to life, and for technological disaster when there is no ethical guidance. The fact-value split is foreign to the wisdom tradition, in which both fact and value are gifts of Holy Wisdom. In this spirit, chiasmic cosmology is the attempt to see what *is*, what *should be*, and what it all *means*, in the light of Christ crucified, "whom God made our wisdom, our righteousness and sanctification and redemption" (1 Cor 1:30 RSV).

NOTES

1. Albert Einstein, *Essays in Science* (New York: Philosophical Library, 1934), 12–21.

2. Aaron J. Ihde, *The Development of Modern Chemistry* (New York: Harper & Row, 1964), 310.

3. Claude Bernard, *An Introduction to the Study of Experimental Medicine* (New York: Dover, 1957), 225.

4. Owen Gingerich, "Laboratory Exercises in Astonomy—Spectral Classification," *Sky and Telescope* 40 (August 1970): 74.

5. For discussions from several viewpoints, see the following: John Hedley Brooke, *Science and Religion: Some Historical Perspectives* (New York: Cambridge University Press, 1991); Stanley L. Jaki, *The Road of Science and the Ways to God* (Chicago: University of Chicago Press, 1978); Christopher Kaiser, *Creation and the History of Science* (Grand Rapids, Mich.: Eerdmans, 1991).

6. W. Norris Clarke, S.J., "Is a Natural Theology Still Viable Today?" in *Prospects for Natural Theology* (ed. Eugene Thomas Long; Washington, D.C.: Catholic University of America Press, 1992), 165.

7. Paul Tillich, *Theology of Culture* (Oxford: Oxford University Press, 1959), 206.

8. Siegbert H. Becker, *The Foolishness of God* (Milwaukee: Northwestern, 1982), 196–98.

9. Thomas F. Torrance, *Theological Science* (Edinburgh: T&T Clark, 1996), 106–7.

10. Nancey Murphy, *Theology in the Age of Scientific Reasoning* (Ithaca, N.Y.: Cornell University Press, 1990).

11. Ibid., 60.

12. Paul R. Gross and Norman Levitt, *Higher Superstition* (Baltimore: Johns Hopkins University Press, 1994).

13. Robert John Russell in John M. Mangum, ed., *The New Faith-Science Debate* (Minneapolis: Fortress, 1989), 91–105.

14. A. Einstein, B. Podolsky, and N. Rosen, "Can Quantum-Mechanical Description of Reality Be Considered Complete?" *Physical Review* 47 (1935): 777. N. Bohr, "Can Quantum-Mechanical Description of Reality Be Considered Complete?" *Physical Review* 48 (1935): 696, is a response.

15. A. Aspect et al., "Experimental Tests of Realistic Local Theories via Bell's Theorem," *Physical Review Letters* 47 (1981): 460.

16. Peter Gabriel Bergmann, *Introduction to the Theory of Relativity* (New York: Dover, 1976), chapter 15 and appendix A.

17. Plutarch set this topic for discussion in his "Table Talk," prefacing it by saying, "While this statement is not made explicitly in any of Plato's writings, it is well enough attested and is in harmony with his character." See Plutarch, *Moralia* (LCL; Cambridge, Mass.: Harvard University Press, 1969), 118–19.

18. English translation with commentary in Francis MacDonald Cornford, *Plato's Cosmology* (London: Routledge & Kegan Paul, 1952).

19. Werner Heisenberg, *Physics and Beyond* (New York: Harper & Row, 1971).

20. Hugo Iltis, *The Life of Mendel* (London: George Allen & Unwin, 1932), 101–75.

21. W. Jim Neidhardt, "The Creative Dialogue Between Human Intelligibility-Relational Aspects of Natural Science and Theology," *The Asbury Theological Journal* 41, no. 2 (1986): 59.

22. George L. Murphy, "A Positive Approach to Creation," *Journal of the American Scientific Affiliation* 32 (1980): 230.

23. Cornford, *Plato's Cosmology,* 28–32.

24. Ilya Prigogine, *From Being to Becoming* (San Francisco: Freeman, 1980).

25. Mircea Eliade, *Cosmos and History: The Myth of the Eternal Return* (New York: Harper, 1959), chapter 4.

26. Brevard S. Childs, *Myth and Reality in the Old Testament* (Naperville, Ill.: Alec R. Allenson, 1960), 72–83.

27. Cornford, *Plato's Cosmology,* 41.

28. George L. Murphy, "Science as Wisdom," *Currents in Theology and Mission* 18 (1991): 198.

29. For general discussions, see Ronald E. Clements, *Wisdom in Theology* (Grand Rapids, Mich.: Eerdmans, 1992); Roland Edmund Murphy, *Wisdom Literature and Psalms* (Nashville: Abingdon, 1983); and Gerhard von Rad, *Wisdom in Israel* (trans. James D. Martin; Nashville: Abingdon, 1972).

30. U. Wilckens and G. Fohrer, "σοφία κτλ," *Theological Dictionary of the New Testament* (Grand Rapids, Mich.: Eerdmans, 1971), 7:465–528.

31. Von Rad, *Wisdom in Israel,* chapter 9. For the phrase "primeval world order," see 161.

32. M. Jack Suggs, *Wisdom, Christology, and Law in Matthew's Gospel* (Cambridge, Mass.: Harvard University Press, 1970), chapter 2.

33. See the list of citations from Prov 8 in the works of Athanasius, *NPNF* 2:4:286. Two modern works are Denis Edwards, *Jesus the Wisdom of God: An Ecological Theology* (Maryknoll, N.Y.: Orbis, 1995), and Elisabeth Schüssler Fiorenza, *Jesus: Miriam's Child, Sophia's Prophet* (New York: Continuum, 1994).

34. *Lutheran Book of Worship* (Minneapolis: Augsburg, 1978), 174.

35. G. Fohrer, "σοφία κτλ," B, The Old Testament, *Theological Dictionary of the New Testament.*

36. George L. Murphy, "Science and Martyrdom," *Perspectives on Science and Christian Faith* 41 (1989): 31.

37. Steven Weinberg, *The First Three Minutes* (rev. ed.; New York: Basic Books, 1988), 154.

38. Friedrich Dürrenmatt, *The Physicists* (New York: Grove, 1962), 93–94.

· 6 ·

GOD'S ACTION IN THE WORLD

CREATION AND PROVIDENCE

Christian faith in creation means trust in the God who has been revealed in the cross and resurrection of Christ as the ultimate source of the universe. Such trust does not require a knowledge of natural science, but we should not conclude that science is of no importance for Christian faith. The first creation story of Genesis repeatedly declares what God has made to be good, and one implication of that is that the world is worth understanding. Science can help us to appreciate God's creative work and deepen our understanding of it. So Aquinas said: "It is, therefore, evident that the opinion is false of those who asserted that it made no difference to the truth of the faith what anyone holds about creatures, so long as one thinks rightly about God, as Augustine tells us in his book *On the Origin of the Soul*. For error concerning creatures, by subjecting them to causes other than God, spills over into false opinion about God, and takes men's minds away from Him, to whom faith seeks to lead them."[1] In particular, those who have pastoral or teaching responsibilities in the church need to know about scientific views of the world and be able to relate them to the Christian faith.

Creation includes the *origination* of the universe from God and God's ongoing relationship with the world, which is described by doctrines of *providence*. Origination is all that some people mean when they refer to creation. Providence, which includes divine preservation of the world and action in it to accomplish God's purpose, is then seen as a matter of keeping the original creation in being. That seems to be a natural way to consider these doctrines, especially in view of the way the Bible begins. But this is not the best procedure if we want science to contribute anything to the way we think about creation. Starting with origination encourages the idea that it is separate from providence, and that while science may need to be consulted when we discuss God's activity in the world today, it must step aside when origins are considered. This has been responsible for much of the tension between science and theology.

It is better to start with God's action in the world today and move from there to the origins of the universe and of life. This is the course that science has taken to gain its understanding of the world. It made progress by first trying to understand phenomena in our neighborhood of space-time, studying moving bodies, light, and living things. The knowledge gained in this manner was gradually expanded until it was possible to speak about cosmology and evolution in ways that were not purely speculative.

But this procedure is also traditional in theology. In the *Small Catechism* Luther explains what it means to believe in God as creator:

> I believe that God has created me together with all creatures. God has given me and still preserves my body and soul: eyes, ears, and all limbs and senses; reason and all mental faculties. In addition, God daily and abundantly provides shoes and clothing, food and drink, house and home, spouse and children, fields, livestock, and all property—along with all the necessities and nourishment for this body and life. God protects me against all danger and shields and preserves me from all evil. God does all this out of pure, fatherly, and divine goodness and mercy, without any merit or worthiness of mine at all![2]

"All creatures" must include things of the past, dinosaurs and distant galaxies, but Luther concentrates on what God is doing for the individual today. The character of creation as *grace* is also emphasized. God preserves and acts in the world freely, and recognition of this is at the heart of the idea of *creatio ex nihilo*.

A similar emphasis is found in the Heidelberg Catechism:

> [I believe] that the eternal Father of our Lord Jesus Christ, who out of nothing created heaven and earth with all that is in them, who also upholds and governs them by his eternal counsel and providence, is for the sake of Christ his Son my God and my Father. I trust in him so completely that I have no doubt that he will provide me with all things necessary for body and soul. Moreover, whatever evil he sends upon me in this troubled life he will turn to my good, for he is able to do it, being almighty God, and is determined to do it, being a faithful Father.[3]

The origin of the universe is mentioned here but the emphasis is still on God's present work for the believer. The Reformed catechism also introduces the difficult matter of God's action through evil occurrences, which I will discuss later in this chapter.

Belief that God provides the necessities of life stems from the Bible. For the sake of definiteness we may concentrate on the provision of food, which Scripture often mentions: "The eyes of all look to you, and you give them their food in due season. You open your hand, satisfying the desire of every living thing" (Ps 145:15–16). This statement expresses the belief that God provides food, but people of faith know that if they don't plant grain, if it isn't watered, and if they don't harvest it, they won't have bread.

With our knowledge today of natural and social processes we can explain in some detail how we get our food. The growth of grain can be explained in terms of genetics, meteorology, solar energy, photosynthesis, and other concepts of natural science. All the technology and the economic structures of agriculture, milling and baking, and distribution systems also play roles in putting bread on our tables. There are things we don't understand at present about the growth of grain, and the economics of the food industry cannot be explained with the same precision that physics achieves, but there is no reason to think that any part of the network of processes involved in food production cannot in principle be described in scientific terms.

Two claims are made here. The first is that provision of food is part of the creative work of the triune God. The second is that science can enable us to understand how we get our food through natural processes. The second explanation is not a rival to the first, as if we were to say, "Ba'al, not YHWH, makes the grain grow" (cf. Hos 2:8). At the same time, faith does not take the place of scientific knowledge: Trust in providence will not enable us to understand photosynthesis or irrigation methods. These claims and their obvious generalizations must be kept together if we are to have a proper understanding of creation.

Divine action has customarily been divided into "ordinary" and "extraordinary" providence, the latter including miracles. Ordinary providence has in turn been divided into preservation, concurrence or cooperation, and governance.[4] God keeps all things with their appropriate powers in existence, concurs with their actions, and directs them to accomplish the divine purposes. The concept of concurrence is defined as follows by Hollaz: "Concurrence, or the co-operation of God, is the act of Divine Providence whereby God, by a general and immediate influence, proportioned to the need and capacity of every creature, graciously takes part with second causes in their actions and effects."[5] The language of God as primary cause operating through created things as secondary causes is like that of Aquinas,[6] and shows the influence of Aristotle on the Protestant tradition.

If things in the world are thought to have more or less static natures, preservation will naturally receive considerable emphasis. If we have the Aristotelian idea that things happen to accomplish some purpose, then governance will be stressed. Both of these ways of thinking may result in concurrence being subsumed under one of the other aspects of providence, and in fact the older theologians often treated it as part of the divine governance.

Today's scientific picture calls for a different emphasis, for the universe on all scales is dynamic. It is not simply a collection of objects with fixed properties moving in different ways. One set of biological species gives way to another over long periods of time. Virtual pairs of particles continually come into being and annihilate one another. This rhythm of creation and destruction has been described by Fritjof Capra, who sees in it the Hindu dance of Shiva.[7] The Christian will see the pattern of cross and resurrection at the basic level of matter.

It makes sense then to emphasize God's cooperation with dynamic processes, and to subsume preservation under cooperation. God preserves by acting. Faith in God as the creator then means confidence that the triune God is continually active through natural processes, and that none of these processes takes part without God.

Traditional doctrines of providence provide some guidance for developing an adequate understanding of divine action, but we need to take seriously the ways in which science has come to understand natural processes if we are to speak about God's actions in conjunction with them. Theological changes are also needed, for doctrines of providence have been weakened by the fact that their deity who acts in the world often does not have the distinctive features of the God revealed in Jesus Christ.[8] I will address both of those concerns together in order to develop a modern doctrine of divine action that is part of a theology of the cross.

GOD'S WORK IN THE WORLD

When the ecumenical creeds call God "almighty," they mean that God is active in everything that takes place in the world.[9] Nothing happens without the one who says, "I form light and create darkness, I make weal and create woe; I the LORD do all these things" (Isa 45:7). But the Bible does not give a detailed description of *how* God is active in the world, so theologies and models of divine action and its relationship with natural processes must be theological inferences rather than dogmatic statements.

Ian Barbour's typologies of theologies and models of divine action form a useful starting point. The following table combines entries from two of his versions, including only the models I want to discuss here.[10]

THEOLOGY	DOMINANT MODEL	CONCEPTUAL ELABORATION
Classical	Ruler-Kingdom	Omnipotent, omniscient, unchanging sovereign
Deist	Clockmaker-Clock	Designer of a law-abiding world
Neo-Thomist	Workman-Tool	Primary cause working through secondary causes
Quantum	Determiner of Indeterminancies	Actualizer of potentialities
Kenotic	Parent-Child	Voluntary self-limitation and vulnerability
Existentialist	None	God acts only in personal life

No single one of these theologies completely accords with our requirements, but a combination of them seems well suited to do so. I will make use especially of the neo-Thomist, kenotic, and existentialist views, though with some nuances.

Barbour's first two entries have serious flaws that disqualify them. The first represents God as the unconstrained dictator of the universe who does all things directly, without the mediation of created agents. This view contrasts with the biblical model of the true king, the one over whom Pilate put the sarcastic title "King of the Jews." Unfortunately, God often has been thought of after the pattern of a despot like Solomon rather than that of Jesus.

This model is also problematic because the direct character of divine action does not allow creatures any role in what happens in the world but makes them simply passive objects of God's work. This would mean that God does not grant creation genuine integrity, and would raise serious questions about the goodness of creation. The successes of science in explaining natural phenomena as if there were causal connections (even of a statistical sort) between them, without any need to speak of divine agency, would then be a puzzle. We would have to think of God moving things about like chess pieces according to arbitrary rules.

Deism, which was more popular in the heyday of the Newtonian worldview than today, makes the opposite error. According to this model, God created the world and set it going initially, and now simply lets it run. It is hard to see how to give any sense to Jesus' statements about God feeding the birds and clothing the lilies of the field (Matt 6:26–29) if God is not actually doing anything in the world.

The God whose action we are trying to discern in the natural world is the God who is paradoxically revealed in the darkness of Golgotha. This appears to us as the absence of God, and if God's activity in nature is to bear the mark of the cross, it too will be hidden. This will be the case if God works through natural processes as instruments, in the way described by the neo-Thomist theology of divine action. If God operates in this way, then what we will observe scientifically will be various combinations of natural processes, and God will never be "seen" by the methods of the natural sciences. As far as purely scientific work is concerned, Laplace was right: God does not need to come into the discussion.

A double metaphor can then be used to describe natural processes theologically. They are the "instruments" of God and, at the same time, are, in Luther's phrase, "masks" of God:

> God could easily give you grain and fruit without your plowing and planting. But He does not want to do so. Neither does He want your plowing and planting alone to give you grain and fruit; but you are to plow and plant and then ask His blessing and pray: "Now let God take over; now grant grain and fruit, dear Lord! Our plowing and planting will not do it. It is Thy gift. . . ."
>
> What else is all our work to God—whether in the fields, in the garden, in the city, in the house, in war, or in government—but just such a child's performance, by which He wants to give His gifts in the fields, at home, and everywhere else? These are the masks of God, behind which He wants to remain concealed and do all things.[11]

Barbour's term "neo-Thomist" is somewhat restrictive. Modern theories of divine action that stem from Aquinas would be included here, but so would other approaches that do not emphasize the ideas of primary and secondary causation. Barth quotes Quenstedt's example of a person writing with a pen: the writing is done wholly by the hand and wholly by the pen, not partly by one and partly by the other.[12] God's action is immediately present to created agencies, concurring rather than precurring, but is mediated through those agencies and does not take place apart from them.

The language of "instruments" calls to mind things like screwdrivers and hammers that function in accord with the rules of mechanics. Such metaphors are appropriate at the level of approximation of Newtonian physics, but at the most basic level God's instruments are the interactions of physics that are described by relativity and quantum theory, and are more subtle than those in the average mechanic's workshop: We would have to use modern inventions such as nanotechnologies for an adequate analogy.

It would be possible to imagine God operating with natural processes in arbitrary ways, having electricity behave one way today and another tomorrow. But the regularities of the world which science discovers and upon which the very possibility of science is based show that God does not work that way. Later I will discuss the possibility of miracles, events in which God acts in ways that science cannot explain, but the laws of physics are respected in the vast majority of situations that we have been able to study.

This suggests that we should make use of the kenotic theology in which God's action is analogous to that of a parent who voluntarily limits her or his work in order to enable children to understand the world and function in it by themselves. This view is closely related to the theology of the cross: The term "kenosis" itself is taken from Phil 2:5–11, which speaks of Christ as one who "was in the form of God" but did not see grasping this as the meaning of deity. Rather, he "emptied *[ekenōsen]* himself, taking the form of a slave."

The use of the kenotic theme in creation has some resemblance to the old distinction between God's absolute and God's ordained power.[13] God could do anything but normally limits divine acts to those fitting a rational pattern that God has freely chosen. The universe is both rational and contingent, as Torrance especially has emphasized.[14] This is consistent with the possibility pointed out in the previous chapter of different mathematical systems that might serve as patterns for universes.

If all kenosis did was to explain why the world can be described without reference to God, then it would be a mere face-saving device for theologians. It is a quite different matter to base such a concept on the theology of the cross and the belief that all God's activity has a cruciform pattern. The ability of science to explain things in the world "though God were not given" is then virtually demanded by theology, and something like the combination of the neo-Thomist and kenotic views will be needed.

A current example is the problem of explaining the origin of the first living systems from nonliving chemicals. Steps have been taken toward a scientific answer to this problem but at present scientists have no detailed theory of the origin of life. Some Christians are elated by this and argue that science's failure to solve the problem shows that only God can create life. Chiasmic cosmology, on the other hand, leads us to expect—or at least hope—*on theological grounds* that a scientific answer to this problem will eventually be found.

God, in Bonhoeffer's phrase, "lets himself be pushed out of the world on to the cross," not only on Golgotha but throughout the universe. The creator is willing to let his creatures get the credit for what is accomplished in the world and does not insist on receiving it himself, just as Christ did not consider divine prerogatives as "something to be exploited" (Phil 2:6). Every knee is indeed to bow to him, but as a consequence of his crucifixion (Phil 2:9–11).

In using the theme of kenosis in a doctrine of creation, it is helpful to be aware of questions it has raised in Christology.[15] To deal with problems in the Chalcedonian doctrine of two natures in one person, some theologians suggested that in assuming human nature the Logos not only gave up the full exercise of some divine attributes but surrendered them entirely. But was the one who brought about atonement on the cross really the Son of God if he did not have all the attributes of God? And if "all things hold together" in him (Col 1:17), what was holding the universe together during the period in which he put aside his divine power?

The difficulty in answering these questions has as much to do with our ideas of power as with the concept of kenosis itself. The language of power usually suggests compulsion, but the image of the suffering servant, which Christ displays and which Paul urges upon the Philippian Christians, is quite different. In another passage Paul says that he was told by God, "My grace is sufficient for you, for power is made perfect in weakness" (2 Cor 12:9). Kenosis does not mean God's abdication but God working in a way that is not recognizable to theologians of glory. The one who had the "form of God" is present and active in "the form of a slave." We recall Bonhoeffer's words quoted in chapter 1: "He is weak and powerless in the world, and that is precisely the way, the only way, in which he is with us and helps us."

The emphasis here on kenosis means that there are similarities between our treatment and the work of Nancey Murphy and George F. R. Ellis.[16] Their attempt to view all the natural and social sciences with theology and ethics "in a specific Christian context"[17] is similar to that of the present discussion. Differences are due in part to the fact that their contribution is in the tradition of the Radical Reformation while this work is in the tradition of the conservative reformation. Their statement that "kenosis is the underlying law of the cosmos"[18] is not identical with "the *cross* alone is our theology," but chiasmic and kenotic cosmologies have a good deal in common.

The combination of neo-Thomist and kenotic views speaks about God's action in the world, but intentionally adds nothing to a scientific description in terms of physical interactions. What justification is there then in talking about divine action if we do not "need" God in order to understand what happens in the world? If the claim is that natural processes and God do just the things that science explains in terms of natural processes, can we not simply eliminate God with Occam's razor?

Here Barbour's "existentialist" theology is helpful. What is needed is not use of the philosophy of existentialism but the crucial element of faith. Faith is not just believing things that we are unable to prove, but personal trust and commitment, and it is in view of such a commitment to the God revealed in the cross of Christ that we can discern God's activity in the world. The explanations of creation in terms of God's provision for the life of the believer, as expressed in the Reformation catechisms quoted earlier in this chapter, are expressions of such faith.

A narrowly existentialist theology may concentrate so single-mindedly on personal commitment that it has no place at all for God's action in the natural world. Rudolf Bultmann, for example, says that a person can only speak of God as the creator of his or her life: "First, only such statements about God are legitimate as express the existential relation between God and man. Statements which speak of God's actions as cosmic events are illegitimate. The affirmation that God is creator cannot be a theoretical statement about God as *creator mundi* in a general sense. The affirmation can only be a personal confession that I understand myself to be a creature which owes its existence to God."[19] The mistake here is the idea that we can understand ourselves adequately as individuals isolated from the rest of the universe. We exist only as parts of humanity and of the whole world. Life is possible only because of the evolution of stars, which makes available the carbon formed by fusion reactions in their interiors. In the last analysis I must be able to speak of God as the creator of the world if I am to understand myself as a creature that owes its existence to God.

A quantum theology of divine action focuses on God as the one who "collapses the wave packet" and produces a definite result for an observation out of an array of possibilities. How this collapse takes place is still debated by physicists. If God cooperates with, and limits himself to, processes described by the present laws of quantum theory, then God leaves some indeterminacy in nature. An alternative model of God as "determiner of indeterminacies" was used by William Pollard.[20] This goes further and argues that God is the one who brings definite outcomes for observations from arrays of quantum probabilities. Robert John Russell has suggested that we should think of God's involvement in the genetics of the evolutionary process at the quantum level.[21] "With this approach," he argues, "God can be understood theologically as acting purposefully within the ongoing processes of biological evolution without disrupting them or violating the laws of nature."[22] God then would direct evolution by means of changes in DNA molecules in accord with the statistical laws of quantum mechanics.

The idea that results of *all* observations are directly determined by God in a way that the laws of physics cannot describe is a return to the rejected classical model of divine action. If we instead pursue the kenotic theme to the end, then it seems that chance would play a fundamental role in the universe, and that God's sovereignty would have to be understood as eschatological: In the end, the House always wins.

THE CHRISTOLOGICAL PATTERN OF DIVINE ACTION

The terms "concurrence" and "cooperation" are both used for God's activity through created things. "Concurrence" suggests that God and creatures accompany one another. "Cooperation" gives further insight with its suggestion that God literally "works with" creatures. The energy concept provides an interesting way of looking at this relationship.[23]

Uses of the Greek *energeia*, "operation," in theology are related to its Aristotelian meaning, "the activity that transforms potentiality into actuality."[24] In classical theology there are energies proper to each nature, so that it is necessary to speak of both divine and created energies. The concept came to prominence in the christological debates following Chalcedon. Those who felt that the two natures doctrine led to too great a separation between the human and divine in the incarnation proposed that while there were two natures in Christ, there was only one will and one operation. But if there were only a divine operation in Christ, then nothing distinctively human was done in the work of salvation. The Sixth Ecumenical Council rejected these ideas and stated that in Christ there are two natural wills and operations, which are in accord in everything that he does.[25]

Energeia is also the root of the scientific term "energy." We cannot simply identify this with the theological concept, but there are interesting connections. Energy is defined in elementary physics as "the ability to do work." It includes the energies of motion and interaction of bodies, heat, and energies of fields. Einstein's $E = mc^2$ identified energy and mass, dynamic "happening" with inert "stuff." Ordinary matter can be converted into forms of energy such as radiation, and all forms of energy have mass.

Energy in these senses can be measured and quantified: A process can transfer so many calories from one physical system to another, and the law of conservation of energy says that the total amount of all types of energy for an isolated system remains constant over time. Another aspect of energy is used in quantum theory where energy is represented by a mathematical operator that alters the waves representing the states of systems. Schrödinger's equation of quantum mechanics is a statement that the energy of a system produces the change of the system's state in the course of time. In other words, energy generates the evolution of the physical world. The fact that energy itself is conserved while it produces temporal change in the world is reminiscent of the polarity of constancy and change in process thought.[26] In traditional doctrines of providence, the constancy of energy would be associated with the divine work of preservation while its role in generating change would be connected with cooperation.

Providential cooperation means that the divine operation acts with and through the physical energies of the universe. God does not add some new type of physical energy to the world but cooperates with the energies of the world. Divine action is then described in language similar to that of the sixth Ecumenical Council about the divine and human operations in God incarnate so that God's work in the world conforms to a christological pattern.

KENOSIS AS GIFT

All the things that sustain and improve our lives are gifts of God. God's providential work through natural processes is such a gift, an expression of the graciousness of the creator and part of the goodness of the world that the first creation account of Genesis emphasizes. Prayers from the simplest table grace to the most exalted liturgies express this belief: "You are blessed, Lord our God, King of the universe, you who have brought bread forth from the earth."[27] Divine action involves another more subtle gift, which is inherent in the way in which God works. We recall Hollaz's statement that God "graciously takes part with second causes in their actions and effects." God's cooperation with natural processes obeying rational laws and the limitation of God's work to what can be achieved through those processes is itself grace.

Creation means that God wills for something to exist that is not God: The universe is not part of God, an emanation from the divine being. "For God is good, or rather is essentially the source of goodness: nor could one that is good be niggardly of anything: whence, grudging existence to none, He has made all things out of nothing by His own Word, Jesus Christ our Lord."[28] The world is able to exist as something that is not God and to function in a way that is not identical to God's action. God's endowing of the world with a rational pattern for its functioning means that things can take place with some completeness without any divine corrections. Howard Van Till has called this the functional integrity of creation,[29] and it implies a rejection of any "God of the gaps" arguments or claims that "only God can create life" (or carry out any other action) in the sense that God must do that directly and not mediately.

With integrity comes some freedom, a point that is significant when we remember the limits that quantum theory and chaos have placed on Laplacian determinism. God does not correct or complete the course taken by natural processes by simply overriding them. Divine self-limitation enables the universe to be a coherent cosmos, not just a collection of objects.

This grace is displayed before humanity comes on the scene, but the functional integrity of creation takes on new meaning with the development of intelligent life. The existence of regularities in natural phenomena is probably necessary for the evolution of intelligence, for intelligence would confer no survival value if thinking in terms of repeatable connections between different types of events did not mirror the way the world actually is. The existence of these regularities makes it possible for rational creatures to understand their world and to live in it as adults rather than as children. If God supplied everything needed for life through miracles that followed no discernible patterns, then we would continually be in the position of babies in a nursery who have no idea where their food and clothing and toys come from. As it is, we are able to operate as parts of creation who are responsible agents.

In fact, all animals need some sense of regularity: Unless the lioness "knows" the habits of her prey, she and her cubs will starve. "The young lions roar for their prey, seeking their food from God" (Ps 104:21), and God supplies it by making it possible for them to find their food.

The ability to understand the world comes to fullest expression in science, where human comprehension of the rational patterns of the world is made explicit. The very possibility of scientific understanding is grace. We might conceive of God acting in accord with some higher rationality that cannot be grasped by creatures within the world. What is critical for the existence of scientific understanding is that God voluntarily limits the divine action to be in accord with the rationality that God has conferred upon the world, so that creation can indeed be understood "though God were not a given." The scientific enterprise is possible because of the divine kenosis, and thus ultimately depends upon the fact that the creator is the crucified.

SUFFERING AND EVIL

"The most difficult problem in the science of Theology is that of exhibiting the method of the divine concurrence in the evil actions of men, without at the same time in any wise throwing the blame of the evil upon the first cause, *i.e.,* upon God. The Dogmaticians employ for this purpose the two formulae: 'God concurs in producing the effect, not the defect; God concurs as to the materials, not as to the form.'"[30] We can agree on the difficulty of the problem described by Schmid. Whether or not the two formulae that he quotes solve it is debatable.

The challenges of evil and suffering, and of God's relationship with them, are ancient but no less difficult because of that. Job still forces us to ponder the question, "If God is both good and almighty, why do evil things happen?" The atrocities and sufferings of the twentieth century have renewed and sharpened discussions of the question.[31]

This problem is more serious than "How can God let evil things happen?" If God is active in everything that takes place, then there is a sense in which God *participates* in actions that result in evil. The Bible does not try to absolve God of all responsibility for evil. It never makes God the cause of human sin, but it does ask, "Does disaster befall a city, unless the LORD has done it?" (Amos 3:6), and has God say, "I make weal and create woe" (Isa 45:7).

It is helpful to distinguish between natural and moral evil. Sufferings caused by disease or earthquake are in the former category while those owing to human malice are in the latter. The distinction has often been blurred in Christian thought because of the belief that all suffering and death were due finally to the primordial sin of Adam. Romans 5:12–14 does link sin with the entry of death into the world, but the fact that organisms were dying for millions of years before the first humans walked the earth keeps us from saying that all physical suffering and death is due to human moral evil in any straightforward causal fashion.

There is nothing intrinsically bad about a volcano, and we may even consider its eruption beautiful if we are at a safe distance. Vulcanism is connected with movements of plates of the earth's crust, which have brought the planet's surface to its present form, and is an effect of divine creation. But for creatures too close to Krakatoa, its eruption meant death. Physical death is even necessary for the continuation of life on Earth, which would be buried in insects if they didn't have short life spans. The concept of natural selection sees death as crucial for the evolutionary process. We call death a natural evil because it is unpleasant for us, but it seems to be the price that has to be paid for a universe in which physical life exists.

This is not true of moral evil. Intelligent creatures do not *have* to choose to cause pain and death for one another. It is only a possibility, though a possibility that humanity has chosen and continues to choose. The concept of original sin means that individuals cannot free themselves from the general moral evil in which all participate, but each sin that a person commits is a sin that he or she could have chosen not to commit.

The question of theodicy is literally that of "justifying God." How can an all-good and all-powerful God concur in evil actions? The question is presumptuous. "But who indeed are you, a human being, to argue with God?" (Rom 9:20), Paul asked. However, the canonical status of the story of Job, in which a man *does* raise the question and in so doing speaks "what is right" (Job 42:7), allows and perhaps even encourages the question.

The argument is sometimes made, as in the passage I quoted from the Heidelberg Catechism, that God brings about evil for the sake of the greater good that will result. Luther made a distinction between God's "proper work" and God's "alien work."[32] The former is work that is suitable to God's real character, work of blessing, forgiveness, and life, while the latter work of condemnation and destruction is foreign to God's character. But God does this alien work for the sake of his proper work.

An alternative pursued in process thought is to abandon omnipotence, and to say that evil occurs because God is not omnipotent, and thus cannot prevent it.[33] There is a serious problem with such a position if we want to maintain that God works through natural processes and that the divine action is voluntarily limited to those processes. The same physical interactions are involved in phenomena that result in both good and evil. Fire can save life or end it, and it is hard to see how we could say in any consistent way that one but not the other takes place by God's cooperation with natural processes. Human actions that are morally evil generally involve the use of good things—sex, food, wealth, knowledge—for evil ends.

Formulae such as those cited by Schmid try to explain how God can concur in the processes that maintain the goodness of creation without concurring, other than permissively, in their evil use. They stand in the tradition stemming from Augustine that sees evil as fundamentally negative.[34] Evil has no separate existence but is a defect in things that are in themselves good. We may wonder if an approach that denies that evil "exists" in the strict sense takes it seriously enough, but such an approach does bring out the important truth that there is a basic senselessness and pointlessness to evil. In some cases we can explain why a natural disaster has happened, or why one person rather than another develops cancer, but this is not always the case. People often suffer for no reason that we can discern.

The basic Christian response to the problem of evil cannot then be an explanation of *why* bad things happen to good people. The only real Christian theodicy is the passion of Christ. This is not an explanation of evil but a claim that God suffers *with* the world from whatever evil takes place. Luther's statement about the cross as the essence of theology can be paraphrased as "The cross alone is our theodicy." The world's pains are God's stigmata.

We begin with the fact that God suffered on the cross, but we do not have to stop with that. God's voluntary self-limitation that enables the world to have its own existence and integrity keeps God from simply preventing all evil in miraculous ways. Evil is then the "dark side" of an aspect of the goodness of creation, its functional integrity. Alluding to the "free-will defence," which is often made for God in debates about theodicy, John Polkinghorne argues for a "free-process defence," the claim that evil must be possible if the natural world is to function with freedom and integrity.[35] If the divine self-limitation is grounded in a theology of the crucified, then we can say that God shares in paying the price that is necessary for the freedom and integrity of creation by going to the cross. I will discuss an important aspect of this point of view when we consider the suffering involved in the evolutionary process in chapter 8.

Finally, none of this absolves us from our responsibility to resist evil, for we are the creatures through whom God often acts. God may be doing the best that is possible with recalcitrant instruments. The question is sometimes asked why God did not stop the Holocaust, but it was stopped through the instrumentalities of Allied armed forces. Not all the Jews of Europe were killed. And if the Holocaust was not stopped sooner, it was because Allied responses to Hitler were not as swift or effective as they might have been. This is not to minimize the radical evil of the "final solution" or to suggest that the question "Where is God?" should not have been asked at Auschwitz, but only to point out that the problem of evil is not simply a theoretical one that we can discuss while avoiding any personal engagement with it.

MIRACLES

What about the extraordinary aspect of providence, miracles? The literature on this subject is extensive and we cannot explore it in detail.[36] In order to decide about any specific putative miracle, we would need to discuss the evidence for it, which for miracle stories in Scripture would mean critical analysis of biblical texts. Our concerns here are limited to two basic questions: What can be the role of the miraculous in a theology of the cross, and how is the possibility of miracles to be evaluated in the light of modern science? In particular, can our discussions earlier in this chapter help us to understand possibly miraculous phenomena?

We can begin with what C. S. Lewis called "The Grand Miracle,"[37] the incarnation. God's self-revelation and work of salvation, the incarnation did not in itself involve phenomena that would inspire wonder. Even virginal conception is something whose facts could be known only by Mary, and which must be taken on faith by others. There was nothing about Jesus himself, apart from his words and actions, that struck his contemporaries as marvelous: "He had no form or majesty that we should look at him, nothing in his appearance that we should desire him" (Isa 53:2). The grand miracle was a concealed miracle.

The miracle stories of the Bible often play a revelatory role. In the Gospel of John, the use of the word "sign" for events like the turning of water to wine at Cana (John 2:1–11) means that these events give indications about who Jesus is. The feeding of the multitudes is a sign that the one who turns a little bread into a great deal of bread in an unexplained way is the creator who every year turns a little grain into a great deal of grain through natural processes.[38] Conversely, Jesus' healings, and the fact that he is moved to do them because of compassion for the sufferers and not simply by a wish to demonstrate power (for example, Mark 1:41), shows the character of God.

The fact that miracles may serve revelation should not, however, obscure the fact that a demand for them as proof of religious claims is a mark of a theology of glory. Jesus made this clear when he refused demands for a sign—other than the sign of Jonah (Matt 12:38–40).

But is it reasonable in a scientific age to believe that miracles have happened? They used to be thought of as one of the strongest supports for Christianity, but the successes of scientific explanation caused many non-Christians to ridicule them, and many Christians to sympathize with the words of Seeberg: "The miracle was once the basis of all apologetic, it then became an apologetic crutch, and today one can call it not infrequently a cross borne by apologetics."[39] Christians today are often more embarrassed than edified by stories of miracles.

The major objection to miracles was given classic form by Hume: "A miracle is a violation of the laws of nature; and as a firm and unalterable experience has established these laws, the proof against a miracle, from the very nature of the fact, is as entire as any argument from experience can possibly be imagined."[40] Uniform human experience testifies, for example, that the dead are not raised, so any reports of resurrections must be mistaken.

It is easy to point out Hume's formal error: The assumed uniformity of nature is arrived at only by rejecting reported non-uniformities. A fundamental principle of science is that one has to pay attention to what is observed. Observations are sometimes incorrect and witnesses may misinterpret or lie about what they have seen, but many scientific discoveries have been made by following up observations that didn't fit into previously established patterns. A serious examination of claims for extraordinary phenomena must examine the evidence.

But there is some truth in Hume's argument. We have some confidence in the uniformity of nature and don't accept all claims for extraordinary phenomena. They have to be evaluated together with their contexts and implications, and it is the latter part of this task that many skeptics omit. A report that an otherwise undistinguished person, with no particular message or connection with any religious tradition, once fed thousands of people with five loaves and two fish, would have no supporting context. We could see it only as a strange, isolated event, coming from nowhere and going nowhere. Such a report made of a man who proclaimed the kingdom of God and love for others, who died for this message and was claimed by his followers to have risen from the dead and to be the Son of God, has to be evaluated differently. That doesn't mean that reports of the event will automatically be taken as historically accurate: The fact that we have no scientific explanation for it remains. But it is the total claim that must be evaluated.

Given that miraculous events have occurred, our emphasis on kenosis will lead us to look for connections between them and natural processes. One approach is to understand miracles as the same things that happen normally in the world, but with special timing or intensity. Explanations of some healings as psychosomatic, the feeding of the multitudes as a "social miracle" in which Jesus got a boy to share his lunch and inspire others to follow his example, and the passage of the Sea of Reeds in terms of the timing of the weather (Exod 14:21) would be examples of this approach. Edward Kessel has even proposed a way in which virginal conception of a male human being would be possible.[41] There are limits beyond which this sort of explanation becomes grotesque. Surface tension allows small insects to walk on water but this cannot be extrapolated to explain Jesus walking on the sea.

A different approach is suggested by a passage in the tractate "Aboth" of the Mishnah: "Ten things were created on the eve of Sabbath between the suns at nightfall: the mouth of the earth, the mouth of the well, the mouth of the she-ass, the rainbow, and the manna and the rod and the Shamir, the letters and the writing and the Tables [of stone]. Some say also: The evil spirits and the sepulchre of Moses and the ram of Abraham our father. Some say also: The tongs made with tongs."[42]

The rabbis faced here the question of the origin of marvelous things in the Bible such as the donkey that spoke to Balaam (Num 22:28). (The last item is different: It seems to have to do with unexplained beginnings, and perhaps with the origins of technology.) They are not mentioned in the works of the six days in Genesis 1, so they must have been made in the moment "between the six days of creation and the nightfall which ushered in the first Sabbath Day."[43] That is based on the assumption that all the types of things that exist were created at the beginning. Somehow then the talking donkey and other marvels must have been created at the start and kept for the time of their use by God.

Miracles were not hard-wired into the universe billions of years ago, for chaos theory shows that the future cannot be orchestrated from initial conditions with that precision. But the basic idea of the passage in the Mishnah may still be useful. We would picture miracles as very rare natural processes whose possibility is inherent in the basic pattern that underlies the universe but which happen so seldom that we are unable to see how they fit into that pattern.

A final way of thinking about miracles makes use of Gödel's theorem, which took the mathematical world by surprise in 1931.[44] It says that any axiomatic mathematical system that is at least as complex as arithmetic is incomplete in the sense that there are questions that can be asked within the system but cannot be answered within it. When this theorem is applied to the mathematical system of the laws of physics, it suggests that there will be phenomena that those laws cannot describe, phenomena that we might identify with miracles.

None of these suggestions really seems adequate to deal with traditional Christian claims about the resurrection of Jesus, a miracle that is essential for the historic Christian faith. This miracle should not be "spiritualized" in a way that amounts to a denial of the value of the material world, but also should not be thought of in a way that makes it just the same type of thing as an ordinary historical event. The raising to new life of the crucified one is seen in the New Testament as the turn from an old order of things to a new, an orientation to the future that cannot be understood entirely in terms of what has gone before. For this reason I defer further discussion of it until I consider the future of the universe in chapter 12.

NOTES

1. Saint Thomas Aquinas, *Summa Contra Gentiles, Book Two: Creation* (Notre Dame, Ind.: University of Notre Dame Press, 1975), 34.

2. Martin Luther, *A Contemporary Translation of Luther's Small Catechism* (trans. Timothy J. Wengert; Minneapolis: Augsburg Fortress, 1996), 21.

3. "The Heidelberg Catechism," in *The Reformed Confessions of the Sixteenth Century* (ed. Arthur C. Cochrane; Philadelphia: Westminster, 1966), 309.

4. Heinrich Schmid, *The Doctrinal Theology of the Evangelical Lutheran Church* (3d ed.; Minneapolis: Augsburg, 1961), 170–94; *CD* 3:3.

5. Schmid, *Doctrinal Theology,* 172.

6. Aquinas, *Summa Contra Gentiles, Book Three: Providence, Part I,* 235–37.

7. Fritjof Capra, *The Tao of Physics* (Boulder, Colo.: Shambhala, 1975), chapter 15.

8. *CD* 3:3:30–33.

9. J. N. D. Kelly, *Early Christian Creeds* (3d ed.; London: Longmans, 1972), 136–39.

10. Two versions are given in Ian Barbour, *Religion in an Age of Science* (San Francisco: HarperCollins, 1990), 244; and *Religion and Science: Historical and Contemporary Issues* (San Francisco: HarperCollins, 1997), 305.

11. "Psalm 147," *LW* 14:114.

12. *CD* 3:3:134.

13. Margaret J. Osler, *Divine Will and the Mechanical Philosophy* (New York: Cambridge University Press, 1994), chapter 1.

14. Thomas F. Torrance, *Divine and Contingent Order* (New York: Oxford University Press, 1981).

15. Donald G. Dawe, *The Form of a Servant* (Philadelphia: Westminster, 1963).

16. Nancey Murphy and George F. R. Ellis, *On the Moral Nature of the Universe: Theology, Cosmology, and Ethics* (Minneapolis: Fortress, 1996). See also John Polkinghorne, ed., *The Work of Love: Creation as Kenosis* (Grand Rapids, Mich.: Eerdmans, 2001).

17. Murphy and Ellis, *On the Moral Nature of the Universe,* 18.

18. Ibid., 251.

19. Rudolf Bultmann, *Jesus Christ and Mythology* (New York: Charles Scribner's Sons, 1958), 69.

20. William Pollard, *Chance and Providence* (New York: Charles Scribner's Sons, 1958).

21. Robert John Russell, "Special Providence and Genetic Mutation: A New Defense of Theistic Evolution," in *Evolutionary and Molecular Biology: Scientific Perspectives on Divine Action* (ed. Robert John Russell, William R. Stoeger, S.J., and Francisco Ayala; Berkeley, Calif.: Center for Theology and the Natural Sciences, 1998), 191–223.

22. Ibid., 193.

23. George L. Murphy, "Energy and the Generation of the World," *Zygon* 29 (1994): 259.

24. Glenn R. Morrow, "Energeia," *Dictionary of Philosophy* (rev. and enl. ed.; New York: Philosophical Library, 1983), 106. .

25. Jaroslav Pelikan, *The Spirit of Eastern Christendom (600–1700)* (Chicago: University of Chicago Press, 1974), 62–75.

26. George. L. Murphy, "Energy and the Generation of the World," 271–72.

27. This Jewish blessing has been taken over into the Roman eucharistic liturgy. See, for example, Lucien Deiss, *Springtime of the Liturgy* (Collegeville, Minn.: Liturgical Press, 1979), 5–6.

28. Athanasius, "On the Incarnation of the Word," *NPNF* 2:4:37.

29. Howard J. Van Till, "Basil, Augustine, and the Doctrine of Creation's Functional Intergrity," *Science and Christian Belief* 8 (1996): 21.

30. Schmid, *Doctrinal Theology,* 185.

31. Douglas John Hall, *God and Human Suffering: An Exercise in the Theology of the Cross* (Minneapolis: Augsburg, 1986), is helpful.

32. *LW* 2:134 and 14:335.

33. Charles Hartshorne, *Omnipotence and Other Theological Mistakes* (Albany: State University of New York Press, 1984).

34. A brief discussion of Augustine's view is in "Enchiridion," *NPNF* 1:3:239–43.

35. John Polkinghorne, *Science and Providence: God's Interaction with the World* (London: SPCK: 1989), 65–67.

36. Barnabas Lindars, "Miracle," *WDCT,* 370–72, provides an overview and references.

37. C. S. Lewis, *Miracles* (New York: Macmillan, 1947), chapter 14.

38. Ibid., 140–44.

39. R. Seeberg, "Wunder," in *Realencyklopädie für protestantische Theologie und Kirche* (Leipzig: J. C. Hinrichs, 1908), Dritter Auflage, 21:562. (My translation.)

40. David Hume, "Of Miracles," section 10 of "An Enquiry Concerning Human Understanding," in *Enquiries Concerning Human Understanding and Concerning the Principles of Morals* (3d ed.; Oxford: Clarendon, 1975), 114.

41. Edward L. Kessel, "A Proposed Biological Interpretation of the Virgin Birth," *Journal of the American Scientific Affiliation* 35 (1983): 129.

42. Herbert Danby, ed., "Tractate Aboth 5.6," in *The Mishnah* (Oxford: Oxford University Press, 1933), 456.

43. Ibid., n. 8.

44. Kurt Gödel, *On Formally Undecidable Propositions of Principia Mathematica and Related Systems* (New York: Dover, 1992).

· 7 ·

THE ORIGIN OF THE UNIVERSE

❧

SCIENCE AND THEOLOGY ON ORIGINS

I have dealt with scientific understandings of the world and theological concepts of divine action in a relatively small region of space-time, and now want to expand our view out in space and back in time. Those dimensions are connected because of the finite speed of light. Photons that enter our eyes when we see the galaxy in Andromeda on a clear moonless night left there about 3 million years ago. We also get other information from the past, "time capsules" such as fossils in the earth's crust or rocks from the surface of the moon.

Although the Bible now begins with the Genesis creation accounts, they are not the first witnesses to revelation. The traditional belief that Moses wrote them meant that they came from a setting in which the God of Israel had revealed himself in the saving acts of the exodus. Belief that it was this God (and not an abstract supreme being) who created the universe is important for understanding what creation means. While few critical biblical scholars today accept Mosaic authorship of Genesis, the thesis of von Rad, that Israel first experienced YHWH as savior in the exodus and saw creation in the light of this event, makes the same point.[1]

The "historical credo" of Deut 26:5–10 contains nothing about the origin of the world. The Israelite who brings first fruits to the sanctuary is to rehearse God's saving acts of the exodus and to conclude with, "So now I bring the first of the fruit of the ground that you, O LORD, have given me." Israel's beliefs about origins developed in the context of this faith. The later context of the Babylonian exile helps us to understand why Gen

1 contains material directed against Babylonian polytheism and cosmogony. In Isa 40–55, which was probably written around the same time, we find faith in the God of Israel as sole creator and redeemer combined with the exodus, return from exile, and polemic against idols.

Sola scriptura does not mean that we must approach Scripture with no knowledge of the conditions from which it comes. The biblical languages are not learned from the Bible alone and a "secular" knowledge of geography is important for understanding the historical narratives of Scripture. By the same token, we must take into account the physical character of the universe if we want to have the deepest understanding of what it means to say that God is the creator of that universe. But we begin now with some of the relevant biblical material.

BIBLICAL CREATION ACCOUNTS

Several passages in the New Testament, John 1:1–5, 1 Cor 8:6, Col 1:15–20, and Heb 1:2, speak of Christ as the agent of creation. The Colossians passage is especially comprehensive. But the New Testament gives us no creation stories. We turn to the Old Testament for these, reading them with the belief that "there is one God, the Father, from whom are all things and for whom we exist, and one Lord, Jesus Christ, through whom are all things and through whom we exist" (1 Cor 8:6).

One group of texts speaks about God as creator in a very dramatic way. For example:

> You rule the raging of the sea;
> when its waves rise, you still them.
> You crushed Rahab like a carcass;
> you scattered your enemies with your mighty arm.
> The heavens are yours, the earth also is yours;
> the world and all that is in it—you have founded them.
> The north and the south—you created them;
> Tabor and Hermon joyously praise your name. (Ps 89:9–12)

Psalm 74:12–17, Isa 51:9–10, and Job 26:12–13 are other texts that use the image of God slaying a sea monster (Rahab, Leviathan) as part of the divine creative work of long ago. The primordial battle with chaos, which is known in other cultures, is used here to express the faith of Israel that YHWH is the creator.[2] Especially in Isa 51:9–10, we see that the motif can also be connected with the exodus.

Battle with chaos is not a fully developed doctrine of creation, but these texts make two important contributions to such a doctrine. They remind us that biblical texts about creation can be true without being historical narratives and they make us aware that creation is costly to God. The story of divine command and fulfillment in Gen 1 gives a picture of a creator who is unscathed by the act of creation. The struggle with chaos is a complementary image.

Turning to those more influential Genesis accounts, the first thing to say is that they are true and authoritative. The second is to ask what kinds of accounts they are and how they are to be read. Failure to ask those questions and an implicit assumption that "true account" must mean "accurate account of historical events" has caused a great deal of grief.

Genesis 1:1–2:4a and 2:4b–25 speak of creation very differently. Attempts to "harmonize" them by fitting the events of the second account into the six-day framework of the first ignore the fact that the order of creation of living things in the second account differs from that of the first. But differences are not simply matters of detail. The whole atmosphere of the story in which God gets down in the dirt of a very dry world to make a man differs from that in which God utters sovereign commands to bring the world into being in a watery environment.

Thus the possibility suggests itself that one, or perhaps both, of these accounts should not be read as a description of events that took place in the early universe. That is to say, there is *internal* evidence in Scripture itself that the Genesis accounts may be read in other ways. But it would be disingenuous to suggest that we have come to this conclusion just by reading the Bible carefully. Equally important is the *external* evidence that the earth is much older than the approximately six thousand years of traditional biblical chronologies and that living things came into being over periods of millions of years, not days. Attempts to read the Genesis accounts as accurate scientific reports conflict with observation of the way the world is. The cosmological picture used in Gen 1 is not that of modern science but of cultures of the ancient Near East.

Thus both external and internal evidence encourage us to read the Genesis accounts as theological statements rather than as modern scientific descriptions or historical narratives. At the same time we should not simply spiritualize or allegorize these texts.[3] Genesis 1 and 2 speak theologically about the real world. The sun and moon created on the fourth day are the real star and satellite that we see today, and the fact that we can identify at least two of the rivers in 2:10–14 means that the text is talking about our world, not some mythical landscape.

What do these texts tell us about God's relationship with the universe? Leaving biological and environmental issues to later chapters, I concentrate here on cosmological aspects of the first Genesis account that are helpful in providing a theological context for a scientific view. Reference should be made to commentaries for more detailed discussion.[4]

Genesis 1:1 can be translated in two different ways, which are found with slight variations in different versions, sometimes with the alternate given in a footnote: "In the beginning God created the heavens and the earth" (RSV, NIV, REB, KJV); "In the beginning when God created the heavens and the earth . . ." (NRSV, NAB, TEV). The second translation implies that God began creation with the condition described in verse 2, and thus is open to the idea that there was some formless material with which God worked. The first translation, on the other hand, indicates a temporal origin of the universe and is consistent with, though it does not require, the traditional idea of *creatio ex nihilo.* The fact that both translations can be defended grammatically should keep us from being too dogmatic about a temporal origin, and open to understanding *creatio ex nihilo* in terms of an eternal dependence of the world on God. As we will see, some scientific cosmologies suggest this idea.

But Claus Westermann has given strong arguments in favor of the first translation.[5] He points out that the first verse of Genesis has no parallels in other ancient Near Eastern creation accounts. It is not part of the creation story itself but "a heading that takes in everything in the narrative in one single sentence."[6] Furthermore, the second translation results in a rather complex sentence that is very different from the simple grammatical style of the rest of the narrative. The traditional rendering of the King James translation, which the *Apollo 8* astronauts read to the earth as they rounded the moon on Christmas Eve of 1968, is thus to be preferred.

"The earth was a formless void, and darkness covered the face of the deep" (1:2a). Did God create the universe from "formless matter" or create prime matter and then give it form?[7] With today's picture of matter composed of patterned interactions, the concept of "formless" matter is close to "nothing." The primordial sea, which originally may have meant material out of which the universe would be made, can be pictured as the formless nothingness *in spite of which* God creates the universe. But "nothing" in "creation out of nothing" does not mean a peculiar "negative something" that has the potential to become a "positive something," but the denial of such a potential. *Creatio ex nihilo,* which is impossible from a creaturely standpoint, is possible only for the God "Who gives life to the dead and calls into existence the things that do not exist" (Rom 4:17). This is why Bonhoeffer, as I noted earlier, says that we know of creation in the beginning because of Easter, and a bit later: "The dark deep—that is the first sound of the power of darkness, of the passion of Jesus Christ."[8]

God creates through his Word, whom Christians identify with Jesus Christ. Here we should note the connection between God speaking the world into existence and the "Word of the LORD," which came to the prophets, the word that is "like fire . . . and like a hammer that breaks a rock in pieces" (Jer 23:29). When God speaks, things happen.[9]

In Gen 1, God creates living things mediately, by commanding the materials of the world to bring them forth. This is in accord with our picture of divine action in which God acts through natural processes. It will be of great interest in our consideration of biological evolution, but there is also an important cosmological aspect to be considered, for it is not self-evident that the material of the world could produce life. All life that we know of requires, among other conditions, the presence of carbon and water. A universe consisting entirely of hydrogen, for example, would not be able to bring forth life as we know it.

The requirement that carbon exist imposes fairly stringent conditions. Only the lightest elements, hydrogen and helium, were formed in significant amounts in the big bang. When stars first condense from clouds of gas, they generate energy from reactions that fuse hydrogen into helium. If the star is sufficiently massive, the temperature in its core can become high enough for helium to fuse into carbon. But this reaction, in which three helium nuclei come together in a fraction of a second, is only possible because the strengths of the electromagnetic and strong forces in the nucleus allow the carbon nucleus to exist in just the right state. If the ratio of these forces were slightly different, the reaction could not occur at an appreciable rate. Carbon would not be formed or would quickly be converted to oxygen by further fusion.[10]

Whether one calls this a "coincidence" or "fine tuning" depends on one's perspective. We can call it fine tuning because we begin with belief that God is the creator of the universe and that the emergence of life is part of the divine purpose. But this is different from claiming that the energy levels of the carbon nucleus are a proof of divine creation.

The creation of sun, moon, and stars on the fourth day is most likely theological polemic against religions in which these bodies were worshiped. During their exile the Jews encountered at firsthand the Babylonian cult with its idea that human beings are slaves of the celestial deities. This religion of the conqueror, with its impressive public ceremonies, was undoubtedly attractive to many of the exiles, and is attacked openly in Isa 2. The criticism in Genesis is more subtle. There the heavenly bodies are made neither first, as if they had precedence, nor last, as if they were the crown of God's work. Sun and moon are made in the middle of the creation week and are given definite purposes—to light the earth and to mark time. They are not divine. The stars are included almost as an afterthought.

Human beings are created on the sixth day, along with the other land animals, but something special takes place with them. God does not simply issue the command for humanity to come into being, but takes counsel. This creature is made in the image and likeness of God, and given dominion over the earth (Gen 1:26–28). Later I will discuss the place of humanity in nature and the meaning of the commission that is given to it. For now I emphasize that the origin of our species is embedded in the story of the creation of the universe, and that this origin is the penultimate creative act of God.

The final act is the Sabbath. God's rest on the seventh day does not mean that God stopped doing anything: "My Father is still working, and I also am working" (John 5:17) was Jesus' response when he was criticized for healing on the Sabbath. The Sabbath was seen by Jews in Jesus' time as a foretaste of the coming kingdom of God.[11] This gives the stories of his healings on the Sabbath special significance, for that is precisely the *right* time for these signs of the inbreaking of the kingdom. The conclusion of the creation account thus points forward toward the goal of creation.[12]

And all the creation, whose parts have been pronounced "good" in God's sight, is said to be "very good" (Gen 1:31). The material world is in accord with God's intention, is harmonious, and contains beauty. It is not said that everything was perfect in the beginning, unable to become better. The fact that "very good" is spoken before the Sabbath, before the promise of fulfillment of God's purpose, suggests that God intends to accomplish this purpose through a process of growth, an idea present in the works of Athanasius and Irenaeus.

THE STRUCTURE AND EVOLUTION OF THE COSMOS

Scientific cosmology, the study of the universe as a whole, began as a coherent discipline in the twentieth century.[13] A hundred years ago there was debate about whether our Milky Way galaxy, a roughly disk-shaped system about 100,000 light years across and containing around 100,000,000,000 stars, was the entire universe. Some astronomers thought that many of the "nebulae" such as the prominent one in Andromeda were galaxies in their own right. Henrietta Leavitt discovered a property of the bright Cepheid variable stars that made it possible to determine the amount of light they emit, and thus to determine their distances. Identification of one of these variables in a region of space made it possible to calculate the distance to that region. Edwin Hubble was then able to show that some of the nebulae lie well outside our galaxy. The farthest galaxies that we can now see are several billion light years away.

The fact that the stellar universe was much larger than had been thought did not in itself demand any radical change in people's view of the world, but Hubble's next discovery did. The overall structure of the universe was changing.

Study of the light from other galaxies found a great predominance of shifts toward the red end of the spectrum. Such changes in positions of spectral lines often indicate an approaching or receding motion of the light source owing to the Doppler shift: When source and observer approach one another, waves are shortened and light is shifted toward the violet end of the spectrum, while recession results in waves being stretched and light being shifted to the red. The galactic redshifts suggested a general recessional motion. In 1929 Hubble announced a correlation between the velocities implied by these redshifts and distances: The velocity of a galaxy is proportional to its distance, the more distant ones moving the fastest.

This statement can be explained with a simple model owing to E. A. Milne.[14] It is *too* simple to explain all we know about cosmology, but is helpful for a first orientation. According to Milne, the fastest galaxies are the farthest away simply *because* they are the fastest. If all the galaxies were ejected at velocities ranging from zero to the speed of light from a gigantic explosion at some time in the past, the ones that were moving fastest would have traveled the farthest. (Since the "edge" of this universe recedes at the speed of light, relativity says that observers on all the galaxies will all see themselves at the center of the expansion.)

Velocity is distance traveled divided by elapsed time, so knowledge of distances and velocities allows us to estimate the time since the initial "big bang." This "Hubble time" is now thought to be about 14 billion years. More sophisticated models take into account variation of the rate of expansion in the past, so that the time from the beginning is only approximately equal to the Hubble time.[15] This is often called "the age of the universe," though it would be more accurate to say "the estimated time since the beginning of cosmic expansion."[16]

From a strict philosophical standpoint there is no way to prove that the universe did not come into existence recently with geological strata, abundance of elements, and receding galaxies arranged to look billions of years old.[17] The world could be six thousand years or fifteen minutes old, with our memories and everything else concocted to give an appearance of great age. But this would mean that the world is fundamentally misleading about its own character, and is ruled out by belief in the goodness of creation.

A more serious alternative was the steady state theory, which was developed in the 1940s by several British cosmologists.[18] At that time there was a problem with the age of the universe. Owing (we now know) to errors in distance measurements, the Hubble time was thought to be only about 2 billion years, less than the age of the earth's crust. But in addition to this difficulty, some scientists wanted to avoid any hint of a cosmic origin at some instant of the past, an idea that seemed too reminiscent of religious concepts of divine creation.

The steady state theorists pointed out that cosmic expansion could be extrapolated back to an initial explosion only if matter is conserved. If matter were continually coming into being, the universe could expand forever and yet always look the same. Matter would appear and condense into new galaxies as old ones moved apart. An infinite universe could exist forever in a steady state, and there would be no unique creation instant.

One point in favor of the steady state theory is that it made unique predictions while the big bang theory has a number of possible models. The basic question is whether or not the universe billions of years ago was significantly different from the way it is today. In big bang models the universe began in a state in which all matter was much more concentrated than now, while the steady state theory said that no matter how far one went back into the past, the universe as a whole would have looked as it does today.

George Gamow developed the big bang theory far enough to make predictions that would eventually allow a decision.[19] He and his coworkers showed that fusion reactions in a mixture of free elementary particles and radiation would have been important in the big bang's extremely hot early stages. These reactions would have produced various light nuclei until the temperature dropped too low for them to proceed. The radiation would have also cooled, losing energy and shifting to longer wavelengths, but should still pervade the universe.

In 1965, microwave radiation with the characteristics of emission from a body at about three degrees above absolute zero was detected from all parts of the sky. Other observations at different wavelengths have confirmed that interpretation, and the expected small variations in temperature owing to lack of smoothness in the early universe have been detected. Most cosmologists now believe that the microwave background is a relic of the "primordial fireball," and that the steady state theory should be abandoned.[20]

Production of atomic nuclei in the early universe can also be confirmed. The big bang theory cannot explain the abundance of all nuclei: Elements heavier than helium were formed later in stellar interiors. But theory predicts that about 25 percent of the mass of atoms in the universe should be helium, and this agrees well with observations. We have good reasons to believe not only that the universe is expanding, but that this expansion began in a hot big bang.

THE EARLY UNIVERSE

Einstein first applied his general theory of relativity to cosmology in 1917, when it was still thought that the universe was static. The gravitation of an initially static collection of matter would make it collapse, so Einstein added a "cosmological term" to his equations. This term represented a repulsive force effective at large distances, which could balance gravitational attraction and make a static universe possible. The resulting "Einstein universe" was finite but unbounded, like the three-dimensional surface of a four-dimensional sphere.

Theorists soon found solutions of Einstein's equations representing other types of space and universes that expanded or contracted in the course of time. Thus when Hubble announced his discovery and it was realized that the universe was expanding, there were a number of relativistic models available to represent it. Einstein then dropped the cosmological term and many other cosmologists followed his example, though we will see in chapter 12 that this decision was apparently too hasty.

All of the viable cosmological models resulting from Einstein's theory seem to have something that looks like a moment of origin. If we use Einstein's equations to extrapolate cosmic expansion back in time, we find that the density of matter and the curvature of space-time increase without limit as we approach a certain time in the past. The equations seem to break down at this event, which may be labeled "t = 0", and we cannot use the equations to get beyond it. This has suggested to many people an identification of the beginning of cosmic expansion with a moment of divine creation. As we saw, distaste for such interpretations was one of the driving forces behind the steady state theory.

But the big bang theory seems to be correct and the temptation to tie this fact to some religious concept of creation has been strong. Astronomer Robert Jastrow put it this way: "For the scientist who has lived by his faith in the power of reason, the story ends like a bad dream. He has scaled the mountains of ignorance; he is about to conquer the highest peak; as he pulls himself over the final rock, he is greeted by a band of theologians who have been sitting there for centuries."[21] The implication that the doctrine of creation has to do only with the beginning of the universe, and that scientists never encounter theological issues anywhere else, is problematic. But first we should examine what we know, or may know, about the early universe from science.

When we observe the microwave background radiation we are already getting signals from close to the beginning, at a time when the universe had cooled enough to allow electrons and nuclei to combine into atoms so that the universe became transparent to radiation. This was when the universe was about half a million years old, a small fraction of the total time since the expansion began until now. An analogy will give a feeling for the scope of our observations. Suppose that the present is noon of a day that began at midnight when the universe started its expansion. A galaxy receding at half the speed of light is then observed as it was around 6:30 A.M. Distant quasars emitted their light a few minutes after 1 A.M. And the microwave background gives us information about the universe at one *second* after midnight.

That is not the end of the story. While we cannot receive radiation from earlier epochs, we do get other types of signals. The nuclei formed in the first minutes of the big bang are fossils that carry information to us about that time. The title of Weinberg's book *The First Three Minutes* refers to the first minutes of the universe in real time, not in our analogy.

We understand the basic physical processes that took place in the universe back to about a billionth of a second after the beginning of the expansion. This does not mean that we know the details of everything that happened from that time on. The spatial variations we see in the background radiation indicate the presence of regions of condensations that began to form into galaxies and clusters of galaxies because of their enhanced gravitation. But the formation of galaxies is a complicated problem involving fluid mechanics, gravitation, and magnetic fields, and we do not yet have a fully developed and tested theory of how this took place.

What was God doing during all this time? With our theology of divine action we can give a very simple answer: God was doing all of these things we have just described. In the first minutes God was acting through the strong and electroweak interactions to bring about the formation of the light elements. God acted through gravitation in the general expansion of the universe and the condensation of matter into galaxies and stars. The fundamental processes that were involved in all of these things are the same processes that we observe today in the shining of the sun, the fall of bodies to the earth, and the chemical reactions of our metabolisms, and we say in the First Article of the Nicene Creed that we believe God to be active in all these things. As we have extrapolated our scientific understanding of processes from the present to the first millionth of a second, we extrapolate our theological understanding of God's involvement with those processes as well.

God's kenosis means that we do not expect to observe astronomical phenomena that science *cannot* explain. Of course, this doesn't mean that we won't ever observe things that are unexpected: The expansion of the universe is a counterexample. But the scientific response will be to search for a broader understanding of natural processes, not to consider the phenomenon to be a miracle. There is no distinctive "creation science" or "origins science." Divine self-limitation also means that there are limits on the kind of universe God could create. Life, for example, could not have come into being until the universe was at least several million years old, when matter and radiation had cooled and stars and planets could form.

Cosmologists are not content to stop at a billionth of a second, but want to get as close to t = 0 as possible. The further back we go in imagination, the more speculative the theories become. We reach epochs when the density and temperature would have been high enough to bring into play new aspects of matter predicted by the theories that attempt to unify the basic interactions. In these theories the fields that describe matter can exist in different phases, much as water displays the phases of steam, liquid, and ice. At high enough temperatures there would have been complete symmetry between basic interactions and thus no real difference between them. As the universe cooled, during a tiny fraction of a second this symmetry would have disappeared and the different forces would have emerged, a bit like what happens when steam condenses to liquid and then freezes. Water can be supercooled carefully so that it remains a liquid below zero degrees Celsius. However, a slight disturbance could cause it to freeze suddenly. The idea that a similar thing could have happened in the early universe is the basis for *inflationary* cosmologies.[22] The excess energy in the supercooled phase would have driven an extra-fast expansion, which could explain features of the present universe such as its large-scale uniformity.

We would like to find evidence of this very early period.[23] The great preponderance of matter over antimatter in the present universe may have originated then. Negative evidence is provided by the absence of isolated magnetic poles, which always occur in north-south pairs. Some theories predict that monopoles should have been produced in the very early universe, but inflation would have greatly diluted their concentration to the point that we can find none.

As we approach even more closely to t = 0, the rapidly changing curvature of space-time in the initial stages of expansion would affect the quantum fields that describe matter and could result in particles being created from the quantum vacuum.[24] Thus physical processes might have been able to bring forth the material content of the universe.

That suggestion may seem strange and even self-contradictory: How can physics describe something coming from nothing? A simple model, however, suggests how this might work.[25] Imagine a state in which there are no particles, no mass, and no energy, and a process by which two particles come into being. This would be impossible in prerelativistic physics with its law of conservation of mass, but Einstein's $E = mc^2$ means that mass is subsumed under the energy conservation law. Thus the process could happen if the energy of the two particles were equal to the zero energy of the initial state. This would be possible because the energy of gravitational interaction between the two particles is negative. (Positive work has to be done to pull them apart.) The transition between the no-particle state and the two-particle state would have to be a discontinuous process, but quantum theory allows such jumps.

This is a greatly oversimplified model. General relativity links matter and space-time, so an adequate theory must explain not just the origin of matter in a preexisting space-time framework, but a way in which matter and space-time could come into existence together. The simple model does, however, suggest that the idea is worth pursuing.

The proposal that origin of matter and of space-time itself might be explained by a scientific theory naturally raises the question, "What's left for God to do?" But if we eschew the use of God as a stop-gap, we will have no good reason to halt at this point. If the suggestion of the previous paragraphs is correct, God did indeed bring matter and space-time into being, but did so through processes that might be described by a suitable quantum theory of matter and gravitation.

This suggestion is perhaps startling but it is not new. Before the rise of modern science, the medieval Jewish philosopher Gersonides gave an "account of creation [which] is remarkable in the history of medieval cosmological theories . . . particularly with regard to the rigor with which he insists that the laws of physics are so universal as to be retrojected to the very beginning."[26] Emil Brunner made the connection between God's self-limitation in the origination of the universe and the divine kenosis of Phil 2: "This, however, means that God does not wish to occupy the whole of Space Himself, but that He wills to make room for other forms of existence. In doing so He limits Himself. . . . The κένωσις, which reaches its paradoxical climax in the Cross of Christ, began with the Creation of the world."[27] Moltmann has developed this idea in some detail, using Isaac Luria's concept of *zimsum*, "a withdrawing of oneself into oneself," to say that "God makes room for his creation by withdrawing his presence."[28] The basic idea of kenosis in creation does not, however, have to depend as strongly on the spatial metaphors of withdrawal and making room as Moltmann's presentation does.[29]

Kenosis means that God does not cling to privileges of divinity and insist upon credit for creative work, just as Christ did not think equality with God "something to be exploited."[30] God is willing to let his own creatures get credit for the divine work, and to be upstaged by them, to be, in Bonhoeffer's phrase, "pushed out of the world on to the cross."

It is natural to imagine the creative word of Gen 1 as an authoritative shout that evoked the world as a faint echo. But when the Word comes into the world, he can be ignored (John 1:11), and when Jesus speaks to still the storm at sea (echoes of Gen 1:2), it is merely to say "Peace! Be still!" (Mark 4:39.) Perhaps Haydn captured the right note in *The Creation*. In it, God's initial command for the creation of light is almost a whisper: "Und Gott sprach: Es werde Licht! Und es ward"—and then comes a powerful "LICHT" and a joyous blaze of music. The thunder of creation drowns out the still, small voice of the creator.

But we do not at present have a full scientific theory of the origin of the material world. (And if such a theory were achieved, it might be beyond our abilities to test.) In the model universes we have described, the density of matter and curvature of space-time go to infinity as we approach the zero of time and Einstein's equations seem to reduce to the useless statement "infinity equals infinity." In the 1960s Penrose and Hawking proved that, under fairly general conditions, such a "singularity" is inevitable.[31]

A space-time singularity implies something more radical than that a strange thing happens at some instant, and even to say "infinity equals infinity" is misleading. A more precise statement is that there is no t = 0: Space-time is incomplete. Einstein's equations do not fail to tell us what happens "at" the singularity for there is no time and place at which anything may happen. A singular space-time is one from which an event or events have been torn out. The initial cosmic singularity is not unique, for space-times that represent black holes are also singular.

The breakdown of Einstein's theory indicates the need for a satisfactory theory of quantum gravity that combines general relativity and quantum mechanics, something that has not yet been achieved.[32] We do know, however, that the combination of these two fundamental insights of twentieth-century physics places a limit on ordinary concepts of space and time. General relativity says that gravitation changes the rate at which a clock runs, while the uncertainty principle says that an increase in a clock's precision also increases the uncertainty in its energy, and thus in its gravitational field. Increasing the precision of a clock will eventually distort the rate at which it runs, so that there will be a limit to the size of intervals it can measure.[33] This limit is the "Planck time," about 10^{-43} seconds. It is determined by the speed of light, Planck's quantum constant, and the strength of gravitation. For time intervals less than this or for lengths less than the distance light can travel in this time, 10^{-35} meters (vastly smaller than atomic sizes), time and space lose the significance we usually attribute to them.

Conditions during an initial Planck instant in which the whole observable universe would have been compressed into a region a few hundred current atoms across can hardly be imagined. Some progress has been made toward understanding such a state by studying simplified model universes. The proposal that has gotten the most attention is that of Hartle and Hawking, which describes a universe without either spatial or temporal boundaries. The whole of space-time would be like a four-dimensional hyperspherical surface.[34] This is accomplished by using a time variable that is imaginary in the mathematical sense. In this way an attempt is made to transcend the idea of a universe coming into existence in favor of one that simply is. This theory is provocative, but it should be emphasized that it is a very simple model that has not yet been developed into a realistic representation of the universe we inhabit.[35]

THE WORD OF GOD AND THE LOGOS OF THE UNIVERSE

"All things came into being through" the Logos, who would become flesh in Jesus (John 1:3, 14). The primary root of the Johannine Logos concept is the Old Testament's "Word of the LORD," the Word that has creative power. It is likely that the "utterance" (*memra*) of the Aramaic Targums played a role in mediating the idea to the Fourth Gospel.[36] But the concept also gave Philo and early Christian apologists such as Justin Martyr contact with ideas about a cosmic Logos or world reason in the philosophies of their culture.[37] The Logos concept can also be useful today in dealing with questions about cosmology and the laws of physics.[38]

Suppose that the origin of the material universe can indeed be understood in terms of known laws of physics, though perhaps laws that differ considerably from present theories. (Explanations of space-time and matter in terms of stringlike or membranelike entities at the Planck scale are thought to be promising by some theorists.[39]) We would then comprehend the natural processes by which matter came into being or, in the case of models like that of Hartle and Hawking, by which matter simply is. These processes would be continuous with those taking place in our world today. We would then know the means of God's ongoing work of creation from the beginning. There would be no "gaps" at the level of scientific questions, no phenomena in the world that would necessitate unmediated divine action.

Such a "theory of everything" will require the existence of *something*—quantum fields, superstrings, or perhaps entities we know nothing of at present. The vacuum of quantum field theories from which particles may have been pulled in the very early universe is not "nothing," the *nihil negativa* of the traditional *creatio ex nihilo*. Moreover, the laws of the fields themselves must be operative. "Something" exists, and we can ask, "Why something rather than nothing?" One can simply refuse to ask questions that science can't answer. But if we do ask them, we must be willing to consider theological answers.

The concept of the uncreated divine Logos or Wisdom of God provides a way to answer such questions in conjunction with the "inverted Platonism" that I discussed in chapter 5. The pattern of the world lies on the creature side of the fundamental creator-creature division, and originating and preserving this pattern is part of the divine work of creation that takes place through the Logos. This means that the Logos must in a sense be "larger" than the ancients thought. It is the source of *all* possible patterns for universes, and not merely of our universe. Why one pattern is "activated" rather than others is determined by the divine will.

The Hartle-Hawking proposal attempts to do away with a temporal origin of the universe, an idea that may be consistent with some approaches in the Judeo-Christian tradition.[40] This would mean that the Logos precedes and originates the pattern of the universe in a causal, rather than a temporal, sense.

The Logos I am speaking of here is the preexistent "unfleshed Word" (*logos asarkos*) who is active in the origination of the universe in which he will become incarnate. The idea of the preexistence of Christ has been discussed extensively in modern theology,[41] and the concept of an unfleshed Word has received some criticism in modern christological and trinitarian discussions. It seems clear, however, that this is what John's prologue is talking about.[42] It is not just the *existence* but the *activity* of the Logos in the creation of the universe that is important. Such an activity of divine Reason seems to be required by our scientific understanding of the world, but it is not something imposed upon theology by science. The Bible and the Christian tradition provide this concept for an understanding of the meaning of science beyond what science itself can reach.

Wolfhart Pannenberg's criticisms of the *logos asarkos* concept are germane to the issues we are discussing: "A contemporary analogy to the Apologists' Logos Christology perhaps would have to look something like this: Jesus Christ would be conceived as the embodiment of Einstein's theory or of some other inclusive physical law. . . . The laws of contemporary physics are inherent in the processes they describe; they do not transcend them and are hardly mediators of divinity!"[43]

In the first place, this involves too narrow a view of the laws of physics. They are not merely descriptions of observed phenomena but approximations to the fundamental pattern of the world. The mathematical pattern does not depend upon the physical world for its reality. Secondly, the unfleshed Word cannot be seen merely as the pattern of something like Einstein's general relativity, but would contain the patterns corresponding to *all* consistent gravitational theories—Einstein's, Newton's, Whitehead's, and others.

We would, however, not know *who* the Logos is without the incarnation. Augustine said that he found in the Platonists some of the concepts of the Johannine prologue, but not that "the Word was made flesh, and dwelt among us."[44] Without the incarnation the Logos would be only a speculation about a catalogue of contingency plans for possible universes.

The Christian claim is that the divine Logos through whom the pattern of the world comes into being and is sustained is incarnate as Jesus of Nazareth. The theology of the cross rejects attempts to know the mind of God from science alone and insists that we must begin with the Word made flesh and crucified. The statement in John 1:14 that the Word became flesh and "we have seen his glory" points toward the "hour" when Christ is "glorified," the hour when he is lifted up from the earth and draws all people to himself (John 12:23–33).

"In him the whole fullness of deity dwells bodily" (Col 2:9). Jesus incarnates the Logos, not just a part that contains the pattern of our universe. He has the particularity of an organism of our universe, a Jewish male *Homo sapiens* born approximately two thousand years ago on this planet. In this regard he embodies the pattern of our universe and not another. But our abilities to compose fiction and do pure mathematics show that every human has the capacity to know the patterns of worlds that do not exist. This gives us a hint of how the finite human may incarnate the whole Logos. We might think of a computer that has access to a much larger computer as a model to illustrate how the human mind of Jesus might be united with the mind of God, as Thomas Morris has suggested.[45]

If all things have been created not only "through" Christ but "for" Christ (Col 1:16), then the universe exists in order for life to come into being so that the Word may be incarnate. I discuss possible connections of this idea with scientific anthropic principles of physics in chapter 12. First, however, I must turn to the development of life and the character of our lives in the world, the subjects of the next chapters.

NOTES

1. Gerhard von Rad, *Old Testament Theology* (New York: Harper & Row, 1962), 1:136–39 and 175–79.

2. Hermann Gunkel, *Schöpfung und Chaos in Urzeit und Endzeit* (Göttingen: Vandenhoeck & Ruprecht, 1895). John Day, *God's Conflict with the Dragon and the Sea* (London: Cambridge University Press, 1985). Bernard W. Anderson, *Creation versus Chaos* (Philadelphia: Fortress, 1987).

3. Colin E. Gunton, "Between Allegory and Myth: The Legacy of the Spiritualizing of Genesis," in *The Doctrine of Creation* (ed. Colin E. Gunton; Edinburgh: T&T Clark, 1997), 47–62.

4. Claus Westermann, *Genesis 1:1–11* (Minneapolis: Augsburg, 1984); Walter Bruegemann, *Genesis* (Atlanta: John Knox, 1982); Gerhard von Rad, *Genesis* (Philadelphia: Westminster, 1972). Also helpful is Dietrich Bonhoeffer, *Creation and Fall,* (vol. 3 of *Dietrich Bonhoeffer Works;* trans. Douglas Stephen Bax; Minneapolis: Fortress, 1997), 34–35.

5. Westermann, *Genesis 1–11,* 93–101.

6. Ibid., 94.

7. Thomas Aquinas, *The "Summa Theologica" of St. Thomas Aquinas* (Chicago: Encyclopedia Britannica, 1952), Q.66, Art.1, pp. 343–45 of volume 1 discusses the views of Augustine and others.

8. Bonhoeffer, *Creation and Fall,* 34–37.

9. Cf. Westermann, *Genesis 1–11,* 110–11.

10. John D. Barrow and Frank J. Tipler, *The Anthropic Cosmological Principle* (New York: Oxford University Press, 1986), 250–54.

11. A. G. Hebert, *The Throne of David* (London: Faber and Faber, 1942), chapter 6.

12. Westermann, *Genesis 1–11,* 170–73.

13. Steven Weinberg, *The First Three Minutes* (rev. ed.; New York: Basic Books, 1988); Joseph Silk, *The Big Bang* (3d ed; New York: W. H. Freeman, 2001). J. D. North, *The Measure of the Universe* (New York: Dover, 1990) is a history of cosmology to 1960. Milton K. Munitz et al., *Theories of the Universe* (New York: Free Press, 1957), contains writings from antiquity to the publication date.

14. See, for example, E. A. Milne, "The Fundamental Concepts of Natural Philosophy" in Munitz, *Theories of the Universe,* 354–76.

15. C. H. Lineweaver, "A Younger Age for the Universe," *Science* 284 (1999): 1503. Recent cosmological data obtained from studies of the microwave background radiation can be found at the online Legacy Archive for Microwave Background Data: http://lambda.gsfc.nasa.gov/

16. Stanley L. Jaki, *Cosmos and Creator* (Edinburgh: Scottish Academic, 1980), chapter 2.

17. Malcolm Acock, "The Age of the Universe," *Philosophy of Science* 50 (1983): 130.

18. See the contributions of Hermann Bondi, "Theories of Cosmology," D. W. Sciama, "Evolutionary Processes in Cosmology," and Fred Hoyle, "Continuous Creation and the Expanding Universe," in Munitz, *Theories of the Universe,* 405–29.

19. George Gamow, *The Creation of the Universe* (New York: Viking, 1957).

20. Stephen G. Brush, "How Cosmology Became a Science," *Scientific American* 273, no. 8 (August 1992): 62.

21. Robert Jastrow, *God and the Astronomers* (New York: Warner, 1980), 105–6.

22. Alan H. Guth and Paul J. Steinhardt, "The Inflationary Universe," *Scientific American* 250, no. 5 (May 1984): 116. Martin A. Bucher and David N. Spergel, "Inflation in a Low-Density Universe," *Scientific American* 280, no. 1 (January 1999): 63.

23. Paul Davies, "Relics of Creation," *Sky & Telescope* 69, no. 2 (1985): 112.

24. N. D. Birrell and P. C. W. Davies, *Quantum Fields in Curved Space* (New York: Cambridge University Press, 1982).

25. George L. Murphy, "Einstein + Newton + Bohr = Quantum Cosmology," *The Physics Teacher* 35 (1997): 480.

26. Jacob J. Staub in David Novak and Norbert Samuelson, eds., *Creation and the End of Days* (Lanham, Md.: University Press of America, 1986), 250.

27. Emil Brunner, *Dogmatics II* (Philadelphia: Westminster, 1952), 20.

28. Jürgen Moltmann, *God in Creation* (San Francisco: Harper & Row, 1985), 87.

29. Ibid., 87–89.

30. Cf. the discussion of a kenotic ethic by Nancey Murphy and G. F. R. Ellis, *On the Moral Nature of the Universe* (Philadelphia: Fortress, 1996), 120, citing Simone Weil: "It is to renounce our rights to rewards."

31. S. W. Hawking and G. F. R. Ellis, *The Large Scale Structure of Space-Time* (New York: Cambridge University Press, 1973), chapter 8.

32. Lee Smolin, *Three Roads to Quantum Gravity* (New York: Basic Books, 2001).

33. George L. Murphy, "The Fundamental Length of Quantized Gravitation," *American Journal of Physics* 42 (1974): 958.

34. Steven W. Hawking, *A Brief History of Time* (London: Bantam, 1988), chapter 8.

35. For a philosophical and theological critique, see Joseph M. Życiński, "Metaphysics and Epistemology in Stephen Hawking's Theory of the Creation of the Universe," *Zygon* 31 (1996): 269.

36. Raymond E. Brown, *The Gospel According to John (I—XII)* (Garden City, N.Y.: Doubleday, 1970), appendix 2.

37. L. W. Barnard, *Justin Martyr* (London: Cambridge University Press, 1967), chapter 7.

38 George L. Murphy, "Cosmology and Christology," *Science and Christian Belief* 6 (1994): 101.

39. Brian R. Green, *The Elegant Universe* (New York: W. W. Norton, 1999).

40. Willem B. Drees, *Beyond the Big Bang: Quantum Cosmologies and God* (LaSalle, Ill.: Open Court, 1990), 69–75 and 141–50.

41. Karl-Josef Kuschel, *Born Before All Time?* (New York: Crossroad, 1992).

42. Ibid., 366.

43. Wolfhart Pannenberg, *Jesus: God and Man* (2d ed.; Philadelphia: Westminster, 1977), 166.

44. "The Confessions of St. Augustin, Book 7," *NPNF* 1:1:107–8.

45. Thomas V. Morris, *The Logic of God Incarnate* (Ithaca, N.Y.: Cornell University Press, 1986), 88–107 and 153–62.

· 8 ·

EVOLUTION AS CREATION

"THE LORD, THE GIVER OF LIFE"

Chiasmic cosmology is well suited to deal with the most controversial topic in science-religion discussions, biological evolution.[1] Its view of divine action allows us to be open to the idea that evolution is the means by which God creates life, and the belief that God is revealed in the cross helps us to see God sharing in the suffering that evolution entails. At the same time, we can resist attempts to make evolution by itself into a religious message.[2]

Before we consider the evolution of living things, let us consider what the Bible has to say simply about *life*. Science sees complexity, flows of energy and matter, and storage and transmission of information as characteristics of all life. The Bible does not define "life" in the abstract but has a distinctive way of speaking about human beings and other higher animals: They are the creatures "in whose nostrils was the breath of life" (Gen 7:22).

The account in Gen 2 in which the first human is made from "dust of the ground" is consistent with our belief that God creates mediately. Humanity, however, is not just dust but *animated* dust, for God "breathed into his nostrils the breath of life; and the man became a living being"(2:7). We are not unique in this regard. The story goes on to speak of God creating the animals from the ground (2:19) and they are described there with the same phrase that is used for the human, *nephesh ḥayah*, "living creature." In Ps 104, human beings together with cattle, storks, lions, and sea creatures look to God for life.

111

> When you hide your face, they are dismayed;
> when you take away their breath, they die and return
>   to their dust.
> When you send forth your spirit [or "your breath", *ruḥᵃkha*], they
>   are created;
> and you renew the face of the ground. (Ps 104:29–30)

It is by God's spirit that matter becomes a living creature, and in Ps 104:30 the verb *bara'*, expressing uniquely divine creative action, is used.

The Hebrew Scriptures thus include in their understanding of life the observation that taking in and expelling air is necessary for its maintenance. But the biblical idea of spirit goes deeper than the importance of breathing. The Hebrew *ruah* and Greek *pneuma* can mean both moving air and some reality that is imperceptible to our physical senses, a fact that must be kept in mind if we are to get the full sense of passages such as Ezek 37:1–14 and John 3:1–8.

We speak of the "spirit" of a community or a "team spirit" as the intangible reality that expresses the meaning of a group and holds it together. The spirit is the dynamic atmosphere that enables the different parts of a complex structure to function in a unified way. Pannenberg has pointed out that this concept resembles the idea of the field in physics.[3] The Christian understanding is that the spirit that makes life possible is none other than the Holy Spirit of God who is, as the Nicene Creed says, "The Lord, the giver of life." The Spirit of the Father and the Son is the "atmosphere" of all living systems. The scope of Gen 1:2 is even broader, suggesting a role of the Spirit in the creation of the entire universe.

But there is a distinctive activity of the Spirit among the people of God. In the Fourth Gospel (John 7:39) we are told that "as yet there was no Spirit, because Jesus was not yet glorified." On the cross Jesus "gave up his spirit" (John 19:30) and, risen, "breathed on them and said to them, 'Receive the Holy Spirit'" (John 20:22). The gift of life to the Christian community and the world comes from the cross.[4]

THE ORIGINS OF LIFE

A theological understanding of relationships between creation and evolution must be based on Scripture. We view the Bible, however, through the lenses of twenty centuries of Christian interpretation, and that gives us an opportunity to avail ourselves of tradition in the best sense of the word. It is important to know what the texts meant in their original setting, but also to be aware of how the community of faith has understood them at later periods. It is easy for the debates about the early chapters of Genesis that have taken place since Darwin to obscure understandings from the early church that may not be what we have come to expect.

The first creation account of Genesis is remarkable for the way in which it speaks of the mediated character of the origin of life.

> Then God said, "Let the earth put forth vegetation: plants yielding seed, and fruit trees of every kind on earth that bear fruit with the seed in it." And it was so. . . . And God said, "Let the waters bring forth swarms of living creatures, and let birds fly above the earth across the dome of the sky." So God created the great sea monsters and every living creature that moves, of every kind, with which the waters swarm, and every winged bird of every kind. . . . And God said, "Let the earth bring forth living creatures of every kind: cattle and creeping things and wild animals of the earth of every kind." And it was so. (Gen 1:11, 20–21, 24)

God does not cause living things to appear out of a vacuum. Instead, the earth and the waters are to "put forth" and "bring forth" vegetation and animals. This is still divine creative action, as is shown especially in verse 21 where the verb *bara*, "create," of which only God can be the subject, is used to describe the "bringing forth" of aquatic animals and birds. The second account complements this by speaking of the mediated creation of humanity.

The ideas of the church fathers about the creation of the world, and especially of living things and humanity, were studied by Ernest Messenger in connection with the post-Darwinian debates over evolution and decrees of the Vatican's Biblical Commission on the Pentateuch.[5] The strongest single point that emerged was the consensus of the fathers that God's creation of life took place through secondary causes, by means of powers that God had placed in the materials of the world. A statement by Ephrem of Edessa on the creation of plants in his commentary on Genesis is typical: "Thus, through light and water the earth brought forth everything. While God is able to bring forth everything from the earth without these things, it was His will to show that there was nothing created on earth that was not created for the purpose of mankind or for his service."[6] In chapter 11, I will address the anthropocentrism expressed here. For now it is the goodness of created things as divine instruments that is significant.

The idea that nonliving things developed through natural processes has not aroused nearly the degree of controversy as has the concept of organic evolution. The reverse tends to be the case for these early theologians.[7] Genesis 1 explicitly states that living things came from the materials of the world at God's command, while such an idea about the inorganic world can only be a theological deduction. Here the fathers paid stricter attention to the literal sense of the text than have some more recent theologians.

The thought of Gregory of Nyssa is perhaps of the most interest for the present subject.[8] He has a challenging overall concept of God's creative work. According to his view, God created all things in the first instant of time in their active causes (Gen 1:1), and the account of the six days of creation describes the unfolding of these causes in accordance with God's will. In his "Apologetic Treatise on the Hexaemeron" Gregory says, on Gen 1:2, "all things were virtually (τῇ δυνάμει) in the first Divine impulse for creation, existing as it were in a kind of spermatic potency, sent forth for the genesis of all things. For individual things did not then exist actually."[9]

This concept is similar to the suggestion in the last chapter that God's creative action in the beginning was the putting into operation of the rational pattern that we approximate by our laws of physics. This pattern is not merely a passive template but is the dynamic aspect of matter itself, corresponding to Gregory of Nyssa's "spermatic potency." Our insistence that the rational pattern of nature is intimately connected with God's own Logos is similar to Gregory's idea that the divine commands in Gen 1 are powers implanted in creation as an expression of the divine will. But Gregory gives no attention to the possibility that such potencies given to nature are "masks of God" concealing the creator of the universe.

Both creation accounts of Genesis describe the origin of humanity in special ways, pointing to a peculiar dignity and role that human beings are to have. In particular, God's declaration in Gen 1:26 that humanity is to be created "in our image, according to our likeness" distinguishes human beings from other living creatures. The fathers believed that human beings possess an immaterial and immortal soul as a distinguishing characteristic, and this meant that the "ensoulment" of the first human had to be part of God's creative work. This leads to the kind of distinction made in Pius XII's *Humani Generis* of 1952.[10] The pope said rather cautiously that the status of the theory of evolution of human beings as physical organisms could be discussed, but that it was necessary to believe that at some point God supernaturally joined rational souls with the first humans. In 1996, John Paul II stated, "new knowledge has led us to realize that the theory of evolution is no longer a mere hypothesis," but that theories that "consider the mind as emerging from the forces of living matter, or as a mere epiphenomenon of this matter, are incompatible with the truth about man."[11]

While Gregory's statements on the creation of humans do not constitute a scientific theory of evolution, they do describe a *development* of humanity that has room for evolution. He held that there were three types of souls in terrestrial creatures, the vegetative, the sensitive, and the rational. The first is found in all living things, the second in animals, and

the third only in human beings. The distinction of these, and their relationship in human beings, is set out in the treatise "On the Making of Man."

> [L]et no one suppose on this account that in the compound nature of
> man there are three souls welded together, contemplated each in its own
> limits, so that one should think man's nature to be a sort of conglomer-
> ation of several souls. The true and perfect soul is naturally one, the
> intellectual and immaterial, which mingles with our material nature by
> the agency of the senses; but all that is of material nature, being subject
> to mutation and alteration, will, if it should partake of the animating
> power, move by way of growth: if, on the contrary, it should fall away
> from the vital energy, it will reduce its motion to destruction.[12]

The vital activity of human beings is unified, containing aspects common
to plants and other animals, but going beyond them.

How does this human type of life come to be? First, Gregory sees
embryological development to be a working out of the powers implanted
within the human germ.

> [W]e suppose the human germ to possess the potentiality of its nature,
> sown with it at the first start of its existence, and that it is unfolded and
> manifested by a natural sequence as it proceeds to its perfect state, not
> employing anything external to itself as a stepping-stone to perfection,
> but itself advancing its own self in due course to the perfect state; so that
> it is not true to say either that the soul exists before the body, or that the
> body exists without the soul, but that there is one beginning of both,
> which according to the heavenly view was laid as their foundation in the
> original will of God; according to the other, came into existence on the
> occasion of generation.[13]

The embryological development of each human being parallels the development of the universe, not in the sense that "the human is a microcosm"
but in the manner of God's working. The order of events in Gen 1 is seen
in a sense as a *historical* development of the same kind.

> [T]he lawgiver says that after inanimate matter (as a sort of foundation
> for the form of animate things), this vegetative life was made, and had
> earlier existence in the growth of plants: then he proceeds to introduce
> the genesis of those creatures which are regulated by sense: and since,
> following the same order, of those things which have obtained life in the
> flesh, those which have sense can exist by themselves even apart from the
> intellectual nature, while the rational principle could not be embodied
> save as blended with the sensitive,—for this reason man was made last
> after the animals, *as nature advanced in an orderly course to perfection.*
> (Emphasis added.)[14]

Nature did not "advance" independently of God, but it was a natural process, the unfolding of spermatic potencies placed in nature, that led to humanity. This philosophical and theological argument can be accommodated to some scientific theories of evolution.

It should certainly not be implied that there was anything like a common evolutionary understanding of human nature in the early church, though the force of passages sometimes quoted against human evolution can be overstated.[15] Our point here is that there is considerable scope for an evolutionary understanding in the ideas of these theologians.

We should not read the Genesis accounts as historical chronicles. If we did, we would see their statements of mediated creation as meaning that plants and animals sprang full-grown from the waters and the earth, as Ephrem apparently thought.[16] That is not the kind of thing evolutionary theories speak of. What is of interest in these patristic discussions of Genesis is simply that God's creation of life is understood to be mediated through created things.

Theories of biological evolution attempt to explain the origin and development of life in terms of natural processes, and thus may be understood theologically as accounts of mediated creation. That they are also compatible with the idea of a hidden creator is shown by the label "atheistic," which is often attached to them, sometimes proudly by their proponents and sometimes as a dire warning by Christian opponents. A scientific theory *should* be "a-theistic" in the precise sense that the concept of God does not appear as an element of the theory itself.

But theories of evolution must be more than the general idea that somehow living things have changed over the course of time. We have to ask whether or not they can actually explain what has happened in this universe. At the same time, theology does not insist that a theory explain all phenomena before it is accepted as a possible description of God's instruments. While belief in God's cooperation with secondary causes is part of the Christian tradition, no specific mechanism of secondary causation has dogmatic status. Whether God makes the sun shine by chemical combustion or nuclear reactions is not of basic theological importance.

The great majority of biologists are convinced that the evolutionary paradigm provides a correct description of the history of life on Earth. At the same time, there are significant unsolved problems, the most important being chemical evolution.

The problem is to explain how simple molecules on the primitive earth could have formed complex systems able to utilize flows of material and energy and to store and transmit information.[17] In a classic 1952 experiment Stanley Miller passed an electric discharge, representing lightning, repeatedly through a mixture of methane, ammonia, water vapor, and hydrogen to simulate the early atmosphere of the earth.[18] A water trap played the role of seas or pools in which products of the reaction could gather. Miller found that several amino acids, as well as other organic molecules, were formed. Since that time the experiment has been repeated with many variations. Most of the amino acids needed for proteins, as well as all the bases in DNA and RNA, have been positively identified as products of such experiments.

These results are encouraging and have led some scientists and popularizers of science to say that the problem of the formation of life is close to a scientific solution and that "only the details remain to be unraveled."[19] But that is a vast overstatement. One thinks of Wolfgang Pauli's comment when Heisenberg was reported to have made a similar statement after he published a unified field theory. Pauli sketched a blank rectangle with the caption, "'This is to show the world, that I can paint like Titian:' Only technical details are missing."[20]

Proteins and nucleic acids are formed today by living systems that have information already encoded in their nucleic acids to tell how they are to be made. The problem is to form living systems without a preexisting blueprint by a process through which both basic structures and information storage mechanisms could develop together. To code information we have to bring elements into a particular order, like the sequence of bases in DNA. The second law of thermodynamics says that the *dis*order in an isolated system always increases. Biological processes run in the opposite direction—"like a sailor who runs up the rigging in a sinking ship," as Sir James Jeans said.[21] This does not violate the second law because living systems are not isolated. A decrease of disorder in a system can be overbalanced by an increase in the disorder of its environment, so evolution of living systems from nonliving constituents is not ruled out. But the probability for such evolution may be very low.

The number of proteins of reasonable size that could be formed by stringing together the twenty amino acids in all possible ways is huge, and the odds against forming a given protein at random out of all possible sequences are far worse than those for choosing a specific atom out of the entire universe. The formation of a protein from amino acids also requires free energy, and there were originally no enzymes (some of the very proteins we are trying to account for) to catalyze the reactions. Standard chemical calculations show that the concentration of even a small chain of amino acids in a "prebiotic soup" would be minute.[22]

Such results are discouraging but not disastrous, for they assume that the reactions take place in such a way that the state of the system is one of thermal equilibrium. Reactions that proceed *via* states far from equilibrium may produce very different results. I pointed out earlier that the existence of *dissipative structures* like convection cells shows that energy flowing through a system can lead to highly structured types of order. This suggests that life itself arose as a dissipative structure. In addition, nonequilibrium chemical reactions can show an *autocatalytic* effect in which reactions proceed more rapidly than equilibrium considerations suggest.[23] Nonequilibrium thermodynamics seems to be a promising approach to the problem of chemical evolution, though there remains a great deal of work to be done.

Science has made some steps toward understanding chemical evolution, but we do not know yet what a successful scientific theory of the origin of life will look like. There are claims, as I noted, that the problem is much closer to solution than it really is. Other people, however, argue that a special "origin science" that recognizes divine creation is needed to solve the problem.[24] In recent years proponents of "intelligent design" have presented claims based on information theory.[25] Their basic idea can be put simply. Life involves "complex specified information," such as that encoded in DNA, and the probability of this information arising by chance is too slight to take seriously. Complex specified information shows design, so that there must be an intelligent designer. It is a small step to identify this designer with God.

The understanding of creation that we are exploring enables us to resist the temptation to seize upon unsolved problems as an excuse to introduce God as an element of scientific explanation, and to hope that science will be able to explain how life has developed. We cannot rule out miracles, but belief in God's kenotic action through natural processes can see no reason for the initial development of life on Earth to be any exception. God is indeed the source of the information in living things, but we expect that God puts that information there as God does other things in the world, through natural processes.

A reminder of the limitations of current science can be a helpful corrective to hubris. The scientist who is a Christian and who believes that God acts in such a way that the world is knowable "though God were not given" should approach the work of trying to understand that world with humility in the face of the divine condescension rather than with pride. We should be willing to say, "We don't know" without concluding that "we are not meant to know."

God's "almightiness" means that God does all things, not that God is a specialist who can do some special thing—create life—that no one else can do. There is no theological basis for the idea that a special type of science is needed to deal with biogenesis and nothing in Scripture to suggest that life as such is created in a miraculous way. On the contrary, it is precisely of living things that Gen 1 asserts mediated creation. The nineteenth-century Anglican clergyman and author Charles Kingsley stated the matter very well: "We knew of old that God was so wise that He could make all things; but behold, He is so much wiser than even that, that He can make all things make themselves."[26]

THE RANDOMNESS OF EVOLUTION

Einstein's objection to the idea that God "plays dice" was connected with his belief in the pantheism of Spinoza and its deterministic view of the world.[27] Christians have been equally opposed to "chance" because it seems to diminish God's sovereignty.[28] Perhaps this position needs to be rethought, not only because of indeterminacy in quantum and chaos theories but also because of our kenotic understanding of God's action in the world.

The study of chemical evolution has shown that the development of complex systems needed for life in thermal equilibrium is very unlikely. We already know that there is a fundamental element of probability in physical laws, and thus some basic freedom in the world. Scientists can't shrug off every observation they don't understand by saying "Strange things happen," but the undeniable existence of life and the fact that strenuous effort has not yet been able to explain its origin suggest that life may be due to very improbable occurrences.

Once life has come into being, evolutionary theory holds that the ways in which it will continue to develop will also have a random character. Natural selection works because there are chance variations among members of a species, some of which will be more favorable for survival than others. Mutations due to changes in DNA by radiation or chemical agents take place at the molecular level and have the statistical character described by quantum theory. The uncertainty of survival of an organism is magnified by the fact that its variations from the average do not have a value for or against survival by themselves, but only in relation to an environment that itself is changing in ways that may be unpredictable.

In the Bible, the casting of lots to make decisions (e.g., Acts 1:21–26) and the use of Urim and Thummim (e.g., 1 Sam 14:41)[29] shows that God's will was supposed to be made known through chance phenomena. This concept finds expression in the idea that the Holy Spirit is connected with "the spontaneity of natural process."[30] It comes together with the creedal claim that the Spirit is the life-giver to suggest that the origin of life and the way it evolves is rooted in the world's freedom, which manifests itself as "chance."

It is tempting to think that God is active behind the scenes, determining the outcomes of all the events that seem to us to be random—that the Holy Spirit makes the dice fall in the right way. But if we pursue the parallel between Spirit and field, we must remember that the fields of modern physics are quantum mechanical entities and thus have uncertainties associated with them. The Spirit-field analogy suggests a kenotic aspect of the activity of the Spirit, who does not strictly determine the outcome of all events.[31] This tentative conclusion is consistent with the picture of divine action that we have developed from the theology of the crucified, a picture in which divine action is voluntarily limited for the sake of creation.

NATURAL SELECTION AS AN EXPRESSION OF CHIASMIC COSMOLOGY

Given that the first living things did somehow come to be, how have they developed over some three and one-half billion years into the tremendous variety of organisms on Earth today? What mechanisms make evolutionary change possible? It was the answer given to this question by Darwin and Wallace that made evolution a major part of biological science. But it is of equal importance for us to note the theological significance of their idea.[32]

It will be helpful to reflect on two possible explanations for evolution. Neither needs to be adhered to in its purity, and theories combining the two types are possible. Darwin himself made use of both concepts, but the basic ideas are quite different. The first is natural selection, which has already been sketched. A well-worn "Just-So Story" illustrates this theory by explaining the long necks of giraffes with the suggestion that some members of the giraffe's ancestral species had slightly longer necks than others, and that the presence of foliage high up on trees made long necks a trait that helped in survival. Those with slightly longer necks were better able to live and reproduce in this environment. Over many generations this led to a long-necked species.

The other idea of "inheritance of acquired characters" is usually associated with the name of Lamarck. It suggests that properties that an organism develops during its life can be passed on to its descendants. The corresponding giraffe story is that animals that stretched their necks more to reach leaves on higher branches would survive better in times of food shortage. They would pass on their stretched and slightly longer necks to their offspring.

The Lamarckian idea suggests that effort is rewarded and that evolution is a gradual process of improvement. This is an attractive idea because we like to be rewarded for our work, and in fact is a kind of biological works righteousness. Systems of thought as different as the liberal theology of the nineteenth century, the Roman Catholic thought of Teilhard de Chardin, and the Marxist-Leninist ideology of Michurin and Lysenko all prefer Lamarckian evolution.[33] It is consistent with liberalism's belief in progress, the Roman Catholic idea that "grace perfects nature," and the notion that "the new Soviet man" could be developed by education after revolution had "shattered" old class structures.

Natural selection is not nearly as congenial with the type of moral views that we would like to see embodied in the world. With natural selection, the only sense in which we can speak of one organism being "better" than another is in terms of survival and propagation of its genes. The tapeworms that have evolved to live as intestinal parasites in human beings are just as "advanced" from this standpoint as are human beings themselves.

More ominous is the basic point I noted in the opening chapter. Natural selection involves privation, competition, and death, and it gives a picture of the world that has been described with phrases such as "nature red in tooth and claw." Actually, extinction may often result from a slow process of one group producing fewer and fewer offspring as another takes over its territory rather than from bloody extirpations. Nevertheless, extinction is death.

However congenial Lamarck's idea may be, it is not the way evolution takes place. It is difficult to see how this mechanism *could* work. The DNA in an organism's sex cells must be altered in order for any mutation to be passed on to its offspring, and the stretching of an animal's neck will not change its sperm or ova. Natural selection may not be the whole story of evolution, but it seems to be the primary mechanism. Deprivation and death are fundamental to the development of life on Earth, and human life in particular. This presents a serious problem for theologies of glory. Darwin himself, who began his university studies to prepare for the ministry, reached the end of his life uncertain whether or not he could believe in God, and the acceptance of Darwinian evolution has often been represented as a triumph of science over Christianity.[34] It does represent a defeat of commonsense religion, for the development of life out of death is not the way that ordinary religious people expect God to operate.

Even before Darwin, the discovery of the extinction of species posed a serious threat to commonsense theologies that accepted the idea of a "great chain of being" maintained in static perfection from the highest angels to the meanest worms.[35] God was supposed to maintain this hierarchy with no breaks or deletions, so that species could never become extinct. It was a shock to discover from the fossil evidence that large numbers of species that had once lived were no longer extant. Loren Eiseley has given a good description of the impact of this discovery of the "naturalness" of the death of species.[36] The abandonment of belief that God maintained the status quo meant for many people an elimination of the whole idea of God.

But the God of the Bible is not the deity of commonsense religion. To quote Sanders again on the destruction of Jerusalem and the exile,

"Nobody in his right mind could possibly believe that God would want us to die in order to give us life again."[37] Even less could they believe that God himself would die in order to give life to the world. The two events are closely connected, for destruction and exile bear the mark of the cross. We can extend that insight to say that extinction and natural selection are the mark of the cross placed on the biosphere.

The fundamental problem that evolution poses for theology is not any conflict with Genesis but the difficulty of reconciling natural selection with commonsense religious ideas of the way God ought to work. The theology of the cross avoids that problem because from the outset it rejects the approach of commonsense religion. It insists that God's self-revelation takes place in situations of suffering, loss, and apparent hopelessness, exactly the situations to which evolution through natural selection directs our attention. Cooperation and symbiosis may play a significant role in evolution, but we do not need to shy away from the harsher features of the picture. As we look back on the whole process, we can see how further development of life and consciousness came from the deprivation and extinction of species that allowed the mammals to become dominant. But if the dinosaurs had been intelligent, they would have seen no natural cause for hope as they moved toward extinction.

Transmission of acquired characters would suggest that life possesses in itself some possibility for advancement and reaching out to God. As Teilhard de Chardin puts it: "Human suffering, the sum total of suffering poured out at each moment over the whole earth, is like an immeasurable ocean. But what makes up this immensity? Is it blackness, emptiness, barren wastes? No, indeed: it is potential *energy.* Suffering holds hidden within it, in extreme intensity, the ascensional force of the world."[38] Contrast this with the statement of Bonhoeffer, cited previously in chapter 3: "The fact that Christ was dead did not provide the possibility of his resurrection but its impossibility; it was nothing itself, it was the nihil negativum. There is absolutely no transition, no continuum between the dead Christ and the resurrected Christ, but the freedom of God that in the beginning created God's work out of nothing."[39]

It is, of course, possible for human beings to develop the idea of natural selection as a scientific theory of processes within our world. Darwin and Wallace did precisely that, and the majority of biologists today accept some variant of this as a scientific theory. But the idea clashes with common ideas of the goodness of God, and for that reason it is hard for many people to see how God could be at work in such a process. An understanding that it *is* possible comes from God's revelation in Israel, which culminates in the cross and resurrection of Christ. However, that revelation does not give us Darwinian evolution as a scientific theory. It is the task of theology to see the meaning of the processes discovered by science in the light of the cross, not to deduce scientific results from theological principles.

Stephen Jay Gould's contribution to discussions about the significance of evolution should especially be noted. In his book *Wonderful Life* he focused on a critical period in the development of life on Earth, the early Cambrian explosion.[40] This was when, after about 3 billion years of relatively undramatic existence primarily in the form of unicellular organisms, terrestrial life really took off. A fascinating fossil deposit in the Canadian Rockies, the Burgess Shale, contains vital evidence about this period. The remains of bizarre animals, in some ways unlike anything now living, are found there.[41] By exploring this evidence and considering the role of sudden catastrophic events such as the asteroid impact that may have doomed the dinosaurs, Gould removes some comfortable ideas that we may have had about evolution.

When we talk about "survival of the fittest," we should not mean that the organisms that survive and produce offspring are in any absolute sense better than those that don't. The extinct organisms of the Burgess Shale were not inferior to those that survived 500 million years ago: they *may just not have been as lucky.* Even after we have shaken off our Lamarckian illusions, we may imagine that evolution favors organisms that are clearly smarter or stronger than others. But a smart one could have been killed by a falling tree, while her stupid sister survived. Natural selection involves the environment as well as the organism, and survival requires the good luck not to be under falling trees!

Evolution deals with populations and not just the fortunes of individuals, but the same idea applies. The dinosaurs could not have "adapted" for an asteroid impact. (The development of intelligence changes the situation, as I will note later.) We couldn't have examined the species that existed half a billion years ago and determined accurately which would eventually evolve into the dominant species on the planet. The development of life has, as far as science is concerned, been radically contingent: it could have happened in other ways. (This is why Gould titled his book in tribute to the classic film *It's a Wonderful Life.*[42])

Such ideas do not fit very well with conventional pictures of a wise and benevolent God directing the process of evolution. But the biblical God does not operate in conventional ways. God tells the Israelites that they were not the obvious choice to be his people. "It was not because you were more numerous than any other people that the LORD set his heart on you and chose you—for you were the fewest of all peoples. It was because the LORD loved you and kept the oath that he swore to your ancestors, that the LORD has brought you out with a mighty hand, and redeemed you from the house of slavery, from the hand of Pharaoh king of Egypt" (Deut

7:7–8). And from this people comes "Christ, who is God over all, forever praised!" (Rom 9:5 NIV).

Because "survival of the fittest" has been capitalized upon by movements such as Social Darwinism and Naziism, we need to emphasize that God's use of natural selection does not mean that God is "beyond good and evil" or that Christianity sanctions exploitative systems of ethics. God's alien work is done for the sake of his proper work. The enslavement of the Israelites in Egypt was evil, but God brought good out of it. God takes no pleasure in death (Ezek 18:32), but uses death to bring forth life.

In spite of that caveat, the picture of a creator manipulating countless organisms and species through want, suffering, and death in order to accomplish his purpose has an unpleasant look to it. But we have to go on to consider the central aspect of the Christian claim: God is not just a transcendent creator who manipulates terrestrial life, but himself becomes a participant in evolution and dies as the dinosaurs and Neanderthals died.

THE INCARNATION AND THE EVOLUTIONARY PROCESS

Theories of evolution would have raised only minor concerns for theology if they had excluded human beings from the process, but we share so many features with other animals, from chemical composition and anatomy to behavior, that an evolutionary explanation for animals almost demands the same for ourselves. *Homo sapiens* has no qualitatively different place in a scientific theory of evolution by natural selection than does any other organism.

But from the theological standpoint humanity does have a unique role. Human beings are created in the image and likeness of God, open to divine revelation and knowledge of God's will, and are given a position of responsibility. Human evolution must therefore be given special theological attention in order to see how these claims can be correlated with our physical origins. God's creative work is concurrent with the processes of genetic variation and natural selection, but this does not end God's involvement with evolution. Jesus of Nazareth, a member of this species who shares in its evolutionary history and relationships, is the eternal Word of God, and all of those evolutionary relationships are assumed in the incarnation.

The details of human evolution are not as well understood as we would like, but appearances of uncertainty about our family tree are due in part to the fact that we are naturally more interested in this aspect of evolution than in the development of a particular species of tree or fish. Humanity's place in evolutionary history is fairly clear.[43] The closest living relatives of *Homo sapiens* are the great apes—chimpanzees, gorillas, and orangutans. But present-day humans did not "descend from apes."

Instead, both humans and apes descended from a common ancestor, which has not yet been identified with certainty. The branching of the two lines took place between 10 and 25 million years ago, depending on the dating method that is used. The ancestral species within our genus, *Homo erectus* and *Homo habilis,* are now extinct, as is the subspecies *Homo sapiens neanderthalensis.*

The emergence of *Homo sapiens* took place between one hundred and two hundred thousand years ago. It is difficult to tell precisely when the creatures whose remains we study became *human,* in the sense of possessing reflective consciousness and self-awareness. This probably was a process spread over some period of time. In any case, the first hominids among whom this change took place can be thought of as playing the theological role of Adam and Eve in the Genesis accounts. (This need not mean that we could pinpoint a single male and a single female as the ancestors of all humanity.) The evolution of intelligence meant that humans could understand, trust, and obey—or mistrust and disobey—God's word.

In Western Christianity the traditional picture of Adam and Eve in paradise was one of perfect human beings with tremendous wisdom, ability, and beauty. Luther's exaggerated description of Adam is a fair representative.[44] But the Bible does not tell us anything of the sort. It says that humanity was created without sin and with the ability to avoid sin, but gives no information about the intellect, culture, or appearance of the first humans.

Eastern Christianity has had a more modest view of the original state of humanity, with the first humans sometimes pictured as having been created in an immature state. Theophilus of Antioch, commenting on the prohibition of the tree of knowledge, says, "Adam, being yet an infant in age, was on this account as yet unable to receive knowledge worthily."[45] "The man was a young child, not yet having a perfect deliberation" according to Irenaeus, and "It was necessary for him to reach full-development by growing in this way."[46] Genesis 3 is then a story of humanity taking the wrong road in its development rather than one of a "fall" from an already given state of perfection.[47] Athanasius saw in the early chapters of Genesis a humanity with a potential for progress toward final union with God, and seems to have thought that the first humans, even if they had not sinned, could have died physically.[48] The penalty for sin would have been something more than death, "abiding ever in the corruption of death."[49]

We could move at this point to the incarnation, seeing it as the purpose of creation and thus, from a theological standpoint, of evolution. In chapter 12, I will pursue the old question of whether the incarnation would have happened if humanity had not sinned. But humanity *has* sinned, and much of the theological reflection of the church has had to do with sin and the way in which God deals with it in Christ. Thus we need to consider how this can be thought of in view of evolution. There are two basic issues that have to be addressed.

A Christian understanding of evolution must deal with the existence of suffering and death for millions of years before there were human beings, and thus before there could be sin in the world. The focus in Rom 5:12, "death came through sin, and so death spread to all because all have sinned," is on the human situation, and there is no need to extend "all" beyond the human race. We have seen that Athanasius apparently did not think that even humans would have been completely exempt from physical death if they had not sinned. But how are we to understand the connection that Scripture makes between sin and death?

Perhaps the best way to think of this is in terms of the *meaning* of death. Auschwitz, Dresden, and Rwanda show that human sin has had major influences on the world since it first occurred, but it has also had an effect on the meaning of what had happened *beforehand.* As an analogy, one can argue that the Civil War is the most important thing that has happened in American history. What took place between 1861 and 1865 still affects society today in profound ways. But many things that happened *before* 1861—the slave trade, the Constitution, the invention of the cotton gin, and the Missouri Compromise, for example—have meanings that are only understood fully in light of the Civil War. The war did not cause those things, but it helped to give them their significance.

Perhaps we can speak in a similar way about the effects of sin. Physical pain and death were in the world before humanity, but there was no willful turning away from God, and therefore no sin. When the first humans chose to disobey God, their action put a new and disastrous meaning upon the death that had gone before them. It was no longer a purely physical process, the stopping and dissolution of the bodily machinery, but separation from God and an assault on God's intention for the world.

Speaking about the first humans "choosing" to disobey God introduces a second issue. It seems very likely that our prehuman ancestors would have been prone to sexual promiscuity, theft, and some violence directed against one another, behaviors that were not "sin" for creatures who were not moral agents but that would be sinful for human beings. This is suggested by the nature of natural selection, for such behaviors sometimes will be conducive to survival and propagation of one's genes, and it is also indicated by the behaviors of the closest surviving relatives of our species.[50] The earliest humans would have been subjected to strong influences inclining them to behaviors that the biblical tradition would consider sinful.

We will have to understand the traditional idea that the first humans possessed an "original righteousness," so that it was possible for them to avoid sinning, in a very limited way. Given what we know about evolution, the first sin, like the sin of every succeeding human being, seems inevitable, yet it would have been something for which the agents would have been responsible, and not something that was strictly necessary.[51]

Sin is not, however, simply one or another immoral act. In Rom 1, Paul speaks of the fundamental human problem as the refusal to acknowledge God as creator and all other sins as consequences of this. The story of Gen 3, in which disobeying the divine command is the first sin, makes the same point. How we are to think of the first human beings as knowing God's will and yet acting contrary to it, or when this might have happened for the first time, are questions that we can't answer scientifically. But this is not just speculation about some bizarre possibility. It is what human beings have been doing throughout history.

If sin was inevitable for the first humans, yet something for which they were responsible, how much more is that the case for their descendants born into an atmosphere of sin. Original sin or sin of origin means that all human beings from the beginning of their lives are without true faith in God and inclined to evil.[52] It is not necessary to think of this as a condition that is determined by our genes. The analogy of something like fetal alcohol syndrome may be more helpful than a condition that is genetic in the precise sense of the word.[53]

It is as a member of this species that had become conscious and open to God but that had turned away from God and toward spiritual death that Jesus is born. If we want to know what it means to be truly human, this is the one to whom we are pointed—not the Adam and Eve of the biblical story (about whom Scripture tells us very little) or some paleontological data. In Jesus we see the human who is in the right relationship with God and therefore with the world. The Letter to the Hebrews quotes part of Ps 8 that reflects in amazement on the dominion given to human beings, and then says: "As it is, we do not yet see everything in subjection to them, but we do see Jesus, who for a little while was made lower than the angels, now crowned with glory and honor because of the suffering of death, so that by the grace of God he might taste death for everyone" (Heb 2:8b–9).

The fundamental concern of Christology has been to express together the full divinity and the full humanity of Jesus. Divinity is necessary because only the creator of the world can be its redeemer. "The renewal of creation has been the work of the self-same Word that made it at the beginning" is the way Athanasius put it.[54] This can be taken as a first soteriological axiom. If the savior of the world were not its creator, then creatures would have two sources of life to look to, and would really have two gods.

The full humanity of Jesus is of equal importance. Beginning with the assertion that "he had to become like his brothers and sisters in every respect" (Heb 2:17),[55] the Christian tradition came to realize that nothing proper to humanity could be omitted from what God had assumed in the incarnation. If any aspect of the human had not been assumed by God, then that aspect of humanity would have remained outside the range of salvation. Thus suggestions like that of Appolinarius, that the divine Logos had taken the place of the rational soul in Christ, had to be rejected.[56] A second soteriological axiom, usually connected with Gregory of Nazianzus, is "That which He has not assumed He has not healed."[57]

In order to do justice to both the full humanity and the full divinity of Christ, classical Christology holds that he exists in two natures, divine and human, which are united in the divine Second Person of the Trinity. There is no separate human person in Christ, for human nature subsists in the person of the Word. This could be expressed by saying that the Second Person of the Trinity assumed impersonal (anhypostatic) human nature, which was "enpersoned" from its conception in Mary's womb in the Second Person of the Trinity.[58] The idea was put succinctly by Newman: "Though Man, He is not, strictly speaking, *a* Man."[59]

This idea seems very odd to modern westerners, accustomed to nominalism and individualism. The biblical view is different. The Bible does not use the concepts of "nature" and "person" as later theology would do, but it does have its own ways of speaking that seem to express some of the same ideas. The Hebrew idea of "corporate personality" and the Pauline concept of "the body of Christ" both speak of a sense of community that goes well beyond the idea of a collection of individuals.[60]

Irenaeus argued that Christ recapitulated the history of humanity, passing through all the stages of human life in order to sanctify them.[61] Ernst Haeckel, the German champion of Darwin and vocal opponent of Christianity, emphasized a concept of embryological recapitulation.[62] His idea that a human embryo actually passes through the forms of the adult ancestors of humanity in a speeded-up fashion is much too simplistic. It is true, though, that at appropriate stages of development, a human embryo cannot be distinguished above the molecular level from those of other mammalian species, and in a sense repeats the evolutionary history of its ancestors' embryos.[63] C. S. Lewis saw the significance of that for the incarnation: "He comes down; down from the heights of absolute being into time and space, down into humanity; down further still, if embryologists are right, to recapitulate in the womb ancient and pre-human phases of life; down to the very roots and sea-bed of the Nature He had created."[64] The *Te Deum's* "You did not abhor the Virgin's womb" *(Non horruisti Vir-*

ginis uterum) includes the fact that the Son of God did not despise the bestial ancestry of the human race.

In assuming human nature, God also assumes humanity's relationship with all other species, living and dead. The embryological illustration of this may be the most dramatic, but other aspects of Jesus' humanity display it as well. For Jesus, being fully human, has the same relationships with apes and fish that all other human beings have. His gross anatomy has the same features homologous to those of other vertebrates, and his DNA and proteins show the same similarities to their chemistry, as do those of other humans.

It is offensive to some Christians to think that Jesus would have such a relationship with other animals, and this feeling of revulsion can be made into an argument against evolution: "Theistic evolution . . . makes man a half-evolved, half-created being who is a remodeled ape, so to speak. It also makes the Lord Jesus Christ into a very specially made-over ape. But the Bible says that He is the Creator of the universe. . . ."[65] But the idea that Jesus is a "specially made-over ape" (passing over the fact that human beings are more like "cousins" of apes than their descendants) is a magnificent expression of chiasmic cosmology. It is part of the same scandal as God born in a stable and being executed as a powerless criminal, the scandal of the cross. The idea that Jesus is a "specially made-over ape" is not an *alternative* to the idea that he is the creator of the universe. *As* a "made-over ape" he is the incarnation of the one through whom all things were made.

Humanity's evolutionary relationships with the rest of the biosphere and the history of life on Earth, together with our theological insistence on the full humanity of Jesus, *require* us to recognize that he shares our evolutionary relationships. What has not been assumed has not been healed, and this includes whatever tendencies to sin result from our evolutionary history. For him, as Barth said, "'Without sin' means that in our human and sinful existence as a man He did not sin."[66] It is because that history has been assumed and those tendencies overcome by Christ that we have hope for our complete healing.

The argument can go in the other direction as well to help us to understand how "all things" can be reconciled to God through the cross (Col 1:20). In assuming human nature, God also assumed our relationships with all other life forms. Other species can participate in God's salvation in the way and to the degree appropriate for them (as Isa 11:6–9 hints) because, through the relationship that humans have with the biosphere, they are included in the incarnation.

Natural selection does not set the standard for human behavior.[67] The early church saw Hos 4:6a, "My people are destroyed for lack of knowl-

edge," as meaning that ignorance is a basic part of the human predica-
ment, and the coming of the Logos in the flesh was for the education of
erring humanity.[68] There is also the opportunity, and even the demand,
for ethical change. Survival of the fittest is not the highest ethical standard
for human beings. The demand for unlimited vengeance of Gen 4:23–24
is restricted by the "eye for eye" of Exod 21:23–24, and that in turn is tran-
scended by Jesus' teaching in the Sermon on the Mount (Matt 5:38–42).
We are called to look to God's future, and not only to what worked for our
ancestors in the past, when we deal with other people and with the rest of
creation. In the next three chapters I will spell out some of the ethical
aspects of chiasmic cosmology in greater detail.

NOTES

1. For aspects of the history, see Ernest C. Messenger, *Evolution and Theology: The Problem of Man's Origin* (New York: Macmillan, 1932); Ernst Benz, *Evolution and Christian Hope: Man's Concept of the Future, from the Early Fathers to Teilhard de Chardin* (trans. Heinz G. Frank; New York: Doubleday, 1966); and Ronald L. Numbers, *The Creationists* (Berkeley: University of California Press, 1992).

2. George L. Murphy, *The Trademark of God: A Christian Course in Creation, Evolution, and Salvation* (Wilton, Conn.: Morehouse-Barlow, 1986).

3. Wolfhart Pannenberg, *Toward a Theology of Nature: Essays on Science and Faith* (ed. Ted Peters; Louisville, Ky.: Westminster/John Knox, 1993), 123–61.

4. For a discussion of "cosmic Spirit," see Robert W. Jenson, "Eighth Locus," in *Christian Dogmatics* (ed. Carl E. Braaten and Robert W. Jenson; Philadelphia: Fortress, 1984), 2:165–78.

5. Messenger, *Evolution and Theology*.

6. St. Ephrem, "Commentary on Genesis," in *St. Ephrem the Syrian: Selected Prose Works* (ed. Kathleen McVey; Washington, D.C.: Catholic University of America, 1994), 82.

7. Messenger, *Evolution and Theology*, 36–37.

8. Ibid., part 1, chapter 5, and part 2, chapters 8 and 9.

9. Ibid., 25–26.

10. Benz, *Evolution and Christian Hope*, 103–6.

11. John Paul II, "Message to the Pontifical Academy of Sciences," in *Evolutionary and Molecular Biology* (ed. Robert John Russell, William R. Stoeger, S.J., and Francisco Ayala; Berkeley: Center for Theology and the Natural Sciences, 1998), 2–9. The cited passages are from, respectively, pages 4 and 6.

12. Gregory of Nyssa, "On the Making of Man," *NPNF*, Series 2, 5:403.

13. Ibid., 421.

14. Ibid., 394.

15. Messenger, *Evolution and Theology*, part 3, chapter 14.

16. *St. Ephrem the Syrian: Selected Prose Works*, 90.

17. Charles B. Thaxton, Walter L. Bradley, and Roger L. Olsen, *The Mystery of Life's Origin* (New York: Philosophical Library, 1984). John Maynard Smith, *The Problems of Biology* (New York: Oxford, 1986), chapter 10. P. C. W. Davies, *The Fifth Miracle* (New York: Simon & Schuster, 1999).

18. Stanley L. Miller, "Production of Amino Acids under Possible Primitive Earth Conditions," *Science* 117 (1953): 528.

19. Eric Chaisson, *Universe* (Englewood Cliffs, N.J.: Prentice-Hall, 1988), 6.

20. George Gamow, *Thirty Years That Shook Physics* (Garden City, N.Y.: Doubleday, 1966), 162.

21. Dorothy L. Sayers, *The Mind of the Maker* (London: Methuen, 1941), 112.

22. Thaxton et al., *The Mystery of Life's Origin,* chapter 8.

23. Ilya Prigogine, *From Being to Becoming* (New York: W. H. Freeman, 1980).

24. Thaxton et al., *The Mystery of Life's Origin,* epilogue.

25. William A. Dembski, *Intelligent Design* (Downers Grove, Ill.: InterVarsity, 1999).

26. Colin A. Russell, *Cross-Currents* (Grand Rapids, Mich.: Eerdmans, 1985), 167–68.

27. Max Jammer, *Einstein and Religion* (Princeton, N.J.: Princeton University Press, 1999), 221–40.

28. For example, John Calvin, *Institutes of the Christian Religion* (Philadelphia: Westminster, 1960), book 1, chapter 16.2, 198–99: "There is no such thing as fortune or chance."

30. I. Mendelsohn, "Urim and Thummim," *The Interpreter's Dictionary of the Bible* (Nashville: Abingdon, 1962), 4:739–40.

30. Jenson, "Eighth Locus," in Braaten and Jenson, eds., *Christian Dogmatics,* 2:170–73.

31. Ernest L. Simmons, "Toward a Kenotic Pneumatology: Quantum Field Theory and the Theology of the Cross," *CTNS Bulletin* 19, no. 2 (1999): 10.

32 George L. Murphy, "A Theological Argument for Evolution," *Journal of the American Scientific Affiliation* 38, no. 1 (1986): 19.

33. Lyman Abbott, *The Theology of an Evolutionist* (New York: Houghton Mifflin, 1897). Pierre Teilhard de Chardin, *The Phenomenon of Man* (New York: Harper & Row, 1959), especially 149–50. Zhores A. Medvedev, *The Rise and Fall of T. D. Lysenko* (New York: Columbia University Press, 1969).

34. For a description of the nineteenth-century opposition to Christianity that centered on Darwinism, see Russell, *Cross-Currents,* 188–96.

35. Arthur O. Lovejoy, *The Great Chain of Being* (New York: Harper Torchbooks, 1960).

36. Loren Eiseley, "How Death Became Natural," in *The Firmament of Time* (New York: Atheneum, 1962), 33–58.

37. James A. Sanders, *Torah and Canon* (Philadelphia: Fortress, 1972), 87.

38. Pierre Teilhard de Chardin, *Hymn of the Universe* (trans. Gerald Vann; New York: Harper & Row, 1965), 93–94.

39. Dietrich Bonhoeffer, *Creation and Fall* (vol. 3 of *Dietrich Bonhoeffer Works;* trans. Douglas Stephen Bax; Minneapolis: Fortress, 1997), 34–35.

40. Stephen Jay Gould, *Wonderful Life: The Burgess Shale and the Nature of History* (New York: W. W. Norton, 1989).

41. Ibid., chapter 3.

42. Ibid., 287–88.

43. Richard E. Leakey and Roger Lewin, *Origins* (New York: E. P. Dutton, 1977), and *Origins Reconsidered* (New York: Doubleday, 1992), give a good survey of human evolution.

44. "Lectures on Genesis," *LW* 1:62.

45. Theophilus of Antioch, "Theophilus to Autolycus," *ANF* 2:104.

46. St. Irenaeus of Lyons, *On the Apostolic Preaching* (Crestwood, N.Y.: St. Vladimir's Seminary, 1997), 47.

47. Timothy Ware, *The Orthodox Church* (Baltimore: Penguin, 1964), 223–30.

48. Athanasius, "On the Incarnation of the Word," *NPNF,* Series 2, 4:38–39. See also the prolegomena to this volume, lxxi.

49. Ibid., 38. The Hebrew *moth tamuth* in Gen 2:17 is emphatic: "Thou shalt surely die" (KJV). But the over-literal *thanatō apothaneisthe,* "dying ye shall die," of the Septuagint supported Athanasius's idea of a two-fold death.

50. Leakey and Lewin, *Origins Reconsidered,* chapter 16. Carl Sagan and Ann Druyan, *Shadows of Forgotten Ancestors* (New York: Random House, 1992), chapters 14 and 15.

51. Reinhold Niebuhr, *The Nature and Destiny of Man* (New York: Charles Scribner's Sons, 1964), vol. 1, chapter 12.

52. "The Augsburg Confession," Article 2, in *The Book of Concord* (ed. Robert Kolb and Timothy J. Wengert; Minneapolis: Fortress, 2000), 36–39.

53. Other useful discussions are Philip Hefner, *The Human Factor: Evolution, Culture, and Religion* (Minneapolis: Fortress, 1993), chapter 8; and Craig L. Nessan, "Sex, Aggression, and Pain: Sociobiological Implications for Theological Anthropology," *Zygon* 33 (1998): 443.

54. Athanasius, "On the Incarnation," 36.

55. "His brethren" of the RSV is a literal rendering of *tois adelphois.* But the implications of the passage require that male and female be included if women are to be saved through the incarnation. See George L. Murphy, "For the Ordination of Women," *Lutheran Forum* 24 (Advent 1990): 6.

56. Aloys Grillmeier, *Christ in Christian Tradition* (2d ed.; Atlanta: John Knox, 1975), vol. 1, book 1, chapter 6.

57. Gregory Nazianzen, "To Cledonius the Priest against Appolinarius," *NPNF,* Series 2, 7:440.

58. Jaroslav Pelikan, *The Spirit of Eastern Christendom (600–1700)* (Chicago: University of Chicago Press, 1974), 75–90.

59. D. M. Baillie, *God Was in Christ* (2d rev. ed.; New York: Charles Scribner's Sons, 1955), 15.

60. H. Wheeler Robinson, *Corporate Personality in Ancient Israel* (Philadelphia: Fortress, 1980); John A. T. Robinson, *The Body* (Philadelphia: Westminster, 1952).

61. Irenaeus, "Against Heresies," *ANF* 1, book 2, chapter 22, par. 4; book 3, chapter 18, par. 7; and book 5, chapter 21, par. 1.

62. Ernst Haeckel, *The Riddle of the Universe* (London: Watts & Co., 1929), chapter 4.

63. Stephen Jay Gould, *Ontology and Phylogeny* (Cambridge, Mass.: The Belknap Press of Harvard University Press, 1977).

64. C. S. Lewis, *Miracles* (New York: Macmillan, 1947), 115–16. I have corrected what appears to be a typographical error.

65. Robert E. Kofahl, *Handy Dandy Evolution Refuter* (San Diego: Beta Books, 1980), 17.

66. *CD* 4:2:92–93.

67. Murphy, *The Trademark of God,* chapter 11.

68. Maurice Wiles, *The Christian Fathers* (London: Hodder & Staughton, 1966), 86–89.

· 9 ·

TECHNOLOGY AND ETHICS

☙

"THE WORK OF OUR HANDS"

The human, according to Philip Hefner, can be considered theologically as "the created co-creator."[1] *Homo sapiens* is God's creation through the processes of evolution "whose purpose is to be the agency, acting in freedom, to birth the future that is most wholesome for the nature that has birthed us—the nature that is not only our own genetic heritage, but also the entire human community and the evolutionary and ecological reality in which and to which we belong. Exercising this agency is said to be God's will for humans."[2] Technology makes the concept especially vivid and raises penetrating questions about it. Technological ability will tell us neither what is "most wholesome" for nature nor "God's will." The ability to do things raises questions about what *should* be done and calls for scientific reflection on the consequences of actions, theological reflection on God's will, and ethical reflection on right and wrong.[3] In the conclusion of the somber Ninetieth Psalm we pray,

> Let the favor of the Lord our God be upon us,
> and prosper for us the work of our hands—
> O prosper the work of our hands! (Ps 90:17)

Our efforts to change the world will come to nothing if God does not establish them.

One of our most profound myths is Prometheus's theft of fire from the gods and gift of it to humanity. Other animals use rocks and sticks but only human beings have developed technology, which requires both the intelligence and the opposable thumb that together have often been seen as distinguishing human features.

The differences between recent technologies and those of antiquity are obvious. Not only can we do things that people centuries ago could not dream of, but technologies are now developed deliberately by scientific research rather than through accidents and trial and error. There is, nevertheless, some continuity between ancient times and today. While early technologies were primitive in comparison with ours, the ways in which the Bible speaks about the technologies of its time can help us to assess technology in general.

In the second creation story of Genesis, humanity is called to the practice of agriculture. God places the human in the garden "to till it and keep it" (Gen 2:15). The human vocation is not to live idly in paradise but to do manual and mental work. Genesis 4 has hints about the origins of human culture—domestication of animals, musical instruments, and metalworking (vv. 20–22). When evil reaches such a pitch that God resolves to wipe out humanity with the flood, Noah is saved by building a ship.

But in the story of the tower of Babel, the use of technology brings a response from God that confuses language, aborts the project, and scatters humanity. This is not one of the myths of an attempt to scale heaven and overthrow the supreme god. The builders don't mention God at all.[4] A kind of youthful exuberance motivates them, but there is also a note of anxiety: "Let us make a name for ourselves; otherwise we shall be scattered abroad upon the face of the whole earth" (Gen 11:4). There is not a little resemblance here to modern secular cultures that see humanity itself as responsible for its own survival and salvation by its own powers.

The Bible may speak of technology in negative ways as something in which people put trust and confidence that should be placed in God. In relying on what they can do, people worship "the work of their hands" (Isa 2:8). It is especially tempting to make idols of weapons systems (Ps 20:7, Isa 31:1). But positive references predominate. Agriculture, building, metalworking, and medicine are used as metaphors for God's activity,[5] and in Exod 31:1–11, all the crafts needed for the tent of meeting are said to be inspired by God.

Jesus is called "the carpenter" by the people of his hometown (Mark 6:3): The Greek *ho tektōn* can mean a worker in wood, metal, or stone. This verse was an embarrassment to early Christians in a culture in which manual laborers were not held in high regard: Celsus ridiculed Christianity because its founder was only "a carpenter by trade." That type of criticism may be why some manuscripts of Mark have assimilated this verse to Matt 13:55 in which Jesus is "the carpenter's son."[6] If a Greek philosopher could have conceived of the Logos becoming incarnate, it would probably have been as a philosopher, and certainly not as a carpenter. The biblical view, however, is not one of the superiority of pure thought. Work in which knowledge is applied in order to effect change in the world is part of the human vocation to care for creation in Genesis and is given God's blessing in the incarnation.

Technology has developed rapidly in recent centuries. Watt's steam engine made possible new and more abundant consumer goods and faster communication and travel, but also led to urban squalor, child labor in factories and mines, and pollution: The smog of London and the stench of the Thames were early signs of the negative environmental impact of science-based technology.[7] Automobiles and airplanes changed traditional structures of society and required exploitation of the earth's petroleum.

Connections between electricity and magnetism provided ways of generating electric current and of using it to run machinery. Electromagnetic technologies have impacts on the physical environment, such as the damming of rivers for hydroelectric power, and the social environment, such as the profound influence of radio and television on popular culture.

Chemical research led to materials such as new alloys, modern dyes, plastics, and drugs. The understanding of atoms and crystals by quantum mechanics made possible developments in electronics, which made computers and the internet feasible. Deeper research into the structure of matter led to the discovery of nuclear energy with potential for both peace and destruction.

The earth sciences have assisted in the development of energy sources and raw materials. A technological society does not simply "find resources" that are already present in the world. Bauxite is a very common mineral, but it was of no use until an intelligent species evolved and, in 1886, developed the electrolytic Hall process, which made it possible to extract aluminum from it. There is an important sense in which a culture with science-based technology cooperates in the creation of the resources that it uses.

Biotechnologies have in many ways taken the lead in recent years. In the next chapter, I will look at some of the new biomedical techniques. At the same time, the successes of "old-fashioned" medical science in the prevention and in some cases eradication of infectious diseases, and in the treatment and cure of other conditions, should not be forgotten.

Agricultural science has led to great increases in food production. New crop strains, chemical fertilizers, and irrigation produced the "Green Revolution" of the 1960s and it seemed for a time that widespread hunger and malnutrition might be eliminated, but this was too optimistic. Losses of food-producing land by erosion, construction, and the growth of non-food crops contribute to these problems.[8]

THE CONTEXT FOR DECISIONS

Many issues posed by technology require reflection on social ethics. This is especially so when we consider the impact of technology on the environment. Even individual decisions like those involved with abortion or organ donation are influenced by the framework of society and its laws. Thus a technological ethic must involve ethics of a society—but what society? Is it a Christian community or the nation? What should be the relationship between the ethics of the Christian community and that of the larger society?

For a good deal of Christian history the two were thought to be much the same. Church and state were to be mutually supportive as one operated in the spiritual realm and the other in the secular. The society to which Christian social ethics applied was coterminous with the civil realm. What was expected from most Christians was the ethics of good citizenship.

It is easy to criticize this "Constantinian settlement" with its alliance of throne and altar. The automatic administration of baptism, subtly or blatantly coerced professions of faith, church support for the interests of those in power, and religious compromises for political expediency now seem obvious problems. But the idea of Christendom should not be viewed in an entirely negative way. Is the gospel not to change the world? Is Christ not really king of kings?

In any case, the idea of a "Christian society" in the sense in which it was understood from the fourth through the nineteenth centuries is now outdated in virtually the whole world. The assumptions accompanying that idea, however, still strongly influence Christian thought.

We have developed a view of the scientific world centered on the cross and resurrection of Christ and now want to deal with technology in that same spirit. But for the foreseeable future the ethics of society as a whole will not be centered on the cross. An ethic of the cross cannot be expected of or imposed upon the adherents of other faiths and largely secularized populations of today's industrialized societies. The United States is not a Christian nation in the medieval sense: The president could be a Muslim or Buddhist.

The history of the United States, however, has been pervaded by aspects of the Judeo-Christian tradition. Many Americans are members of Christian churches. Unfortunately, the type of Christianity prevalent in America is more comfortable with theologies of glory than with the theology of the cross.[9] This is most evident in the optimism of American religion. The cross is often displayed in public and sometimes becomes the subject of legal disputes, but it is almost always the *empty* cross rather than the crucifix. It is a sign of triumph over adversity, with no reminder of the one who hung on the cross.

One popular American saying is "God helps them who help themselves." Many people think that it comes from the Bible but it is actually from Benjamin Franklin's *Poor Richard's Almanac*.[10] God does cooperate with creatures, and Paul could say, "Anyone unwilling to work should not eat" (2 Thess 3:10). But Franklin's proverb is often used to justify ignoring the needs of those who *can't* help themselves, and to validate those who help themselves at the expense of others. And at a fundamental level it is contrary to the gospel message that God saves those who are unable to save themselves.

These attitudes are relevant for us because of their connection with the technological optimism of American culture. It is no accident that Franklin was the first important American scientist and inventor. While most of the development of pure science in the nineteenth century took place in Europe, the United States was especially the land of inventors. Mechanical and electrical devices for farm, factory, and home transformed American society and gave it the lead among industrial nations. The continent-spanning telegraph and railroad and the building of the Panama Canal with its associated conquest of yellow fever show that there were solid reasons for the "can-do" attitude of American inventors, engineers, and doctors. Positive attitudes toward technology have produced many benefits. But unchecked technological optimism that follows from the popular theology of glory has a great deal of trouble in dealing with the possibility that there are some things that technological ingenuity *can't* do.

The earth's resources are finite. We will run out of oil, and the only question is "When?" The laws of thermodynamics place limits on the extent to which we can use energy resources. Antibiotics save lives, but natural selection, exacerbated by overuse of some antibiotics, has produced strains of bacteria that are resistant to current antibiotics. Humanity has not "lost" to bacteria but the battle against infectious disease will be an ongoing one.

A genuine ethic of the cross is possible only within a community that understands itself to be Christian. Such an ethic would be directed first toward formation and nurture of the community as the body of Christ, and only secondarily to the civil righteousness demanded in the secular realm. It would have some of the characteristics of the ethics of the Radical Reformation. Mennonite theologian John Howard Yoder expresses the view of that tradition:

> There is no self-evident reason to assume that the obligations of Christians and non-Christians are the same in the New Testament when one decides and acts within the reestablished covenant of grace and the other does not. There is no reason to have to assume that the moral per-

formance of which God expects of the regenerate [God] equally expects of the unregenerate. Of course, on some much more elevated level of abstraction, our minds demand that we project a unique and univocal ultimate or ideal will of God. But it is precisely the nature of [God's] patience with fallen humanity that God condescends to deal with us on other levels.[11]

One strength of this view is that it does not need to compromise with standards of civil righteousness that are feasible in society as a whole.

A weakness of this tradition is its tendency to withdraw from participation in the affairs of the larger society. This is stronger in some parts of the tradition than in others, and some Quakers, Mennonites, and others try to influence public policy. But wariness about participation in civil government limits the effectiveness of such action. Christians ought to take the lead in humanity's vocation to represent God in creation and must participate with people of other faiths, or with no religion at all, in determining and carrying out public policy without remaining silent about the cruciform pattern that motivates them.

KENOSIS AS PATTERN

How shall we live? That question has faced people at all times throughout the world. Traditional moral codes and principles were developed long before the growth of scientific knowledge, which began in the sixteenth century. Since then the work of scientists, engineers, and physicians has been rewarded with qualitatively new capabilities and has greatly expanded the scope of those the human race already had. What are we to do with those abilities?

Not all of the moral issues we now face are complicated, and traditional ethics is not simply invalidated by modern discoveries. Nazi doctors in concentration camps performed medical experiments on Jews and other prisoners that resulted in their deaths. Many of these were simply excuses for sadism, but others had some real scientific purpose. For example, at Dachau prisoners were placed in a decompression chamber to simulate the atmospheric conditions at high altitude that were experienced by flyers, and many of the subjects of these experiments died.[12] A quite adequate ethical judgment on such practices is "You shall not murder" from the Ten Commandments or its equivalent in any other moral code.

But some new discoveries raise questions that are not addressed by traditional ethics. The Bible says nothing about organ transplants or the disposal of waste from nuclear power plants. Scripture is relevant to these concerns, but we cannot read from it answers to them in the same straightforward way that we can with Nazi experiments.

An understanding of the scientific and technological world in the light of the cross should be accompanied by an ethic of the cross. Important contributions toward such an ethic may be found in Bonhoeffer's unfinished *Ethics* and other writings, and Larry Rasmussen has developed Bonhoeffer's ideas further.[13] The kenotic ethic proposed by Murphy and Ellis, especially as it relates to scientific understanding of the world, is closely related to such a project.[14]

Philippians 2:5–11 has already played important roles in our discussions. It is not simply a doctrinal statement on Christology but a description of the kind of attitude toward life that Christians are to have, a summons to think and act in ways that are patterned after Christ's kenosis and cross: "Do nothing from selfish ambition or conceit, but in humility regard others as better than yourselves. Let each of you look not to your own interests, but to the interests of others. Let the same mind be in you that was in Christ Jesus . . ." (Phil 2:3–5).

On the one hand, the kenosis of Christ shows what God is really like: It was not simply a stratagem practiced by a deity who is really selfish and domineering. On the other hand, it had a purpose: God's goal is not emptiness and suffering for their own sake, but for the good of the world. The cross shows that God is willing to go to any lengths, even death, for God's own creation, for that which is other than God.

The kenotic aspect of divine action means that God cooperates with things in such a way as to preserve their integrity and freedom. They are instruments and masks but not puppets, and God does not override even the misguided actions of people that result in moral evil. But God does not simply let go of creation, for then the universe would cease to exist. An important part of this grant of freedom and integrity to creation is the delegation of authority to humanity: "The heavens are the LORD's heavens, but the earth he has given to human beings" (Ps 115:16). If our exercise of this relative degree of authority follows God's example, then we will take action and not be passive in the face of suffering and evil. We will try to turn our abilities toward enabling other creatures to fulfill God's creative purpose for them.

Kenosis modeled on the example of Christ is directed toward "the interests of others." Pain, loss, and death are not ethical goods to be pursued for their own sake but they are to be accepted and welcomed for the interests of others. When Jesus tells a man to sell all that he has, he is not to throw the money away but to give it to the poor (Mark 10:21).

Kenosis is a not a striving for nirvana, but it is also not a utilitarian acceptance of present hardship for the sake of future profit, the sort of thing encouraged by slogans like "No pain, no gain." The gain that is the goal of Christlike kenosis is the gain of others, not of the one who gives or suffers. The cross is accepted in hope of the resurrection, but it is accepted first because it is the way of solidarity with God. C. S. Lewis put the matter well in a letter to a friend:

> I believed in God before I believed in Heaven. And even now, even if— let's make an impossible supposition—His voice, unmistakably His, said to me, "They have misled you. I can do nothing of that sort for you. My long struggle with the blind forces is nearly over. I die, children. The story is ending"—would that be a moment for changing sides? Would not you and I take the Viking way: "The Giants and Trolls win. Let us die on the right side, with Father Odin."[15]

Jesus' way to the cross began with acceptance of human existence under conditions of weakness and vulnerability: He took the form of a slave. His whole earthly career is given as a pattern, and in the Gospels he is pictured as one who speaks and acts "as one having authority, and not as their scribes" (Matt 7:29). He commands, heals, forgives, and defies those in power. Jesus does not disclaim the exercise of power but uses it for others. He does not turn stones into bread to satisfy his own hunger but in some surprising way provides food for others because "I have compassion for the crowd" (Matt 15:32).

Attempts to practice "the imitation of Christ" have a long history and are subject to some dangers.[16] The most naive mistake is to think that we are to mimic the activities of Jesus two thousand years ago. It would be neither feasible nor helpful for all to be carpenters. At the same time, we have no accounts of Jesus deciding how to balance protection of an endangered species and jobs of workers. In many ways it would be better to speak of conformation to the pattern of Christ rather than the imitation of Christ.

A more serious error is the idea that a person gains salvation by imitating Christ. Paul's words in Philippians are directed to a Christian congregation and, moreover, to Christians with whom he is quite pleased. Having the attitude of Christ is not a way for them to be saved but the way that they are to live as people who have been saved.

Rasmussen argues that the imitation of Christ "has been frustrated by continued Constantinian assumptions on the part of those who have held a theology of the cross."[17] But many issues raised by technology have to be dealt with politically, and Christians should not overreact to the compromises of the past by abdicating responsibility for effective action today. Christians can abstain from exercise of political authority when they are a minority in society and others can do the necessary tasks. But if they are in a majority, if they have the character and abilities to exercise authority, and if public welfare requires action, then a refusal to participate in civil government, and even to use force, may be irresponsible. Failing to help a person who is attacked because of a commitment to nonviolence may amount to placing abstract doctrine above the needs of the other. Kenosis means a willingness to give up the exercise of power for the sake of the other, not for the sake of one's own moral purity.

From the beginnings of modern science there was a drive not only to understand the world but also to control it: Human beings were to be "the lords and masters of nature."[18] Nature was to be of benefit to humanity, and the only limits on what could be done with it were technical rather than moral. Deleterious effects of technology on the environment generally escaped the attention of people in Western societies until well into the twentieth century, and the technological superiority of European and American nations could be used to justify colonialism and other exploitation in the name of the advance of civilization. All of these attempts to exercise control of the world for our own benefit run counter to the kenotic theme.

Who are the "others" to whose interests we are to look? Jesus' story of the Good Samaritan (Luke 10:30–35) suggests that there are to be no limits to concern for members of the human family. He has just cited Lev 19:18, "You shall love your neighbor as yourself," and has been asked in turn, "And who is my neighbor?" There is a natural tendency to want to draw some boundaries on neighbor-hood so that we know where our responsibilities end. Jesus' parable stops that attempt by making it clear that every encounter between human beings has the potential to bring forth the response of the neighbor. Whenever I have the possibility of aiding anyone in any way I have the possibility of loving that person as myself—or refusing to.

"You shall love your neighbor as yourself" is given special force by God's identification with the neighbor: "Those who oppress the poor man insult their Maker, but those who are kind to the needy honor him" (Prov 14:31). That identification is greatly strengthened with the incarnation, so that charity or lack of it shown to "the least of these" is equated with a person's actions toward the King himself (Matt 25:31–46). As Barth put it:

> There is a general connexion of *all* men with Christ, and every man is His brother. He died for all men and rose for all men; so every man is the addressee of the work of Jesus Christ. That this is the case, is a promise for the whole of humanity. And it is the most important basis, and the only one which touches everything, for what we call humanity. He who has once realised the fact that God was made man cannot speak and act inhumanly.[19]

Moreover, the Bible does not portray God as being concerned only for the welfare of humanity: The Lord's response to Job (chapters 38–41) concentrates on the divine care for the creatures of the wilderness that live apart from humankind and are not under human control, and Jesus speaks about God's care for the birds and the lilies (Matt 6:26–30). If our attitude is to reflect the manner in which God values things, then we will show a proper regard for other animals, plants, and the inanimate creation.

TECHNOLOGICAL WAR

The Old Testament does not renounce all warfare, but even when the king rides out to battle, he and his people are reminded of where their confidence is to lie:

> Some take pride in chariots, and some in horses,
> but our pride is in the name of the LORD our God. (Ps 20:7)

When Zion's true king comes he will be riding a donkey rather than a warhorse, and chariot and bow and other implements of war will be "cut off" (Zech 9:9–10).

Modern weapons systems provide the sharpest example of the threat that technology can pose for the world. The problem of technological war is part of the larger question of how to deal with issues of war and peace. Pacifism, adhered to especially by those in the Anabaptist and Quaker traditions, has a good deal to recommend it as a Christian position in accord with an ethic of the cross. It need not imply a passive acceptance of evil. Effective forms of nonviolent resistance such as those practiced by Gandhi and Martin Luther King Jr. are ways in which evil is opposed without recourse to violence.

Other nonviolent techniques may be useful in dealing with modern military technology. When the possibility of a full-scale nuclear exchange between the United States and the Soviet Union was very real, James Burnham suggested that the two nations agree upon "the reciprocal introduction of each side's strategic experts into the other side's strategic system."[20] This would have given both sides access to information that would have made a surprise attack virtually impossible. The proposal was both imaginative and realistic. It would be worth exploring ways in which this proposal could be adapted to current situations of potential conflict.

But nonviolent means may not be effective in preventing injury to innocent people, and the only way of preventing or stopping something like the Holocaust may be military force. The just war doctrine holds that in some situations war may be the lesser of evils. A just (or better, justifiable) war may be seen as God's alien work carried out through the instrumentalities of human beings and their military technologies.

Yoder has given a helpful treatment of this doctrine as a challenge to those who claim this position.[21] The criteria for a just war include conditions for going to war and those concerning the means used in war. The conditions relevant for us here are as follows:

7. The means used must be indispensable to achieve the end.
8. The means used must be discriminating, both
   (a) quantitatively, in order not to do more harm than the harm they prevent ("proportionality"), and
   (b) qualitatively, to avoid use against the innocent ("immunity").[22]

It is here that issues of technology are important. The criteria of proportionality and immunity have been eroded seriously by the development of weapons of mass destruction. In 1983 the Roman Catholic bishops of the United States used the just war criteria to argue that there can be virtually no morally acceptable uses of nuclear weapons in warfare.[23]

The impact of modern war on the environment can be so severe that it should be taken into account in determining whether or not some means of war are justifiable: Deuteronomy 20:19–20 provides a biblical precedent for adding an environmental criterion to the list. This would prohibit such practices as the American defoliation of the jungles in Vietnam or Iraq's deliberate oil spills and firing of the Kuwaiti oil fields in the First Gulf War.

The science and technology that make possible modern weapons cannot be eliminated. They are expressions of energies in creation that from a theological standpoint have to be considered good. Nor is that a purely theoretical judgment. Even if all nations turned to peace and wanted to beat their swords into plowshares in accord with Isa 2:4/Mic 4:3, it would be wise to maintain a stockpile of nuclear weapons as a defense against the type of asteroid impact that destroyed the dinosaurs. The best way to prevent worldwide disaster in such a situation might be to use nuclear explosives to deflect or to break up the asteroid before impact.[24]

That is not intended to suggest that science and technology can always save us. But it does bring out the fact that the way to deal with technological threats is not simply to get rid of technology. It is rather to use technology for the defense and the welfare of creation.

FREEDOM FOR DECISION

When a situation calling for decision has been evaluated and rights and wrongs have been considered, we are often left in some ambiguity about the best action to take. This is so even if behavior is supposed to be governed by an absolute moral code. Christians and those of other faiths have developed casuistic systems to deal with such ambiguities, but situations brought about by new technologies may require further decisions: Does turning on an electric light on Saturday violate the prohibition on lighting a fire on the Sabbath?

If we have to decide whether or not to continue life support for a terminally ill patient or where to place a repository for nuclear waste, the Decalogue or the example of Jesus will give us some guidance but will not provide us with certainty. And yet the decisions have to be made. The feeding tube will either be put in or not, and the radioactive material has to go somewhere.

Some people have no difficulty in making such decisions but others may be paralyzed by the fear of making the wrong choice. Still others act but are plagued by doubt and guilt if the outcome of the decision remains unclear. (It may be centuries before flaws in a nuclear waste repository appear.) Guilt will be severe if it emerges that a bad choice *was* made, as when an autopsy shows that a doctor's course of treatment was poorly chosen.

There are two objects of this anxiety, our penultimate ends and the ultimate.[25] We may be concerned about the effects that our action or inaction will have upon people and affairs in the world, or about our relationship with God.

What happens within the world to ourselves, other people, and the rest of nature is important. We may be concerned literally with life and death decisions, which should be made as responsibly as possible. Prayer, careful thought, consultation with experts, and the counsel of the church should all be components of such decisions. Our choices will help to determine the future course of events and, in some cases, such as the possibility of modifying the human genome, may have effects far into the future. But these are still penultimate matters.

Our ultimate end is God, and the promise of the gospel is that God freely accepts us for Christ's sake. Our decisions, right or wrong, do not determine our status before God. The choices we make, as long as we are not willfully opposing what we know to be God's will, do not sever this relationship. Thus we can act, free of the prospect of divine condemnation. The God who raises the dead and creates out of nothing is the one who justifies the ungodly (Rom 4:17 and 5). A fortiori, God justifies those who try faithfully to make the best choice but fail.

The gospel's promise of ultimate salvation frees us for penultimate decisions. This does not mean that they can be made lightly. What happens to creation matters to the creator. But nothing that we do or fail to do makes God's grace impossible or compels it. The ultimate work is God's, and our freedom to act is based finally upon the free gift of God, which ensures our ultimate status so that we are able to make penultimate choices.

NOTES

1. Philip Hefner, *The Human Factor: Evolution, Culture, and Religion* (Minneapolis: Fortress, 1993), 23–51.

2. Ibid., 27.

3. Ian Barbour, *Ethics in an Age of Technology* (San Francisco: HarperCollins, 1993).

4. Gerhard von Rad, *Genesis* (rev. ed.; Philadelphia: Westminster, 1972), 148–49.

5. For these and other scientific and technological allusions in the Bible, see George L. Murphy, LaVonne Althouse, and Russell Willis, *Cosmic Witness* (Lima, Ohio: CSS, 1996), appendix C.

6. William L. Lane, *The Gospel According to Mark* (Grand Rapids, Mich.: Eerdmans, 1974), 201–3; Bruce M. Metzger, *A Textual Commentary on the Greek New Testament* (Stuttgart: United Bible Societies, 1971), 88–89.

7. Colin A. Russell, *Cross-Currents* (Grand Rapids, Mich.: Eerdmans, 1985), 226–27.

8. Barbour, *Ethics in an Age of Technology,* chapter 4.

9. Douglas John Hall, *Lighten Our Darkness: Toward an Indigenous Theology of the Cross* (Philadelphia: Westminster, 1976), 145–52.

10. *Poor Richard's Almanack* (Mt. Vernon, N.Y.: Peter Pauper Press, n.d.), no page numbering.

11. Larry Rasmussen with Renate Bethge, *Dietrich Bonhoeffer: His Significance for North Americans* (Minneapolis: Fortress, 1990), 170.

12. William L. Shirer, *The Rise and Fall of the Third Reich* (Greenwich, Conn.: Fawcett, 1962), 1281–83.

13. Dietrich Bonhoeffer, *Ethics* (New York: Macmillan, 1965); Rasmussen, *Dietrich Bonhoeffer: His Significance for North Americans,* especially chapter 8.

14. Nancey Murphy and G. F. R. Ellis, *On the Moral Nature of the Universe: Theology, Cosmology, and Ethics* (Minneapolis: Fortress, 1996).

15. C. S. Lewis, *Prayer* (Glasgow: William Collins Sons, 1966), 120.

16. E. J. Tinsley, "Imitation of Christ, The," *WDCT,* 285–86. .

17. Rasmussen, *Dietrich Bonhoeffer: His Significance for North Americans,* 144.

18. René Descartes, "Discourse on Method," in *Selected Philosophical Writings* (Cambridge: Cambridge University Press, 1988), 47.

19. Karl Barth, *Dogmatics in Outline* (New York: Harper & Row, 1959), 138.

20. James Burnham, "Strike Three and Out," *National Review* 21 (June 3, 1969), 531.

21. John Howard Yoder, *When War Is Unjust* (Minneapolis: Augsburg, 1984).

22. Ibid., 18.

23. National Council of Catholic Bishops, *The Challenge of Peace* (Washington, D.C.: United States Catholic Conference, 1983).

24. Tom Gehrels, "Collisions with Comets and Asteroids," *Scientific American* 274, no. 3 (March 1996): 54.

25. Bonhoeffer, *Ethics,* 120–87.

· 10 ·

MEDICINE AND BIOETHICS

❧

THE ANOINTING OF THE SICK

Surgery and medicine were practiced well before biblical times, and Sir 38:1–15 praises physicians and medicine as gifts of God. One medication was olive oil (Isa 1:6, Luke 10:34), and when Jesus sent disciples out to preach and heal, they "anointed with oil many who were sick and cured them" (Mark 6:13). They would have accompanied this with prayer, and the question of whether cures were "natural" or "miraculous" probably did not occur to them. The Epistle of James gives directions for those who are sick: "They should call for the elders of the church and have them pray over them, anointing them with oil in the name of the Lord. The prayer of faith will save the sick, and the Lord will raise them up; and anyone who has committed sins will be forgiven" (5:14–15).

Anointing of the sick came to be considered a sacrament and in the West became extreme unction for the dying, developments that were criticized by the sixteenth-century reformers. The practice fell out of use for Protestants, while for Roman Catholics it no longer had physical or mental healing as its primary purpose. But Vatican II gave renewed attention to healing in connection with anointing, an emphasis that had always been maintained by the Orthodox, and Protestants have begun to regain appreciation for such ministries of healing.[1]

In such a rite we are, first, asking God for healing. But this prayer takes place with the use of a medicine. Today we have things that are far more effective than olive oil, but it is a representative medicine, and its use suggests that we are asking for God's healing power through the things that

God has created. God may heal in ways that we can't explain, but in the vast majority of cases healing is mediated through doctors, nurses, surgery, drugs, radiation, diet, exercise, and other instruments. The theological basis for the anointing of the sick is the idea of God's cooperation with lawful natural processes.

It is unfortunate that Christians have sometimes thought that going to a doctor or taking medicine betrays a lack of faith in God. A proper balance is found in Stark's *Hand-Book,* a devotional work of German pietism first published in 1728. Under the heading "The Patient Prays on Taking Medicine," there is the following "exhortation":

> If a devout prayer is indispensable even in times of health, how can a patient neglect it, particularly when he takes medicine?
>
> 1. The patient must not despise the physician, nor his medicine, nor think that if he is destined to recover, God can restore him without medicine, and that if he is destined to die, the medicine will be of no avail. No, to think thus were to tempt God. God has not promised to help us without means; and what God has not promised, we cannot ask of him. Those who despise medicine and die, are guilty of their own murder.
>
> 2. Yet he must not set his trust upon the physician and his medicine, but upon God; as it is declared to be one of the sins of King Asa, that in his sickness he did not seek God, but the physicians, and trusted them more than God. 2 Chronicles, xvi. 12.
>
> 3. Between these two extremes, the patient must select the golden mean. With his lips and his heart he must pray, and take the medicine in firm reliance upon the helping hand of God; then he may know that there is a blessing upon it.[2]

The stories of Jesus' healings in the Gospels have a cruciform character. In Matt 8:1–16 several cures are described and are summarized in verse 17: "This was to fulfill what had been spoken through the prophet Isaiah, 'He took our infirmities and bore our diseases.'" I noted earlier Bonhoeffer's statement that this shows "that Christ helps us, not by virtue of his omnipotence, but by virtue of his weakness and suffering."[3] Jesus' healings are not described in terms of supernatural power from above but of the servant who from below bears the sufferings of others. God's work of healing, like all divine action in the world, is kenotic.

Doctors are often tempted to see themselves in "godlike" roles, with superior knowledge and abilities that give them powers of life and death. As medicine comes more and more to involve sophisticated science and technology, and as HMOs, insurance companies, and government agencies come to control health care, medicine becomes increasingly impersonal. The pattern that God gives in the ministry of Jesus is different. Nurses and doctors do need to be objective about, and at times distanced from, patients: accident victims do not want emergency room physicians to be overcome with pity for them. But healers should understand their solidarity with those they are called to heal.

Modern medical practice, especially as it is informed by developments in biology and other sciences, has raised a host of new ethical and theological issues. These have to do with the appropriateness and significance of procedures that were not dreamed of until recently. We are now faced with questions about who we are as human beings as well as about the decisions we should make for our own lives and those of others.

Bioethics only began to emerge as a separate discipline in the 1960s[4] but the scope of the issues with which it deals is now quite large: The 1995 edition of *Encyclopedia of Bioethics* is in five large volumes.[5] I am not going to survey this whole discipline but will look at representative issues brought about by modern science and technology at the beginning, middle, and end of life to suggest the distinctive insights of chiasmic cosmology.

LIFE BEFORE BIRTH

Many new procedures are related to conception and prenatal development, areas in which there is a great deal of religious and ethical feeling. Applications of genetic science begin before conception. Genetic counseling is available for couples who want to have a child but who have reason to believe that their offspring may have problematic genetic conditions. Potential parents can then make decisions about whether to conceive a child in the usual way, make use of some fertility technology, or adopt.

Technologies for assisting conception include fertility drugs, artificial insemination and *in vitro* fertilization (IVF), and surrogate motherhood. Germ line genetic engineering would introduce genetic modifications in a person's sex cells that would be passed on to his or her descendants. (This should be distinguished from somatic cell therapy, which affects the genes only in certain cells of the body and would not be transmitted to offspring.) Many physical conditions have been linked to specific genes, and the results of the Human Genome Project are expanding our knowledge of such linkages. This means that it may become possible to eliminate undesirable traits such as cystic fibrosis at the very beginning of life.

A more radical procedure is cloning, in which the genetic material from a cell of a person who has already been born would replace that of a fertilized ovum before embryonic development begins. A child resulting from this procedure would be a genetic identical twin of the person from whom the genetic material was taken, though of course at a younger age.[6]

The ability to conceive is essential for human existence and it is hardly surprising that it has been ascribed to God. Men and women cooperate in this through sexual intercourse, but there will be no conception or child-birth if God does not bring it about. "When Rachel saw that she bore Jacob no children, she envied her sister; and she said to Jacob, 'Give me children, or I shall die!' Jacob became very angry with Rachel and said, 'Am I in the place of God, who has withheld from you the fruit of the womb?'" (Gen 30:1–2). Yet Rachel responds by having Jacob conceive by her maid Bilhah so that she can have a child who will be legally hers. In modern terms she uses a form of surrogate motherhood!

Technologies to assist conception are now widely accepted, yet a crucial question often goes unasked: Why are we doing this? Why invest a great deal of time and money and engage in some practices that may be ethically problematic in order to overcome difficulties in conceiving?[7] Our desire to have children is one of the most powerful drives we have. But this still does not get to the heart of the matter. Why is it so important for people to have children who are in some sense biologically "their own"? If it were simply a question of having a child, adoption would be a simpler procedure.

The propagation of genes is a crucial feature of evolution, and a species that produces no offspring will not survive. But this, like so many aspects of evolution, has to do with populations rather than individuals. Some types of altruism are not only allowed, but even favored, by evolutionary theory. A person who gives up his or her life to save those of several siblings can increase the likelihood that the hereditary information that they share will remain in the gene pool more than by surviving and allowing those siblings to die. This sort of altruism within kinship groups is fairly easy to make sense of in an evolutionary context.[8]

More difficult to understand and more controversial is *trans-kin altruism* practiced for the benefit of those with whom one has only very distant biological relationships. Why would a Clara Maass risk and lose her life so that people unknown to her might be protected from yellow fever?[9] Why are some people willing to make sacrifices to protect whales or birds? Such behavior is far from universal, but trans-kin altruism is not just theoretical. We practice it every time we show some small courtesy to a stranger, often without thinking about it.

The attempts of sociobiology to explain trans-kin altruism entirely on the basis of kinship are interesting but they do not exhaust the topic or really get to the heart of the matter.[10] Hefner has put it well: "Trans-kin altruism is not simply a scientifically puzzling phenomenon, nor a regrettably neglected virtue; it is a central symbol and ritual of what human beings should be doing with their lives."[11] This is the point of Jesus' story of the Good Samaritan. If we limit the good we try to accomplish to ourselves or to our own tribe, we limit our humanity. We are sometimes called to make sacrifices at the trans-kinship level, foregoing behaviors that might help to propagate our genes in order to benefit those who are not close relatives.

A desire to continue our biological heritage is not wrong, but it should not be absolutized. In particular, the desire of a couple to have its own biological descendants does not validate all uses of technology that might be needed to accomplish it. If the couple has trouble conceiving, there is no fundamental problem with them using IVF. But if they have a high probability of conceiving offspring with a major genetic problem, it might be better to consider adoption rather than conceive in the usual way with the likelihood that they will have to choose between abortion or bringing a severely handicapped child into the world.

But adoption is not merely a way of avoiding the use of fertility technology. If trans-kin altruism really is a central symbol and ritual of what we should be doing with our lives, then a willingness to adopt strengthens this crucial feature of our joint humanity. Adoption processes should be made as simple as possible while retaining adequate safeguards against children being treated as commodities. Pregnant women who do not want to keep their babies should be encouraged to carry them to term and give them up for adoption rather than have abortions.

If the power to conceive is God's, the nature of the person who is conceived is also in God's hands. Since ancient times people have tried to improve plant and animal stocks by selective breeding. The Bible tells of Jacob doing this with the flocks under his care, using the idea that what a female sees during conception will influence the character of the offspring (Gen 30:25–43)—a mixture of practical knowledge about heredity and magic.[12] Plato proposed selective breeding of human beings in the *Republic.* But before Mendel's research there was no real understanding of how heredity worked and thus no possibility of "genetic engineering" in the modern sense. Inheritance was a mystery known only to God.

It is hardly surprising then that assisted conception or genetic engineering would be seen by some as an usurpation of God's role. The phrase "playing God" is often heard in discussions of new technologies, and has often been used in discussions of issues in bioethics. Ted Peters has subjected the slogan to theological analysis and states his view

> that the phrase "playing God?" has very little cognitive value when looked at from the perspective of a theologian. Its primary role is that of a warning, such as the word "stop." In common parlance it has come to mean just that: stop. Within the gene myth it means we should stop trying to engineer DNA. Theologically, however, there is at best only minimum warrant for using this phrase in such a conservative and categorical way.[13]

We first have to ask what is meant by "playing God." Does it mean playing the absolute monarch who exerts unlimited control over the fate of creatures, not allowing them any integrity or freedom? We agree that we should not try to play that role, but also say that the real God revealed in Christ does not play that role either!

But there is another way of "playing God," indeed, a sense in which we *should* play God! Being God's representatives in caring for creation is precisely the human calling. Part of the divine kenosis is that God does not control creation directly but, while cooperating with natural processes and thus keeping the world in being, delegates authority to humanity. God grants creatures their own integrity to be what they are and to develop in accord with the processes of the world, and this includes granting to intelligent creatures the freedom to exercise their intelligence.

Human dominion is to show those same features. Our intelligence and skill are to be used in the care of other humans and of the nonhuman creation, while respecting the integrity of these creatures. God's kenosis does not mean a strict "hands off" policy, and if we follow that model we will exercise an active, but respectful and responsible, care for the world. To refuse to act on the pretext that we do not want to "play God" is to refuse the vocation of created co-creator. It would be a sin at the other extreme from trying to model the divine absolute monarch and using others simply for our own benefit.

Contrary to the "gene myth" to which Peters refers, knowledge of the human genome and the ability to alter it would not give us unlimited ability to determine our future. Genes do determine some properties such as blood type in a straightforward way. Other features have genetic components but are also affected by environmental factors. Severe malnutrition in infants can stunt brain development in spite of any genetic predisposition to intelligence they may have. There is even greater flexibility with behavior. There may be genetic components of alcoholism, but some alcoholics may stop drinking completely while others drink themselves to death. It is neither a denial of the importance of heredity nor an assertion of unlimited free will to say that human beings have some say about what they do. Each of us recognizes that we really can make choices about some things, though a strict determinist may maintain with theory-affirming bravado that this appearance of choice is an illusion.[14]

The criterion that we are to care for human beings in order that they may be themselves, and not so that they can be useful to us, gives some guidance for appropriate genetic intervention and for ways to respond to genetic diagnoses that indicate problems. Pastoral counseling as well as medical information is important in these situations, and there are resources for ministries whose emphasis on cross and resurrection parallels ours.[15]

Debilitating ailments of genetic origin detract from a person's ability to be fully what she or he might be. It would be appropriate to eliminate cystic fibrosis by germ line therapy if that could be done without giving rise to other genetic problems. But as we work to get rid of genetic defects, it will be important not to disparage those who have them. Even the term "defect," with its connotation of something wrong with a product from a factory, should be used with care. (But we need not abandon common sense. Other things being equal, it is better to be able to see than not to see. Otherwise, when blind Bartimaeus said, "My teacher, let me see again," Jesus would have replied, "Why?" [Mark 10:46–52].)

The idea of bringing about *improvements* by genetic engineering is more problematic. There is not a simple one-to-one relation between musical or athletic abilities and genes. Even if such abilities can be enhanced, it may be done to satisfy the needs of others rather than of the genetically modified person, and thus will treat that person as a means to an end. We need not rule out all genetic engineering because of a fear of "playing God," but caution is needed about attempts to introduce genetic improvements. Some person or group will have to make the decisions about what changes constitute desirable improvements, and the old question, "Who will guard the guardians?" always needs to be asked.

Caution also needs to be exercised with reproductive human cloning, though again there is no reason for a permanent and total ban on it. A human clone should be acknowledged to be as fully human as any other person, just as identical twins are recognized as separate and fully human persons. Such acknowledgment would rule out some of the reasons for cloning, such as trying to ensure one's personal survival. In fact, it is not easy to see what good grounds could be given for reproductive cloning if that guideline were observed. There might be exceptional situations in which a person would be of such value to society that it would seem legitimate to produce a clone, with due regard for his or her value as an individual, but the difficulty of reproducing the necessary environmental influences from the womb onward makes the success of such an attempt unlikely.

Different issues are raised by the possibility of bringing embryos into being not to come to birth but to provide stem cells for various therapies. Since some stem cells have the potential to develop into any type of cell of the body, they could be used for the treatment of conditions such as Parkinson's disease or spinal cord injuries. Therapeutic cloning would enable stem cell lines of definite genetic makeup to be produced. Such possibilities should not be pursued before the theological and ethical status of the embryo is considered.

Of course this is not the only reason for discussing the status of the unborn. Abortion may be considered for many reasons, including the fact that a woman may not want a child. Prenatal diagnosis may show that a fetus has some crippling and painful condition that cannot be corrected. The technologies of IVF sometimes result in there being frozen embryos whose parents for one reason or another no longer wish to, or cannot, have them implanted. Abortion is by no means a new practice, but new technologies are creating some issues that are different from those that are involved when abortion is used essentially as a method of birth control.

The earliest Christian condemnation of abortion is in the second century *Didache*.[16] Until recently it was generally considered sinful by churches, though not always morally equivalent to murder. In the Middle Ages a distinction was made between the "formed" and "unformed" fetus, and only abortion of the latter was considered homicide. Furthermore, the practice might be allowed in order to preserve the life of the mother. It was only in 1869 that the Roman Catholic Church completely condemned abortion at any stage of development.[17] The life and health of the mother have long been considered to be factors that might justify an abortion, but new technologies have introduced questions about the health of the fetus.

Debates about abortion often center around the question of whether or not the embryo or fetus is a "person" at a particular stage of development. This is an important question for theology, ethics, and law, but biological science does not use the concept of person. This does not mean that scientific knowledge about conception and embryology is irrelevant for theology and ethics. Conception is a process spread over a period of time. Even after a few cell divisions, up to about a week after an ovum is fertilized, it is still possible for the conceptus to develop into twins rather than a single individual.[18] This forces us to ask critically about identification of a fertilized ovum with "a" person, whose classical definition is "the individual substance of a rational nature."[19]

After fertilization there is distinct human life, genetically different from father or mother but not yet a fully developed and viable human being. It is human life in its most imperfect and vulnerable state. And it is in this state that the enfleshed presence of God began in the womb of Mary. Just as the crucified God is a scandal, so God as an embryo, floating, tiny and fragile, in the womb of Mary, is a strange and offensive idea.

This aspect of the doctrine of the incarnation has sometimes been used to argue for the personal character of all fetuses from conception on, but that conclusion is debatable. Mary's child was, after all, unique. The relevance of the incarnation to the issue of abortion is that God identifies with human life precisely at this stage of weakness and incompleteness.

This is part of the whole picture of the biblical God who cares especially for the poor, for widows and orphans, for those who have no other helper or defender. And if God identifies the divine life with the unborn, we have no business treating fetal life as something that can simply be disposed of if it is inconvenient for us.

That does not mean that opposition to abortion must be absolute. The life and health of parents must be considered as well as that of the child, and there may be disabilities so severe (as when a fetus has no higher brain) that abortion seems to be the lesser of two evils. But that is something quite different from making freedom of choice an absolute.

ORGAN AND TISSUE TRANSPLANTS

The now routine procedures of donation and transplantation of hearts and other organs and tissues are of particular interest for the cruciform ethics in which we are interested here. The Christian life is to be patterned on the one who did not cling to what was rightfully his, and willingness to give part of one's self for others is congruent with that pattern. Blood donation should be seen in that light and there are other situations when a living person is able to donate bone marrow or a kidney that can be used by a person who is in need. This type of sacrifice is profoundly compatible with the Christian calling.

All heart transplants and many other major organ grafts are received from someone who has died. Consequently, there is not the same degree of sacrifice involved, although the feelings that most people have about their bodies, or their respect for the bodies of loved ones, mean that the sacrifice is not negligible. In any case, it is a sacrifice that often provides quite literally a gift of life. But many religious traditions have had special concern for maintaining the integrity of the body and have been opposed to anything that could be considered mutilation of it.[20] Jewish, Christian, and Islamic teachings about bodily resurrection make this an issue that has to be addressed in connection with transplants.

Pascal speculated that "Jesus Christ allowed only his wounds to be touched after the Resurrection,"[21] while Charles Wesley's hymn makes them an object of eschatological hope:

> The dear tokens of his passion
> Still his dazzling body bears;
> Cause of endless exultation
> To his ransomed worshippers:
> With what rapture
> Gaze we on those glorious scars![22]

Organ donation can be an act of self-giving that bears almost literally these marks of the cross, which, like the stigmata of martyrs, will be seen in the resurrection as signs of glory. (St. Bartholomew, who is supposed to have been flayed alive, carries his skin in Michelangelo's *Last Judgment* in the Sistine Chapel.) In this light donation is not only to be approved but should be actively encouraged.

Bodily healing is important for Christian faith because we live in the physical world. Belief in the resurrection of the body, however, goes beyond affirmation of our present existence. Christian faith is not about God performing a "soulechtomy" so that immortal souls can leave bodies behind and go to heaven.[23] Paul speaks in 1 Cor 15:35–57 of a transformation of the body and Dante sings of "the glorious and holy flesh" *(la carne gloriosa e santa).*[24]

Ironically, this very belief in resurrection of the body is an obstacle to organ donation. Some people think that each person will need his or her own body parts, so that organs should not be donated to others. This worry needs to be addressed because it is part of a serious practical problem. The availability of suitable organs is far below the need for them. Less than half of potential organ donors in the United States actually give them, and while in 1996 around fifty-five thousand people nationwide were on waiting lists for organ transplants, only about twenty thousand received them and more than four thousand on the lists died.[25] Part of the shortage is due to lack of awareness of the need, but if only a fraction is due to religious ideas, then those ideas have to be addressed.

The Christian belief in bodily resurrection was challenged in the form of a puzzle about a person whose body was eaten by cannibals. How can the same particles of matter be part of the bodies of both the victim and the cannibals in the resurrection? This is not a practical concern for many people but it is intended as a *reductio ad absurdum* of the whole idea of a general bodily resurrection. If there is even a single case in which that idea cannot be true, then it collapses. Various theologians took the challenge seriously and tried to answer it, but their arguments are not terribly convincing.[26]

Many theologians today would say that material identity is not the crucial aspect of the resurrection, arguing that continuity of experience and history is what is really important for personal identity.[27] Even in everyday life material identity may be less important than continuity of pattern. While a genuine 1804 United States silver dollar is very rare and valuable, if one were melted down it would be worth only a tiny fraction of its original value, even though it contained "the same silver atoms." This seems even more the case for human beings. It is our experiences and our consequent memories of them that determine who we are.

Our experience is, however, bodily experience. If resurrection of the same human person is to mean anything, then it must somehow be possible to speak of bodily sameness. Continuity of experience and history is essential, for Christianity is not concerned with zombies like those who come out of the Caldron of Rebirth in Welsh legend.[28] But that emphasis should not be adopted as a counsel of despair because of an apparent impossibility of any consistent understanding of material identity.

For such an understanding we can look to quantum theory, which says that identical particles really are identical.[29] The equations of this theory allow no change in observable results if identical particles are interchanged. If electrons behaved like billiard balls, then in a collision we could follow each one along its trajectory and keep track of which was which. But electrons don't have classical trajectories, being described instead by probability distributions for position and momentum. When two of them interact, their probability distributions will overlap and there will be no way of telling which is which.

This means that we cannot really speak of a body containing "the same atoms" that composed it at an earlier time, but only of it having the same pattern of the same kinds of atoms. The challenge posed to the idea of bodily resurrection by cannibalism or organ donation thus becomes a nonproblem. The pattern of the body, formed by its experience and history, is crucial, but this is not because we are unable to speak of the risen body itself. The instantiated pattern *is* the body, and in this sense we can affirm the statement of the Fourth Lateran Council that "all rise in their own bodies that they now have."[30]

DEATH AND LIFE

"You are dust, and to dust you shall return." Those words of Gen 3:19 are repeated in many churches every year on Ash Wednesday, accompanied by an imposition of ashes that makes their meaning vivid. It is as much as to say, "Remember that you are dying."

The proclamation of the resurrection of Christ is a claim that death does not have the last word but "has been swallowed up in victory" (1 Cor 15:54b). Athanasius, writing when the church had just gone through severe persecution, could say that death "is despised by all Christ's disciples."[31] But C. F. W. Walther in the nineteenth century was more realistic: "Many preachers picture the Christian as a person who does not fear death. That is a serious misrepresentation, because the great majority of Christians are afraid to die. If a Christian does not fear death and declares that he is ready to die at any time, God has bestowed a special grace upon him."[32] There is a normal fear of death that is not eliminated by belief that it is not an utter end.

Doctors and nurses know more realistically than others about death's inevitability and realize that a person may come to a point at which death should be allowed to happen. But because their calling emphasizes so strongly the preservation and saving of life, they may feel that they have failed when the inevitable takes place. Most people share this ambiguity. We sense that in some situations everything possible should be done to keep a person alive and that in others there is no point in taking extraordinary measures to keep biological processes going. But it is not always easy to know where to draw the line, and people draw it in different places.

The very definition of death has become debatable. In the biblical tradition, as in many others, life and death are associated with the presence or absence of breath. When breathing ceases, the heart soon stops beating and life is over. Until recently, medical and legal views that defined death in terms of cessation of cardiopulmonary functions were in accord with this commonsense understanding of death. But defining death in terms of breathing and blood circulation began to be questioned when it became possible to sustain these functions artificially. With a modern ventilator, a person unable to breathe on her or his own can be kept breathing and the heart kept beating for a long time. In some cases the person is conscious and unable to breathe only temporarily. But others may never regain either consciousness or the ability to breathe on their own. How long then is it appropriate to keep them on this artificial life support? Does a time come when they should simply be allowed to die? When *can* a person really be said to be dead, and then buried or cremated?

The difficulty of answering these questions was exacerbated by the fact that at about the same time that these improvements in life support technologies developed, it also became possible to transplant organs from a cadaver to a living person. Organs should receive oxygen from circulating blood up to the time of their removal for transplant, but the law requires that vital organs can be removed only after the donor has died.[33]

The concept of brain death, which was developed to deal with these issues, reflects a belief in modern scientific culture that the brain is the essential organ whose integrating and controlling function makes it possible for the organism as a whole to live.[34] In accordance, "Brain death is defined as the irreversible cessation of all functions of the entire brain, including the brain stem."[35] Unconsciousness, coma, and vegetative state are not identical with whole brain death. It is when the brain stem stops functioning that spontaneous respiration will cease.

This now widely accepted definition makes it possible for organs to be removed for transplantation while breathing and circulation are maintained, but it has continued to be criticized.[36] One set of issues has to do with whether medical personnel are applying the criteria correctly. A different problem is that reliance on the definition of whole brain death may be driven by the desire to have transplantable organs. These are real concerns, but returning to a cardiopulmonary definition of death is questionable. It is possible to use the criterion of brain death and to require consistent application of well-defined clinical tests for it.

But a careful definition of death does not answer another question that faces more and more people today: When should life support measures be stopped and death allowed to occur? There are few ethical questions about the use of life support measures when there is a reasonable possibility of the return of a patient to conscious, and to some extent active, life. But questions arise in cases such as that of a person in the final stages of a terminal illness or a persistent vegetative state, or an infant with no higher brain. To what extent is it necessary or even proper to "keep the machinery going" when there is no hope for recovery of higher brain function? Alternatively, we may be confronted with a relatively young person who has been paralyzed in an accident, but who is conscious and aware of the situation and does not *want* to be kept alive.

Debate about these questions has sometimes been dominated by slogans—"Sanctity of life" on one hand and "Death with dignity" on the other. These considerations have their places but do not by themselves define an adequate Christian understanding of life and death. A cruciform ethic asks us to keep two considerations in mind at such times, and actual decisions will depend on determining the significance of both of them for the individual situation.

The death of Christ was one from which all dignity had been removed. Suffering is not to be avoided at all costs, for a sufferer need not be hopeless even when no release other than death is in view. On the contrary, that is where the theology of the cross leads us especially to hope for the presence and activity of God. In the complete privation of what is good by human standards, God's work can stand out clearly because it is the only work that can be done. The Christian tradition has said that martyrdom can in a paradoxical way be a special blessing.[37]

Suffering is not to be sought out, for that would be simply another human work to gain God's favor. The church eventually had to condemn the practice of *trying* to become a martyr. And we certainly should not neglect works of mercy that alleviate suffering, or minimize the importance of the efforts of physicians, nurses, and others with healing vocations. But avoiding suffering is not the highest good.

In the present context this suggests that life is not to be terminated or allowed to end simply to end suffering. This is true even when "quality of life" is appealed to. Life does not have to have some minimum quality for it to be valuable to God, and it is impossible for us to tell what influences a person's life may have on others even when it may seem pointless to us.

At the same time, the hope God gives against death is not that it will be possible for our technologies to stave off death and enable us to live forever. There is no promise of turning back the clock. The resurrection of the crucified gives the hope of life *in spite of* death. But maintaining bodily functions by every conceivable means when the possibility of recovery is gone is not an expression of biblical hope. It may in some cases even be a denial of it.

As far as practical answers are concerned, we are left in the middle with what may seem to be simply a commonsense answer to the question about whether life support systems should be withdrawn: Life is not to be terminated actively, and the necessities of life (oxygen, water, food) should be made available in normal ways, but technological means of life support need not, and sometimes should not, be continued when all reasonable possibilities for recovery are gone. This may seem to be mere common sense, in need of no profound theological grounding. But today's common sense may not be that of tomorrow. The increasing tendency for the general public and those in the medical profession to accept practices that tend in the direction of active euthanasia or assisted suicide suggests that an argument for the type of moderate position set out here must continue to be made. Even though it falls between extreme positions, it is not presented here as a compromise solution but as one that attempts to bring out the full implications of chiasmic cosmology.

As with all weighty matters, it is important to emphasize that Christian decision-making stands in the context of the justification of the sinner. It is natural to feel special responsibility when literally life and death decisions have to be made, and to be afraid of the consequences of making the wrong choice. Such decisions should not be made lightly, but with prayer, intelligence, and expert counsel. But in the last analysis we are justified before God for Christ's sake, not because we have made correct choices. And we are justified rather than condemned (cf. Rom 8:33–34), even if we make the wrong choice. Death and life are finally in the hands of the one who raised the crucified Christ from the tomb.

NOTES

1. Robert W. Jenson, "Tenth Locus, Part Two," in *Christian Dogmatics* (ed. Carl E. Braaten and Robert W. Jenson; Philadelphia: Fortress, 1984), 2:375–77.

2. John Frederick Stark, *Daily Hand-Book* (Philadelphia: I. Kohler, 1855), 297–98.

3. Dietrich Bonhoeffer, *Letters and Papers from Prison* (enl. ed.; New York: Macmillan, 1972), 361.

4. Albert R. Jonsen, *The Birth of Bioethics* (New York: Oxford University Press, 1998), is a history of the field.

5. Warren Thomas Reich, ed., *Encyclopedia of Bioethics* (rev. ed.; New York: Simon & Schuster Macmillan, 1995).

6. This is slightly oversimplified. The nuclear DNA would be identical with that of the person being cloned, but the DNA in the extranuclear mitochondria would be that of the ovum.

7. For the following, see George L. Murphy, "Fertility Technologies and Trans-Kin Altruism," *The Journal of Medical Humanities* 17 (1996): 195.

8. W. D. Hamilton, "Altruism and Related Phenomena, Mainly in Social Insects," *Annual Review of Ecology and Systematics* 3 (1972): 193.

9. Mildred Tengbom, *No Greater Love: The Gripping Story of Nurse Clara Maass* (St. Louis: Concordia, 1978).

10. Edward O. Wilson, *Sociobiology* (Cambridge, Mass.: Harvard University Press, 1975).

11. Philip Hefner, *The Human Factor: Evolution, Culture, and Religion* (Minneapolis: Fortress, 1993), 248.

12. Claus Westermann, *Genesis* (Grand Rapids, Mich.: Eerdmans, 1987), 214.

13. Ted Peters, *Playing God? Genetic Determinism and Human Freedom* (New York: Routledge, 1997), 2.

14. Ibid., chapter 2.

15. Ronald Cole-Turner and Brent Waters, *Pastoral Genetics: Theology and Care at the Beginning of Life* (Cleveland, Ohio: Pilgrim, 1996).

16. "The Teaching of the Twelve Apostles," *ANF* 7:377.

17. For a survey of the history, see Jonsen, *The Birth of Bioethics*, 285–93.

18. Keith L. Moore and T. V. N. Persaud, *The Developing Human* (5th ed.; Philadelphia: W. B. Saunders, 1993), 1–7 and 132–33.

19. Anicius Manlius Severinus Boethius, "A Treatise against Eutyches and Nestorius," in *Boethius: The Theological Tractates and the Consolation of Philosophy* (New York: G. P. Putnam's Sons, 1926), 85.

20. James F. Childress, "Organ and Tissue Procurement: Ethical and Legal Issues Regarding Cadavers," *Encyclopedia of Bioethics*, 1857–65.

21. Blaise Pascal, *The Pensées* (trans. J. M. Cohen; Baltimore: Penguin, 1961), no. 734, 252–53.

22. Verse 3 of Charles Wesley's "Lo! He Comes with Clouds Descending," in *A Rapture of Praise* (London: Hodder & Stoughton, 1966), 55.

23. Ted Peters, *God: The World's Future* (2d ed; Minneapolis: Fortress, 2000), 323–25.

24. Dante, *The Divine Comedy*, "Paradise," canto 14, line 43.

25. "Statement of Claude Earl Fox, M.D., Acting Administrator, Health Resources and Services Administration, U.S. Department of Health and Human Services," *Hearing before the Subcommittee on Human Resources of the Committee on Government Reform and Oversight, House of Representatives*, 105th Congress, 2d Session, April 8, 1998 (Washington, D.C.: United States Government Printing Office, 1998), Serial # 105–133, p. 6.

26. Athenagoras, "The Resurrection of the Dead," *ANF* 2:151–53; Augustine, "The City of God," book 22, chapter 20, *NPNF* 1:2:, 498–99; Thomas Aquinas, *The "Summa Theologica" of Saint Thomas Aquinas* (Chicago: Encyclopedia Britannica, 1952), vol. 2, Supplement to the Third Part, Q. 80, Art. 4, pp. 959–63. For the present topic see George L. Murphy, "Quantum Theory and Resurrection Reality," *CTNS Bulletin* 11 (1991): 25.

27. Gerald O'Collins, *Jesus Risen: An Historical, Fundamental, and Systematic Examination of Christ's Resurrection* (New York: Paulist, 1987), 179–87.

28. "Branwen Daughter of Llyr," in *The Mabinogion* (London: J. M. Dent & Sons, 1949), 25–40.

29. J. C. Polkinghorne, *The Quantum World* (Princeton, N.J.: Princeton University Press, 1984), 38–39.

30. Alois Winkelhofer, *The Coming of His Kingdom* (New York: Herder & Herder, 1963), 216.

31. Athanasius, "On the Incarnation of the Word," *NPNF* 2:4:50.

32. C. F. W. Walther, *The Proper Distinction between Law and Gospel* (St. Louis: Concordia, 1929), 313.

33. Jonsen, *The Birth of Bioethics,* 235–44.

34. Ronald E. Cranford, Alexander Morgan Capron, and Karen Grandstrand Gervais, "Death, Definition and Determination of," *Encyclopedia of Bioethics,* 529–49.

35. Ibid., 530.

36. For example, Robert D. Truog, "Is It Time to Abandon Brain Death?" *Hastings Center Report* 27, no. 1 (1997), 29.

37. Dietrich Bonhoeffer, *The Cost of Discipleship* (rev. ed.; Macmillan, 1963), 342.

· 11 ·

THE NATURAL ENVIRONMENT

❦

ATTITUDES TOWARD NATURE

Environmental issues, like evolution, provoke heated debate. Ecological challenges tend to be more practically oriented because some ideas about our proper relationship with nature call for changes in the way we live. Issues connected with protection of the environment and the availability and use of resources have to be dealt with in the economic and political lives of communities, and dealing with them costs time, energy, and money. This may require that we forego some economic development and profits.

Ecology treats *Homo sapiens,* like all species, as part of the natural world, which affects and is affected by other species. Human intelligence and technology enable us to influence the world in far greater ways than can any other species. Agriculture, plant and animal breeding, mining, and other activities are carried out only by humans. We can wipe out other organisms or try to preserve endangered species. These abilities make it easy for us to see ourselves as qualitatively different from other species. They are parts of nature, and we tend to think of nature as an environment that is external to our true selves.

Our potential to have an impact on the world raises ethical issues. Are the nonhuman parts of the world to be used by us whenever it may be beneficial for us, or should we consider other species and the inorganic world as having some value in themselves that it is our duty to respect? We cannot cleanly separate what is good for the rest of the world and what is good for us. Pollution of rivers not only kills fish but poses health hazards for human beings. An enlightened self-interest alone would require that we have some concern for the environment.

162

In many cultures nature has been an object of worship. The fertility deities of Canaan posed a threat to Israel's faith, and the struggles of the prophets with these cults are important parts of the Old Testament. Today some aspects of New Age thought amount to nature worship, and part of the appeal of that rather amorphous movement lies in the connections it claims with care for the environment.

At the same time, our naturally anthropocentric viewpoint encourages us to see God simply as the provider of human needs. The idea that nature is provided for our benefit may be coupled with a belief that God will avert environmental disaster regardless of what we do. Commentator Rush Limbaugh expresses this view in his book, *The Way Things Ought to Be.* The chapter titled "Sorry, but the Earth Is Not Fragile" begins with a section headed "And the Lord Created . . .":

> My views on the environment are rooted in my belief in Creation. I don't believe that life on earth began spontaneously or as a result of some haphazard, random selection process; nor do I believe that nature is oh-so-precariously balanced. I don't believe that the earth and her ecosystem are fragile, as many radical environmentalists do. They think man can come along, all by himself, and change everything for the worse; that after hundreds of millions of years, the last two generations of human existence are going to destroy the planet. Who do they think we are?
>
> I resent that presumptuous view of man and his works. I refuse to believe that people, who are themselves the result of Creation, can destroy the most magnificent creation of the entire universe.[1]

This sounds like a call for a humble attitude toward the creator, and we have to agree that sometimes the claims of environmental doomsayers have been overstated. But "the Lord" seems here to be a creator who will simply keep nature working the way we want it to. This is quite different from the biblical picture of the God who could destroy temple and kingship and still be faithful to the covenant. It is the view of the false prophets described by Sanders in a passage cited earlier, the view of "normal folk, in their right minds, [who] know that hope is in having things turn out the way they think they should—by maintaining their view of life without let, threat, or hindrance. And normal folk believe in a god who will simply make things turn out that way."[2]

In 1967 the historian Lynn White published an influential essay in which he argued that attitudes toward nature in the Judeo-Christian tradition, and especially the idea that humanity was to have dominion over the earth, were at the root of the ecological crisis that was just beginning to be recognized at that time.[3] The thesis that Christian attitudes have *caused* our environmental problems can be debated. Christians do, however, have to confess that there is a good deal of truth in White's statements about their perspectives on nature.

Paul Santmire has provided a valuable study of the history of Christian attitudes toward nature, which shows that the Christian tradition from its beginnings has been ambiguous about ecological matters.[4] The theme of spiritual transcendence of nature has been in tension with the idea of fellowship with nature. While Francis of Assisi and other Christian thinkers have expressed positive views of nature, Santmire's study reveals a pattern of beliefs that the nonhuman world is inferior to humanity, is here only to serve human needs, and will ultimately be dispensed with in God's plan for creation. In chapter 8, I quoted Ephrem of Edessa's statement that all things were created for humankind. That idea was set out at greater length by Gregory of Nyssa, who saw the order of creative works in Gen 1 as due to God's wish to prepare completely the realm that humanity was to rule before it came on the scene.[5]

Santmire argues that two poles of Judeo-Christian thought in this area can be developed from the theme of "the overwhelming mountain,"[6] which is common to many cultures and religions. The mountain can give two different views, depending on whether the mountain climber looks up or down. There can be the view of heaven and the idea of passing beyond the created world, which gives rise to a spiritual motif. But the climber may also look down and see the goodness and fecundity of the created world. This gives rise to an ecological motif. Moses ascends Mount Sinai to be in God's presence, but he also climbs Mount Nebo to see the good land that God will give to Israel.

Until recently the spiritual motif has been dominant, and most Christians assumed that fellowship with God beyond nature was the primary goal of Christian faith. Francis's attitude toward nature was considered eccentric, and followers of Luther or Calvin emphasized their basic theme of human salvation rather than their positive views of the natural world. If this motif is overemphasized and the world is seen as a collection of resources for humanity to use on a temporary sojourn on Earth, then there are no effective checks on exploitation of nature.

Many churches today no longer concentrate in such a restricted way on the spiritual motif. While theological ambiguity remains, Christians are increasingly concerned about ecological issues and about the ability of their tradition to address them. Theology has shifted from the spiritual toward the ecological motif because of the impact that technology has had on the environment and because of scientific awareness of the interconnectedness of life and the finitude of all resources needed for life.

Purely utilitarian views of nature in theology have been due to misunderstandings of the biblical witness. While the Bible itself should not be blamed for environmental damage, we also should not ignore or excuse the mistakes of the past. An overly "spiritual" attitude, which in effect considers humanity to be too good for the world in which God was willing to take flesh, is just another example of a theology of glory. In order to gain an adequate theological view, we have to look at what the Bible has to say about the human place in nature in the light of the cross. But first it will be helpful to reflect briefly on the way science has influenced theology in this area.

THE ROLE OF ECOLOGICAL SCIENCE IN THEOLOGY

Until about three centuries ago concerns about the environment would have been largely theoretical if they had been expressed at all.[7] For a long time, Westerners did not think extinction of species was possible, and there seemed to be no reason to be concerned about the state of the natural world. That has changed with the rise of modern science, the industrial revolution, and techniques of medicine and agriculture, which have resulted in a rapid growth of the global human population. Oil spills, Chernobyl, and extinction of many species are only a few examples of the negative influence that we can have on our environment. Science tells us that our actions *must* have an impact on the world; they are subject to the laws of thermodynamics. And ecology tells us that there are essential interrelationships among species.

Experience of the impact of technology and scientific understanding of relationships among different parts of nature have been critical in forming a modern ecological consciousness. This new understanding, in the context of the conversations among science, theology, ethics, and technology, has moved Christian thought in the direction of the ecological motif.[8]

Science has theological significance in the context of belief about the world as the creation of the God revealed in Christ. Theology teaches that human beings are called to care for the earth, but is unable by itself to tell them how to do this, and must invite input from science about adequate environmental strategies. In allowing itself to be moved by dialogue with science away from an emphasis on the spiritual motif and toward the nature motif, theology is not submitting itself to an authority alien to itself. Though it has often been subdued and even submerged, the nature pole has never been completely absent from Christian thought. Churches are not simply jumping on a politically correct bandwagon when they participate in secular activities on behalf of the environment.

Science does not resolve the ambiguity between the spiritual and ecological poles of Christian theology, but has moved Christian thought in the direction of the latter. Divine transcendence and the reminder that loving God is the greatest commandment and loving neighbors is second (Mark 12:28–34 and parallels) remain crucial aspects of the Christian view of reality. Science and technology, within the total context of Christian thought, do demand that we place much greater emphasis on the ecological aspects of doctrine and practice than previous generations of Christians have done. If this demand is ignored, the spiritual motif simply provides an excuse to escape from responsibility. But it must be retained as long as we hold that the divine reality is not limited to the world that science is able to explore.

TRUE DOMINION

The opening chapter of the Bible makes a powerful statement about the value of creation. Six times, *before* humanity comes on the scene, God saw that parts of the creation were "good" (Gen 1:4, 10, 12, 18, 21, 25). Then, when human beings have been created, everything is declared by God to be "very good" (Gen 1:31). Creation reaches its full goodness, which includes humanity along with light and stars and trees and whales.

Creation is good and the creator's concern is for all of it even after sin enters the world. God makes covenants with Noah and Israel that include other living creatures and the land (Gen 9:1–17, Lev 25:1–24), and God's promise for the future includes a covenant with the animals (Hos 2:18). Psalm 104 is a hymn of praise of the creator in which God's care for human beings is celebrated together with provision for birds and lions and sea creatures, while Pss 96 and 148 show that nature does not exist simply for humanity but to praise God. Human beings are only part of the choir, albeit an important part, which is to praise the creator.

When the Lord responds to Job to make clear to him the difference between creator and creature, he does not speak about his care for humankind but of his creation and knowledge of the inanimate things of the universe and the wild beasts (Job 38–41). The wilderness has a place in God's intention for creation and will not be paved over in the new creation.

Humanity is, however, given a special role in the first Genesis creation account, and the language that describes that role has been the focus of considerable debate. "Then God said, 'Let us make humankind in our image, according to our likeness; and let them have dominion over the fish of the sea, and over the birds of the air, and over the cattle, and over all the earth,[9] and over every creeping thing that creeps upon the earth'" (Gen 1:26). Critics of the Judeo-Christian tradition have seen the phrase "and let them have dominion," *weyirᵉdu*, as the source of unhealthy attitudes toward nature. How, then, should it be understood?

The Hebrew word derives from *radhah,* which can mean to subdue or to tread upon, and has the sense of the English "dominate." It is important to remember that people twenty-five hundred years ago had nothing like our ability to control nature. They saw themselves in a perilous situation with respect to storms, drought, and savage beasts. Israel's neighbors gave religious sanction to the idea that human beings were to be slaves of the gods, who personified the forces of nature. In the Babylonian creation epic, Marduk relieves the other deities of their labors by creating humanity, upon whom "shall the services of the gods be imposed that they may be at rest."[10] In that context the words of Gen 1 were a proclamation of freedom rather than a license for exploitation.

But we must do more than look at the word itself. The immediate context of "let them have dominion" is the preceding phrase, "Let us make humankind in our image, according to our likeness." Having dominion, the commission given to humanity, is connected with what humanity is to be, the image and likeness of God. As von Rad puts it: "This commission to rule is not considered as belonging to the definition of God's image; but it is its consequence, i.e., that for which man is capable because of it. . . . He is really only God's representative, summoned to maintain and enforce God's claim to dominion over the earth."[11]

The world was not made in a condition of static perfection, but rather on the way to the eschaton, which is symbolized in Genesis by the Sabbath, and men and women are called to be co-creators, instruments that accomplish God's purpose for creation. Because human beings can understand the world, because they are capable of responding to God, they are able to carry out the commission that God gives. But they are also capable of disobedience and refusal to trust in God, and therefore of not fulfilling the role that God gives them.

The fact that this dominion is to be carried out by those who are made in the image and likeness of God means that it is to be exercised by ruling *in the way that God rules.* We are to look to God's governance of the world to discern the pattern that humanity is to follow. Not everything that humans do is co-creative. Some actions are destructive and run counter to God's intention for creation. To be co-creators it is necessary for our actions to be directed toward the end that God desires for creation. We must follow the example of the creator.

The way in which Scripture speaks of God's care for creatures is significant. It should not be sentimentalized: God provides both for the wild asses and the young lions (Ps 104:10–11, 21) and sometimes the provision for the young lions is a wild ass. Each has its place within creation, and only God can grasp the whole. "The compassion of human beings is for their neighbors, but the compassion of the Lord is for every living thing" (Sir 18:13).

We see the full extent of God's compassion and care for creation in Jesus, the true *Dominus* after whom all proper human dominion is to be modeled. In his teaching he draws images from nature, such as the growth of plants from seed (Mark 4:1–20, 26–32), and he speaks of God's care for the birds and the flowers (Matt 6:26–30). Even more, he argues, God cares for human beings: "You are of more value than many sparrows" (Matt 10:31). Insistence on "equal rights" among species is unsupported by Scripture. But this does not mean that the birds have no value *at all* for God, or that human beings are to have no concern for their welfare.

Jesus does more than simply speak about nature. In him we see the creator who is willing to die for creation. Because he emptied himself and was obedient to death on a cross, every knee "in heaven and on earth and under the earth" is to bend to him (Phil 2:10). The common Christian assumption has been that the cross only has significance for human beings, and the bulk of the New Testament does show a rather single-minded urgency about the salvation of human beings. But the setting of that concern is the hope of salvation for the entire creation. Colossians 1:15–20, which has been prominent in discussions of theological views of the environment since its use by Joseph Sittler some forty years ago, speaks of God's intention "to reconcile to himself all things *[ta panta]*" through the cross of Christ.[12] The implication of this, that in some sense Christ died for dinosaurs and oak trees as well as for human beings, is admittedly in some tension with the role of faith in justification. But it is not necessary to insist that, since human beings are called to accept the saving work of Christ through faith, the nonhuman parts of creation cannot be saved because they cannot have faith in the same way.

The idea that all creation is the object of God's saving work is not so surprising if we keep in mind the relational character of life. We are not fully human in isolation but only as we interact with other people and with the rest of the world. If we are to be saved as human beings, then there must be some sense in which our environment is saved as well. Romans 8:18–25 speaks of the liberation from "its bondage to decay" of "the creation." How we are to think of such liberation, especially in view of the second law of thermodynamics, is a difficult question, but the *hope* that is announced here is unambiguous.

This interest in the whole of nature does not lose sight of human beings. In Romans, the creation awaits "the freedom of the glory of the children of God" (Rom 8:21), and the reconciliation spoken of in Colossians comes through the cross of the human Jesus. Humanity cannot be considered independently of nature, but nature cannot be considered without the humanity that is assumed in the incarnation.

We can gain further insight if we go back to Genesis and look at the second creation account. Here nothing is said about the image of God or dominion. Instead, "The LORD God took the man and put him in the garden of Eden to till it and keep it" (Gen 2:15). "Till" is 'abhadh, which can also mean "serve," and "keep" is shamar, which means to guard or protect. Humanity is called to work for the good of the earth and to take care it. The same words are used in Num 3:7–8 to speak about the duties of the Levites in God's tent of meeting with Israel in the wilderness.[13] This suggests that the human task is to care for the earth as God's temple just as the Levites took care of the routine custodial work of the sanctuary. We might say that in Gen 2 humans are called to be doorkeepers in the house of God (cf. Ps 84:10).[14]

We also find in the Old Testament specific directives for dealing with the earth and its inhabitants. There are laws for care of the land (Exod 23:10–11; Lev 25:1–24), trees (Deut 20:19–20), and animals (Deut 22:6–7; 25:4). The detailed regulations in Lev 25 require letting land lie unsown in the sabbatical and jubilee years. It is to be given its rest just as human beings and animals are (Exod 20:8–11; Deut 5:12–15). Modern agricultural science provides more effective ways of preserving and restoring the soil's fertility, but it is the principle that is important: Nature is not just for human profit. Care for the land was an imperative for Israel that flowed out of its covenant with YHWH. Moreover, proper treatment of the land in the first part of Lev 25 is linked with justice among human beings in the second part. Both are aspects of the shalom which God wishes for creation.

"The land shall not be sold in perpetuity, for the land is mine; with me you are but aliens and tenants" (Lev 25:23). Land can only be leased until the year of jubilee, when it is to return to its original owner. The Bible recognizes the legitimacy of private property, but the right of individuals to hold property is not absolutized as it often is in modern capitalist societies. Nor is the land the property of the state, as in communism. It is God's, and human beings are its caretakers. The regulations for the jubilee are part of the civil law of ancient Israel and are not binding upon Christians, but again it is the principle that is important. The king cannot claim land that belongs in a family, as 1 Kgs 21 makes clear. At the same time, opposition to any government regulation for environmental protection on the basis of a supposed absolute right to private property is contrary to the biblical spirit.

Israel's response to the covenant by which God, human society, and nature are bound together will have consequences. If God's people are obedient, God will give them the blessings of nature, and if they aren't, God won't (e.g., Deut 11:13–17). This is not simply a matter of promises and threats attached to arbitrary rules, for our knowledge of ecological interrelationships shows us connections between human actions and environmental consequences. Divine self-limitation means that we have no guarantee that irresponsible treatment of nature will not result in disaster. At present we can see, perhaps more clearly than at any other time, the realistic character of the biblical threats (as in Jer 4:23–28) of "desolation" as a consequence of sin.

We cannot thwart God's ultimate plans for creation, but God will not bring those plans to fulfillment by protecting us from the consequences of our actions. The destruction of Jerusalem and the return from exile is the paradigm of how God allows disobedience to work itself out and still fulfills his promises. Our calling, however, is to be obedient to the pattern displayed in Christ. Care for creation may in some cases call for benign neglect, as when wildfires are allowed to burn, and sometimes may call for intervention. Ecosystems are complex and good intentions can go awry. It may be hard to see how to balance economic needs for human beings and the needs of other species. An understanding of the commission that God gives us to care for creation must be complemented by awareness of what the real environmental problems are and intelligent projections of the likely consequences of courses of action.

CARE FOR CREATION

It is important that Christians operate at all the levels available to them, from their own homes and businesses to the whole planet, to carry out the implications of the theology of nature that I have described. The susceptibility of the world to understanding and control "though God were not given" means that non-Christians can have as good insights as Christians about *how* environmental concerns should be addressed, and cooperation among people of different faiths can therefore be fruitful. There are no special Christian methods of conservation or pollution control. Christians do, however, approach the matter with a particular motivation, the belief that the triune God who creates, redeems, and sanctifies the world has called them to care for nature after God's own pattern of love for creation.

Commitment to environmental responsibility does not automatically enable us to understand what is happening in nature or what measures should be taken to care for it. In some cases problems and solutions may be fairly obvious: Dumping toxic wastes into streams is bad, and corporations should stop doing it. But other situations may be far more complicated. The much-discussed problem of global warming is an example.

There is no dispute about the basic physics of the problem, the greenhouse effect. The radiation the earth receives from the hot surface of the sun is strongest in the visible part of the spectrum. The cooler earth radiates energy back into space at longer wavelengths, in the infrared. The glass of a greenhouse allows solar radiation to pass through but absorbs, and reradiates in all directions, the longer wavelength radiation from inside, thus heating the interior. Some constituents of the atmosphere, including carbon dioxide, absorb at particular wavelengths like the glass of a greenhouse. It is plausible that an increase in carbon dioxide owing to the burning of fossil fuels, together with a decline in the rate at which it is exchanged for oxygen because of deforestation, could lead to an increase in the earth's average temperature, changes in weather patterns, melting of polar ice, and other effects.

At this point questions become difficult. It is not easy to determine how the average temperature over the entire earth has changed since the beginning of the industrial revolution. (There seems to have been an increase of a little less than one Celsius degree over the past century.[15]) Then any attempt to explain the data has to deal with the very complex system of the atmosphere, solar energy, the oceans, and respiration by plants in addition to the combustion of wood and fossil fuels. Computer models of global climate change are only as good as the data and knowledge of physical processes with which they are programmed. At present we cannot say that we have a satisfactory understanding of global temperature change.

We are faced with another of the ethical ambiguities of technology. Global warming by a couple of degrees could be catastrophic, with flooding of coastal cities and the reduction of agricultural land to dustbowl conditions. But if we are not sure that this will happen, should we take steps like those proposed in the 1997 Kyoto Protocol, which would require industrialized nations to bear much of the burden of reduction of greenhouse gases and would have serious effects on their economies?[16] It seems fair to ask countries that have received the most benefit from industrialization to make some sacrifices, but can we put people out of work and their families on welfare because of a catastrophe that might happen in fifty years?

It is necessary especially for industrialized nations to make a decision, and it will not do to use the present uncertain state of scientific knowledge as an excuse to maintain the status quo. The best guess at present is that our technology is having some effect in heating the planet, and that it would be wise at least until we have greater certainty to slow the production of greenhouse gases and deforestation. Technology should not be demonized, as if it were always an enemy of some romanticized state of nature, but those who have it should not use it simply for their own short-term benefit. The welfare of other nations, of future human generations of the entire world, and of other species, should be considered.

We can make more definite statements about some other environmental issues. A major concern is stewardship of natural resources. The very fact that the earth contains only so many tons of metal ores, oil, natural gas, and other materials should in itself discourage any simplistic ideas about human triumph over nature. Only solar energy is so plentiful and so constant that it might be considered a practically infinite resource, but our inability to convert solar energy on a large scale into forms needed by industrialized societies limits its value.

Some resources are renewable. Forests can be replanted and topsoil will eventually be replenished, though these processes take a good deal of time and are difficult if trees have been completely cleared and the soil allowed to erode. Some resources can be recycled. The only way of keeping others available is to use less of them now. This is especially true of the vital energy resource. (The recycling of aluminum cans saves not just the metal itself, which is very common in the earth's crust, but the electrical energy needed to extract it from its ore.) In particular, petroleum reserves of the United States are likely to be exhausted as far as feasible extraction is concerned some time in this century.[17] Since oil is also needed for the production of petrochemicals other than fuels, its conservation is doubly important. More energy-efficient cars and elimination of unnecessary driving can contribute to conservation. The problem needs to be addressed at global and national levels but also demands attention from individuals. The reluctance of Americans to use mass ground transportation, an attitude that betrays a need to be in control and to go where one pleases when one pleases, is wasteful of energy.

Steps can also be taken toward decreasing the energy used for heating, cooling, and lighting. Turning down the heat and wearing sweaters, limiting the use of air conditioners, and using low-wattage bulbs and turning off unneeded lights can save significant amounts of energy and money. Here an individual can see immediate short-term benefits of energy conservation efforts.

We also need to be concerned about the wastes that we and our industries produce. To some extent this is another aspect of resource conservation: Sewage dumped in streams ruins fresh water supplies, for example. Some wastes are unavoidable. A human being excretes a certain amount of waste each day and we have to construct treatment facilities to deal with it. Fortunately, it breaks down fairly rapidly and is recycled like other animal wastes in the biosphere. Other materials last longer and pose greater hazards. Radioactive wastes pose special problems, for the half-lives of some reactor products are measured in tens of thousands of years, and the need to deal with materials that will be lethal for longer than civilization has existed is daunting.

That is only one aspect of the issue of nuclear power.[18] The accident at Three Mile Island in 1979 and the much more serious one at Chernobyl in 1986 soured many people on this energy source. The United States gets about 20 percent of its electrical energy from nuclear fission, a figure that has remained roughly constant for several years. Any public utility wanting to put a reactor into operation faces a tremendous amount of expense and public opposition from people who are absolutely opposed to nuclear power.[19]

The dangers that nuclear energy poses to the environment and human health have to be balanced against the damage done by the major alternative, fossil fuels. The use of coal has involved destruction of land owing to strip mining and acid rain, and black lung disease and cave-ins for miners, while the use of petroleum has brought on oil spills and deaths from fires in addition to the effects of internal combustion and diesel engines in transportation. Both contribute to air pollution and global warming. The number of illnesses and deaths due to a large-scale release of radioactive material could be catastrophic, and for fair comparison, we would also have to include such things as health risks to uranium miners and possible use of radioactive materials by terrorists. But the number of casualties that can definitely be attributed to the use of the nuclear power is, so far, relatively small.[20]

There is, however, a great deal of hysteria about nuclear energy or, indeed, anything with the word "nuclear" or "radiation" attached to it. Public outcries whenever the use of gamma radiation to preserve food is proposed, in spite of the fact that it does not make the food radioactive, provide another example.[21] These fears point up a basic problem of technological societies, the fact that many citizens (and officials) are scientifically illiterate. There are reasons to be concerned about nuclear power, but intelligent discussion of it is impossible if people don't know some basic scientific and technological facts. A desire to get rid of troublesome ambiguities is no excuse for ignorance.

Leviticus 25 reminds us that we must be aware of human needs while we try to care for the nonhuman part of the world. In some cases this means trying to balance jobs for workers and the needs of their families with environmental protection: Loggers and spotted owls in the Pacific Northwest are a classic case. Other situations are examples of what is sometimes referred to as "environmental racism," in which minorities have to bear an undue proportion of the burden of hazardous materials and practices.[22] Hazardous waste facilities are often located in African American, Hispanic, and Native American communities. While racism plays a role here, there are economic factors that also make poor white communities, as well as those of other backgrounds, vulnerable to a kind of blackmail in which they have to accept a dangerous environment as the price of jobs and infusion of money into the community.

The long-term goal should be to minimize the need for toxic waste repositories and industrial sites with dangerous environmental impacts, but as long as they exist they will have to be located somewhere. It may be unrealistic to expect residents of prosperous suburbs to accept these facilities in their neighborhoods, but it is simple justice to expect those who get the most economic benefit from them to bear more of their burden. There is a kind of ecology of justice: Fair treatment for people cannot be separated from the way in which nature is treated.

Finally, our responsibility toward other species needs to be addressed in light of the biblical statement that humanity is to "have dominion" over other living things. Christians have expressed widely different attitudes toward animals, from St. Francis preaching to them to Descartes' belief that they were mere machines.[23]

Homo sapiens is undoubtedly having a major impact upon the other species of the world today. Pollution, economic development of wilderness areas and other destructions of habitats, and hunting are making many species extinct: E. O. Wilson has estimated that fifty thousand species may be disappearing each year,[24] and some may play essential roles in ecosystems. We have now reached the point where the survival in the wild even of elephants is not at all certain. This is not a new phenomenon: At the end of the Permian period some 225 million years ago, half of the families of marine organisms became extinct, and the demise of the dinosaurs is well known.[25] But these extinctions were not brought about because of the actions of a single species. We did not invent extinction, but the present state of affairs is not less of a concern because of that.

The human race has a practical interest in the survival of many other species. Large-scale disruption of ecologies owing to the destruction of some critical species will eventually have an impact on the human species. The earth's rainforests are an important case in point. Their destruction would contribute to a greenhouse effect, which might have a devastating effect upon all the species of the world, including humanity.

God sees other creatures as good in themselves, and in the Genesis creation stories gives human beings the task of caring for them. They may, indeed, be used for food (Gen 1:29, 9:3), but even that must be done responsibly. The Jewish regulations for slaughter of animals, especially as they developed in the post-biblical tradition, may have been motivated by desire for humane treatment as well as by concern for ritual significance.[26] To use animals for food in moderation is legitimate, but to treat them with cruelty or indifference in raising, transporting, or slaughtering them is not. The factory approach to the production of meat is open to serious ethical challenge. Americans don't need to eat as much meat as we do. It would be healthier, a better use of grain resources, and more humane if we would eat somewhat lower on the food chain than we presently do.

The use of animals in research to improve human or animal health and welfare, in ways as humane as possible, is proper. Painful and destructive experiments to test products that are not essential, such as cosmetics, cannot be sanctioned. The use of animals in pure research may lead to practical benefits as well as to deeper understanding of biological processes. But the words of Charles Darwin are worth noting: "Physiological experiment on animals is justifiable for real investigation, but not for mere damnable and detestable curiosity."[27]

Hunting is seen as legitimate in the Bible, though the story of Jacob and Esau suggests that Israel placed a low estimate on it. Few people today in Western societies need to hunt in order to get food. But the maintenance of many ecosystems today requires some limitation of animal populations. Controlled hunting is one appropriate way to do this as long as the means used are not unnecessarily cruel.

In Mark's story of Jesus' temptation in the wilderness we are told that "he was with the wild beasts" (Mark 1:13). Some have seen here a suggestion that Christ begins a restoration of the paradisal relation between humanity and the animals shown in Gen 2.[28] The Ruthwell Cross in southwestern Scotland, which dates to about A.D. 700, has one panel representing this scene. Christ stands over two vaguely piglike animals, and the surrounding inscription reads JHS XPS JVDEX AEQVITATIS. BESTIAE ET DRACONES COGNOUERVNT IN DERSERTO SALVATOREM MVNDI: "Jesus Christ, the Judge of Equity. Beasts and Dragons knew, in the desert, the Saviour of the world."[29] The creatures of the wilderness, without ceasing to be of the wilderness, are at peace with the Lord of creation.

We can make no definitive statements about "Dog heaven" and the like, but can say that an eschatological fulfillment that is adequate to the full scope of the Christian message should in some way include nonhuman life. While this salvation comes about through the incarnation, the fulfillment of the lives of animals should not be seen entirely in relation to that of human lives, for other species are of value to God in their own right.[30]

NOTES

1. Rush H. Limbaugh III, *The Way Things Ought to Be* (New York: Pocket Books, 1992), 152.

2. James A. Sanders, *Torah and Canon* (Philadelphia: Fortress, 1972), 87.

3. Lynn White Jr., "The Historical Roots of Our Ecologic Crisis," *Science* 155 (1967): 1203.

4. H. Paul Santmire, *The Travail of Nature: The Ambiguous Ecological Promise of Christian Theology* (Philadelphia: Fortress, 1985).

5. Gregory of Nyssa, "On the Making of Man," *NPNF,* Series 2, 5:390.

6. Santmire, *The Travail of Nature,* chapter 2.

7. R. H. Grove, "Origins of Western Environmentalism," *Scientific American* 267, no. 1 (July 1992): 42.

8. George L. Murphy, "The Science-Theology Dialogue and Theological Ambiguity," *Currents in Theology and Mission* 21 (1994): 246.

9. This is the reading of NRSV margin, a literal translation of the Hebrew text.

10. Alexander Heidel, *The Babylonian Genesis* (2d ed.; Chicago: University of Chicago Press, 1951), 46.

11. Gerhard von Rad, *Genesis* (Philadelphia: Westminster, 1972), 59–60.

12. Joseph Sittler, "Called to Unity," *The Ecumenical Review* 14 (1961–1962): 177. The attempt of Eduard Lohse, *Colossians and Ephesians* (Philadelphia: Fortress, 1971), 60–61, to avoid the full force of *ta panta* and make only human beings the object of salvation is unjustified.

13. This observation is due to Diane Jacobson. See Peter Bakken, Diane Jacobson, George L. Murphy, and Paul Santmire, "A Theological Basis for Earthcare," *Lutheran Forum* 27, no. 2 (1993): 24.

14 Attempts to spiritualize Gen 2:15 appear quite early. For St. Ephrem, it is the law and the commandments that are to be the objects of serving and guarding ("Commentary on Genesis," in *St. Ephrem the Syrian: Selected Prose Works* [ed. Kathleen McVey; Washington, D.C.: Catholic University of America Press, 1994], 101–2). The human vocation was thus allegorized into "religion" instead of responsibility for the natural world.

15. Chris Bright, "Tracking the Ecology of Climate Change," in Lester R. Brown et al., *State of the World 1997* (New York: W. W. Norton, 1997), chapter 5.

16. David G. Victor, *The Collapse of the Kyoto Protocol and the Struggle to Slow Global Warming* (Princeton, N.J.: Princeton University Press, 2001).

17. See Richard L. George, "The End of Cheap Oil," *Scientific American* 278, no. 3 (March 1998): 78, and related articles in the same issue of this journal.

18. A detailed survey is David Bodansky, *Nuclear Energy* (Woodbury, N.Y.: American Institute of Physics, 1996).

19. Ibid., chapter 1.

20. Dorothy Nelkin, "The Role of the Expert at Three Mile Island," in David L. Sills, C. P. Wolf, and Vivien B. Shelanski, *Accident at Three Mile Island* (Boulder, Colo.: Westview, 1982), 145. At Cherynobyl, there were thirty-one deaths of plant personnel and fire-fighers, and estimates of delayed cancer deaths over fifty years range as high as fifty thousand, but the actual figure may be much lower. Bodansky, *Nuclear Energy,* 224–28.

21. Dale Blumenthal, "Food Irradiation: Toxic to Bacteria, Safe for Humans," HHS Publication No. (FDA) 93–2241 (Rockville, Md.: Department of Health and Human Services, 1993).

22. Robert D. Bullard, ed., *Unequal Protection* (San Francisco: Sierra Club, 1994).

23. Andrew Linzey and Tom Regan, eds., *Animals and Christianity* (New York: Crossroad, 1988), is a useful anthology.

24. Brown et al., *State of the World 1997*, 13.

25. Stephen Jay Gould, "The Great Dying," in *Ever Since Darwin* (New York: W. W. Norton, 1977), 134–38.

26. Zvi Kaplan and editorial staff, "Animals, Cruelty to," *The Encyclopedia Judaica*, 6–7.

27. Charles Robert Darwin in a letter to E. Ray Lankester, quoted in *Bartlett's Familiar Quotations* (13th ed.; Boston: Little, Brown & Company, 1955), 530.

28. Cf. D. E. Nineham, *Saint Mark* (New York: Penguin, 1963), 64.

29. John L. Dinwiddie, *The Ruthwell Cross and the Ruthwell Savings Bank* (6th ed.; Dumfries: Robert Dinwiddie & Co., 1975), 15–16. A photograph of this panel faces page 18.

30. C. S. Lewis, *The Problem of Pain* (New York: Macmillan, 1962), chapter 9 focuses on domesticated animals. For Evelyn Underhill's criticism of this in a letter to Lewis, see *The Letters of Evelyn Underhill* (ed. Charles Williams; London: Longmans, Green & Co., 1943), 300–2.

· 12 ·

THE GOAL OF CREATION

☙

ANTHROPIC PRINCIPLES IN SCIENTIFIC COSMOLOGY

Since its abandonment of Aristotelian physics, science has generally eschewed appeals to final causes. A scientific explanation is a statement about a chain or network of events in the past that result in the phenomenon in question, or the probability of it occurring in the future, not a claim that something takes place in order to bring about a certain result.

Parts of an organism do have functions within it. It does not follow, however, that they have been placed there in order to have those functions. The theory of evolution through natural selection suggests a mechanism by which such organs could have arisen without being designed for their functions. And if teleological explanation is scientifically unsatisfactory for parts of organisms, it cannot be invoked to explain features of the entire world.

In the mid-eighteenth century Maupertuis suggested a "principle of least action" to describe physical processes.[1] "Action" is a particular quantity with units of energy multiplied by time that characterizes a system, and Maupertuis's principle says that the motions of a physical system from beginning to end are such as to make the action a minimum. This and related principles can be given precise mathematical expression and have been powerful tools for the formulation of physical laws.

Maupertuis went further to claim that minimizing the action in the world displayed the wisdom of God. The idea that God would design a world in such a way as to keep action as small as possible suggests a supreme efficiency expert who wants to avoid any wasted motion. This is not the extravagant God of the Bible who does not count the cost even to the extent of giving his own Son for an undeserving world (Rom 8:32). The cross reveals a God who is not, in the ordinary sense, very efficient,[2] and that is consistent with what seems to be the tremendous wastefulness of evolution. (And it turns out that the mathematical expression of Maupertuis's principle allows action to be a maximum sometimes rather than a minimum!)

Recent work in cosmology has led some physicists to reassess their attitudes toward ideas of a purpose or goal for physical processes. The so-called anthropic principles (henceforth abbreviated APs) have been controversial. Some scientists are enthusiastic about them while others argue that they are not science at all, and even that they function as thinly disguised religions.[3] If some APs are true, we want to consider their theological significance. Even if they are not true, they still may point to areas of theology that need attention and development. And if APs function as a religion for some people, we ought to ask whether or not Christianity can respond to their concerns.

The basis for APs is the observation that significant change in some physical parameters that characterize our universe would have made it impossible for intelligent life to develop. For example, two masses of one kilogram separated by a distance of one meter attract each other with a gravitational force equal to about fifteen trillionths of a pound, which seems to be a quite arbitrary value. Why should it not be a completely different number? All the equations of physics would continue to work quite well if the strength of gravitation were different.

But if gravity were stronger or weaker, there would be profound changes in the universe. If it were appreciably stronger than it is, then in the big bang the mutual gravitation of matter opposing cosmic expansion would have been greater. The expansion would have stopped, to be succeeded by a collapse, in a relatively short time. There would not have been time for galaxies, stars, planets, and life to evolve before all structure was crushed out. If gravitation were a great deal weaker, expansion would have proceeded even more rapidly than it did. Galaxies, stars, and planetary systems would not have been able to form before the cosmic gas thinned out too much, and again life as we know it could not have developed.

Tinkering with the strength of gravity would have resulted in a universe in which life was impossible. Changes in other cosmic parameters would have had similar effects. I noted in chapter 7 that a significant change in the ratio of the electromagnetic to the strong nuclear forces would have kept carbon from forming in stars. Life then would have been impossible.

We can speculate on the prospects for life forms that have a physico-chemical basis radically different from our own. But at present we know nothing about how life might be able to develop in a cloud of hydrogen. We cannot rule out the existence of life that is not based on carbon, but at present we have to leave that possibility to science fiction. (This would still be the case if computers could become alive in some sense because we know of no way for them to do this without starting as artifacts of carbon-based life.)

There are several versions of APs of varying strength and speculative content. The least demanding version, the weak anthropic principle (WAP), states that the universe is compatible with the existence of intelligent life. There is nothing very controversial about this, though some might object to calling it a "principle." Obviously we exist. But it is not obvious a priori that a universe will satisfy the relatively stringent conditions for physical life.

We can go further to assert that the parameters characterizing the universe *must* be such as to allow the development of intelligent life. This is the strong anthropic principle (SAP): "The Universe must have those properties which allow life to develop within it at some stage in its history."[4] The strong anthropic principle goes beyond the observed properties of the universe to set conditions on how the universe *has* to be. It does not say that life must evolve, only that life can evolve. But we get a fresh lead by noting that evolution of intelligent life in the cosmos means that *the universe has become conscious of itself.* We are not able to stand outside the universe to observe it and think about it, but are ourselves part of the universe of which we are aware.

This can be tied in with the role of observation in quantum theory. There the description of physical processes depends to some extent on the observations we chose to make. Some theorists argue that an event must be observed in order to exist. There is participation between observers and the physical world. *If* observers are necessary in order for events to exist, then there must be observers in order for there to be a universe. The cosmos must bring into being conscious entities who can participate in it. This leads us to Wheeler's participatory anthropic principle (PAP), "Observers are necessary to bring the Universe into being."[5] Intelligent life must not only be *able* to evolve but must actually do so if the universe is to exist.

It is possible also to argue that once intelligent life evolves it cannot die out. This is the final anthropic principle (FAP): "Intelligent information-processing must come into existence in the Universe, and, once it comes into existence, it will never die out."[6] Those who espouse FAP assume that life will evolve toward ever greater knowledge and control of the universe. This might happen by robotic expeditions spreading through the cosmos, so that the far future would be filled with products of intelligent life. The most extreme of these ideas is Frank Tipler's "Omega Point" theory, which claims to predict, purely on the basis of physics, the coming into being of an omnipotent God and the resurrection to eternal life of all who have ever lived in the ultimate future of the universe.[7]

It is often argued that the universe is so big and so old, and that there are so many stars that might have planetary systems, that there must be life in many places besides Earth. If that is so, there should be some civilizations far more advanced than ours, capable of interstellar communication and/or travel. But then where are they? If advanced star-traveling races exist, why have they not reached Earth and made contact? (There is no good evidence for such contacts to date.) Anthropic principles answer the question by denying the premise of a plethora of intelligent life forms. They point out that if the universe were not as big and as old as it is, conditions would not be right for life to have developed at all. The probable number of sites in the universe at which intelligent life should have developed is on the order of one. We know that there is one intelligent life form in the universe and there *may* be others. But APs suggest that we should not be surprised to find that there are only a few others, or perhaps none.

The status of APs as science is hotly debated.[8] They have avid partisans, but criticisms range from "interesting, but not science" to Martin Gardner's satirical completely ridiculous anthropic principle (CRAP).[9] Challenges have to do with whether or not the different versions of APs are able to make predictions that can be compared with observation and whether or not they mix philosophy or religious motives with natural science.

These principles do not make precise numerical predictions, but this does not mean that they are immune from observation. If we were to discover that our galaxy is teeming with intelligent life forms, all of whom evolved on different planets, it would present a significant challenge to APs. It is hard to say what results may be achieved in the future by investigators inspired by APs, and that is the real test of their value. They are proposed not as competitors of theories like relativity or molecular biology but as principles like the rationality of natural processes. Scientists tacitly use that idea without caring that it is a philosophical principle rather than a scientific theory. The principle that one should not mix religion with science is itself a philosophical principle! The separation of scientific practice from metaphysics has in general been healthy, but it cannot be made into a rigid barrier. What we should ask about a proposal is not "Is it science?" but "Is it fruitful?" and "Is it true?"

Religious evaluations of APs have also varied. Some have seen in ideas such as FAP an attempt to provide a nontranscendental religion.[10] Whether or not this is a valid criticism depends, from the Christian standpoint, on where one puts one's trust and what is made a person's ultimate concern. Natural selection or biblical inerrancy can also become objects of worship. The anthropic principle does not necessarily have a religious character, although one can be conferred on it by a person who chooses to place her or his final confidence there.

Others have hailed WAP as a vindication of design arguments for the existence of God.[11] They argue that if the parameters of the universe are so finely tuned for the existence of intelligent life, then there must be a Tuner. There is, however, another way of explaining the fact that our universe is suited for the development of intelligent life. Ours might be only one of a vast number of universes that make up a "multiverse," one whose parameters have allowed us to evolve. Anthropic principles would then be accounted for by a type of selection operating at the level of entire universes rather than species.

The "many-worlds" interpretation of quantum theory was developed by Everett as a way of understanding the measurement process.[12] Another possibility is Linde's version of inflationary cosmology in which our universe is only one of a huge number of bubbles within a multiverse.[13] The properties of space, time, and matter that have developed within our bubble are suitable for the emergence of intelligent life, but there are many other bubble universes that are quite sterile because their conditions do not allow life to develop.

To some people these multiplications of universes will seem highly extravagant. They are not, on that account, wrong, but Occam's razor does have some pragmatic value. At the same time, the idea of a creator God who chose particular parameters for the universe in order to accomplish a goal will seem to some people naive and unnecessary, and to be cut off by Occam's razor. Whether or not design or multiple worlds can be accepted as an explanation is not something that finally can be proven. Again we see that the beliefs and presuppositions with which we approach the question are crucial.

A Theanthropic Principle

Design arguments never constitute "proofs" in a strict sense. From the standpoint of our dependent view of natural theology they can be at best plausibility arguments, providing ways for those who already believe in God as creator to structure their thinking and open up the possibility of such belief for consideration by others. Darwinian evolution vitiated many traditional design arguments, since it suggested that the eye had evolved through natural selection and did not have to be designed by a Master Optician. Similarly, the argument for God from APs has to reckon with the concept embodied in PAP that the universe can tune itself through a kind of quantum-mechanical feedback process, or with the idea that our universe happens to be just one of many universes in which the conditions for life obtain.

In any case, a narrow focus on design arguments misses the possibility of more profound theological insights. The stronger versions of APs do not just speak of design but of a central role played by intelligent life, and especially human life (hence *anthropic* principles), in the cosmos. The Christian doctrine of the incarnation, however, speaks of a central role not simply for humanity but for humanity indwelt by the creative Word of God: "With all wisdom and insight he [God] has made known to us the mystery of his will, according to his good pleasure that he set forth in Christ, as a plan for the fullness of time, to gather up all things in him, things in heaven and things on earth" (Eph 1:8b–10).

The *theanthropos* Jesus Christ is the purpose of the universe, and it is "the blood of his cross" that achieves the reconciliation of "all things" (Col 1:20). The doctrine of the incarnation can be described as a theanthropic principle (TAP).[14] As Barth put it: "The world came into being, it was created and sustained by the little child that was born in Bethlehem, by the Man who died on the Cross of Golgotha, and the third day rose again. *That* is the Word of creation, by which all things were brought into being. That is where the *meaning* of creation comes from, and that is why it says at the beginning of the Bible: 'In the beginning God made heaven and earth and God said, 'Let there be. . . .'"[15]

This is not proposed as a scientific principle, for its basis is not the strengths of physical interactions or a quantum-mechanical theory of measurement but God's self-revelation. But it can be thought of as a theological parallel to AP. We should be open to the possibility that scientific versions of AP could suggest ways in which God implements TAP by natural processes or that the theological principle might help to give deeper insight into the scientific one.

We must not be dogmatic about how divine incarnation could have taken place, for the cross negates any idea that God's self-revelation must conform to our standards of what is fitting or possible for God. Still, it is difficult to see what might be meant by the "personal union" of the Word with a star or a tree. It does not seem too speculative to argue that an incarnation of the Logos would take place in a rational species, and that creation with incarnation in view would be such that evolution of intelligent life could take place. Thus TAP seems to require at least SAP. But as I argued in chapter 8, there is an important sense in which other terrestrial life forms are assumed in the incarnation, and share in the hope given by the incarnation because of their organic relationship with *Homo sapiens.*

The writer of Ephesians wanted "the manifold wisdom of God" to "be made known to the principalities and powers in the heavenly places" through the church (Eph 3:10 RSV). The language is mythological but nevertheless suggests that the Christian community is called to a cosmic mission. The church should be more enthusiastic about space exploration than it has generally been in the past. Of course all connections between Christian mission and military or economic conquest must—this time!—be renounced. Furthermore, we don't yet know if there are any extraterrestrials to preach the gospel to. However that may be, the church is called to be present wherever humanity is as a community gathered around Word and sacraments, and to trust that the Holy Spirit will be at work through those means to accomplish God's purpose.

Thinking in another direction, the incarnation gives us a novel view of Wheeler's PAP, the idea that intelligent entities are needed in order for the universe to exist. It has sometimes been argued that God is the one who ultimately observes the universe, and even that quantum theory requires the existence of God.[16] The Christian doctrine of creation does say that it is God who ultimately calls the universe into being, but it is not clear how one could speak of God's "observation" of the universe in the sense of quantum theory unless we are able to speak of God as a participant in creation as well as its author. But the doctrine of the incarnation says that we must do just that. We can speak not simply of intelligent organisms bringing the cosmos into being by participatory observation, but of God incarnate doing so.

The *purpose* of the universe is then to evolve *caro* in which God could become incarnate. That gives an affirmative answer to a question debated since the Middle Ages, whether God would have become incarnate if humanity had not sinned.[17] The incarnation was not only a solution to the problem of sin (though it was that) but the very reason for there to be a universe.

The Body of Christ as Evolution's Future

God's intention for the world is focused in the crucified and risen Christ. Our lives are not affairs of pure genetic determination, for in and through the incarnation of the Word the entirety of human nature is infected with the divine. Those who believe this cannot help but see it as having a profound effect on the course of evolution.

When we think of the future evolution of humanity, we are likely to be tempted toward ideas of the emergence of some type of individual superhuman having powers that, in one way or another, greatly exceed our own. Science fiction abounds with such portrayals of *"Homo superior"* having vastly improved intellects, new psychic abilities, and so forth.[18] But this idea is probably on the wrong track. One of the important insights of Teilhard de Chardin was that another picture seems more consistent both with evolutionary history and with the New Testament.[19] For a long part of the history of life on Earth, evolution was a matter of the adaptation of single cells to their environments. But at some period—we probably cannot speak of a single time—a qualitatively different development took place. Multicellular organisms evolved. Evolution took the course of uniting individual cells to form more complex orders of life. From that point on, whatever could, from an external standpoint, be called "progress," involved the further development of multicellular organisms.

Not all the cells that joined together were alike and interchangeable. The mitochondria in cells probably were originally independent organisms that somehow took up a symbiotic relationship with others. Today the brain, liver, muscle, and blood cells of a mammal differ from one another. At a higher level, whole organs such as heart and kidneys are unlike, though in a given organism they are made up of cells with the same DNA. And it is only because these different cells and organs function together that they *can* be different. Unicellular organisms of a given type have to be essentially similar to one another, but when cells operate together, they can be different. In Teilhard de Chardin's phrase, "union differentiates"[20]

The biblical picture of humanity suggests that its future course is toward the uniting of individuals into a single super-personal life. This idea has its background in the Hebrew concept of corporate personality,[21] but finds its fullest expression in the Pauline concept of the body of Christ set out in Rom 12:3–8, 1 Cor 12:12–31, Col 1:15–20, and Ephesians. Here the church is the body of which Christ is the head. Colossians and Ephesians put that picture in a cosmic setting, with the body of Christ the nucleus of the whole redeemed universe.

Teilhard de Chardin's principle, "union differentiates," also holds here. In 1 Cor 12, Paul emphasizes that the members of the body play different roles. The body of Christ is not created by abolishing all personal distinctions. Instead, each member of the body becomes most fully what he or she really is through relationship with other members, and especially with the head who is the source of life for the entire body. The body of Christ is formed and fed by the means of grace, the Word that created the universe in audible and visible forms. In this sense the evangelical activity of the church is the most genuine work of co-creation.

The question of whether or not genetic engineering can contribute to the human future must be viewed in the light of this understanding of evolution. Genetic technologies may be able to make helpful contributions toward the true human future, and thus be instruments that God uses in a positive way. But in order to do this, their use must be consistent with God's intention revealed in Jesus Christ. In particular, the body of

Christ is displayed in "the least" of his brothers and sisters, as the parable of the last judgment (Matt 25:31–46) makes clear. J. A. T. Robinson argued that Paul's concept of believers as members of Christ, united with Christ, stemmed from his experience on the Damascus road.[22] There Paul was told that in persecuting Christians, he had been persecuting Christ himself (Acts 9:5).

The belief that Christ is present for us especially in the weak and suffering does not mean that nothing should be done to eliminate or alleviate weakness and suffering. That would be of a piece with thinking that nothing should be done about poverty because Jesus said that we will always have the poor with us (John 12:8). Scientific techniques such as genetic engineering may be ways of bringing God's will for the world to fulfillment. But short of an undesirable and probably unattainable standardization of human genotypes, we will never be able to eliminate all problems that have a genetic basis, and it will be important that those who have to bear the brunt of those problems not be regarded as second-class people. The need for compassion, care, and respect for the weak and helpless will be as great in a technological future as it was in the past when technological resources were more limited.

THE FUTURE OF THE PHYSICAL UNIVERSE

With the development of modern astronomy Christians had to start considering how other intelligent species might fit into God's purpose for creation.[23] Even if we are the only intelligent beings in the physical universe, we cannot limit the scope of our theological reflection to the planet earth. Just a few human beings have walked on the moon and an expedition to Mars is still some years distant. But our space probes have explored much of the solar system, precursors of robotic descendants that may travel to the stars. Human travel to other planetary systems is further in the future. Even the nearest stars are light-years away and a ship that can reach significant fractions of light speed will require a huge technological commitment.[24] The development of starships like those of popular science fiction, able to travel from one stellar system to another in a few days, would require a major breakthrough in physical theory.

Space travel may be a significant feature of human society for a long time in the future. But what can we say about the *really* long term, the far future of the universe, on the basis of present day science? To answer those questions we have to return to the discussion of cosmology that began in chapter 7. There we concentrated on the early universe, and now we turn to look in the other direction.

General relativity offers a great variety of model universes with which theorists work, and the observational task is to determine which, if any, of these correspond to the universe we inhabit. Matter is actually clumped into stars and galaxies but for the most part we can restrict our attention to models in which clumping is averaged out and matter is distributed uniformly.

The ordinary gravitational attraction of matter will slow down the expansion of the universe. Einstein's original equations of general relativity then yield two classes of model universes, those that will continue to expand forever, though at an ever decreasing rate, and those whose expansion will eventually stop, to be succeeded by contraction and collapse to a "big crunch." Neither possibility seems to offer much hope for continuation of life in the long term. Advanced technological civilizations might be able to survive the demise of the central star of their planetary system as it exhausts its nuclear fuel or even the collapse of their entire galaxy to a black hole. But the dynamics of the universe as a whole are inexorable. Either continued expansion will mean thinning out of matter and falling of temperature toward absolute zero or the cosmos will collapse in a big crunch whose unbounded increase in temperature and density will wipe out any kind of structure. We seem to have an unappetizing choice of "freeze or fry."

Closer examination shows, however, that life may continue in both cases, at least if we define "life" broadly enough. There are model universes of both types in which it would be possible for some machines (perhaps at the level of elementary particles) to process an infinite amount of new information. Information processing is closely allied to the performance of work, and requires both a temperature difference within the machine and a sufficient amount of time. Even though time is limited in a model with a big crunch, the growth of temperature without bounds means that it would be possible to arrange things so that an infinite number of new bits of information could be processed. In an ever expanding and cooling model, information processing would be very slow, but the unlimited amount of time means again that an infinite amount of new information could be processed. If the lifetime of a computer (including the human brain) is measured by the number of its new thoughts, there is a sense in which eternal life would be possible in some universes of both types.

Tipler used this possibility for a universe with a big crunch to argue that an artificial intelligence that would evolve in the far future could engineer cosmic evolution and gather enough information about the past to be able to resurrect everyone who has ever lived in a perfect virtual reality.[25] His argument depends upon a "Postulate of Eternal Life," which may be "beautiful" but is nevertheless a postulate.[26] Tipler wants to work entirely from physics, and there is nothing in physics that rules out intelligent species annihilating themselves in full-scale nuclear war before they ever spread into space. The mere hope that that won't happen is a rather precarious foundation upon which to base a scientific proof of immortality. Tipler's provocative ideas have, of course, evoked a number of other criticisms.[27]

Some of Tipler's ideas may help us to develop an eschatology that is both scientifically and theologically adequate. But our fundamental approach requires that that be done within the context of a theology of the crucified, not a triumphalist belief that physical life forms will be able to overcome all obstacles in the way of immortality.

In any case, observations now appear to rule out Tipler's theory. Since the discovery of the general galactic recession in the 1920s, astronomers have been trying to determine how the rate of cosmic expansion has been changing, and thus the type of universe we inhabit. This has been difficult because it requires accurate observations of galaxies at very great distances. The latest answers to the question about the cosmological future have come as a surprise, though a surprise for which cosmologists really should have been prepared. Cosmic expansion is not slowing down at all but speeding up![28] The most natural way to explain this is with the cosmological term that Einstein added to his equations in order to make a static universe possible. This term is equivalent to a universal repulsive force that grows larger as the separation between bodies increases. Its effect is apparently greater than that of the attractive gravitation of ordinary matter, so the net result is ever faster expansion.

The speeding up of cosmic expansion means that there will be no big crunch. The matter that we see will continue to spread out and cool down. Continued life, in the sense of information processing, may be possible, but eventually at a very slow pace, which makes it hard to see much similarity between this extrapolation of the present course of the universe and the biblical picture of the kingdom of God. But the cosmological term may have another surprise in store for us.

The cosmological constant that determines the magnitude of the repulsive force has had a reputation among physicists as a "fudge factor," a mathematical quantity that is introduced artificially into equations of physics to fit in some unknown phenomenon. The fact that Einstein introduced this constant because of a mistaken belief that the universe was static makes that attitude understandable.[29] The evidence that cosmic expansion is accelerating has forced physicists to reexamine this opinion. The energy of the vacuum in quantum field theory can give rise to a term like the one that Einstein added to his equations, but it is far too large. Some new approach may be needed to explain a cosmological term that is very small on the scale of everyday phenomena but that is not zero, and it is possible that new fundamental insights will emerge from a search for this approach.

The cosmological term represents a fluid with the peculiar property of sustaining a large *negative* pressure. In such a material the speed of sound would be an imaginary number, overcoming the limit that the speed of light normally imposes on signals. This suggests that faster than light transportation and even time travel would be possibilities.[30] These may only be mathematical artifacts that do not correspond to the transmission of real signals, but if there is substance to them then some of the possibilities seen in science fiction may not be so fantastic. There may also be some interesting theological implications.

THE COMING OF THE ESCHATON

In their creeds Christians affirm the hope that Christ "will come again." This is often thought of in spatial terms as an entry into the world from outside. But that assumes that Christ is not present in the world now, in contrast to his promise that "I am with you always, to the end of the age" (Matt 28:20). Such an understanding also distorts the temporal dimension of eschatology. It makes the fulfillment of God's promise something to be expected in the future in much the same way that we might await an event within the world like a political revolution or the appearance of a comet. That would mean that the eschaton unfolds out of the present state of affairs, though perhaps in a way that is beyond our ability to predict.

The New Testament, in contrast, speaks of the coming of something new. The promise is "new heavens and a new earth" (2 Pet 3:13; cf. Isa 65:17, 66:22, and Rev 21:1), and at the end of the Bible the one seated on the throne says, "See, I am making all things new" (Rev 21:5). If something genuinely new is to happen, something that is not simply the working out of the old, then it cannot come about in the same way that things develop in our ordinary experience. It must come from the future.

The message of Easter is a claim that something has come into the world from its future. In the time of Jesus, many Jews expected a general resurrection at the end of history, an idea supported by Isa 26:19 and Dan 12:2. Martha testifies to this belief when she says of her brother Lazarus, who has died, "I know that he will rise again in the resurrection on the last day" (John 11:24). But nobody expected the resurrection of a single person in the middle of history—a resurrection that was not merely a temporary revival like that of Lazarus but a new life such that "death no longer has dominion over him" (Rom 6:9). This means that if

Jesus is risen, what was expected at the end of history has happened in the middle of history. As Pannenberg put it, "If Jesus has been raised, then the end of the world has begun."[31]

The resurrection of Jesus is a prolepsis of the eschaton, God's ultimate future coming into the present from the future. Ted Peters has developed a systematic theology around this theme of prolepsis, "the invasion of the present by the power of what is yet to come."[32] The future is not merely *futurum,* the future as it unfolds causally from the past, or even *adventus,* the future as bringing something absolutely new, but also *venturum,* the future as it "has an impact on us before its full advent," literally the future that is coming.

God does not simply dispose of the old, the original creation. The eschaton is also *creatio ex vetere,* creation from the old: "[T]he new creation is the divine redemption of the old."[33] Its center is Jesus of Nazareth, a human being sharing in the life of the historical people of Israel (Matt 1:1–17) and in the death that is the common lot of humanity in the present world. In the closing vision of Revelation, people will bring into the holy city "the glory and the honor of the nations" (21:26). All the good accomplished in the course of history will become part of God's final future, but it will be made new.

How can all this happen? The kenotic character of God's activity through natural processes means that we should try to gain some understanding of how God's eschatological work may be connected with what we know of the physical world. At the same time we have to remember that the eschaton is something new, and not try to explain it entirely in terms of the old. We should not expect a detailed scientific description of how the resurrection will occur, but we also need not be content simply to say, "It's a miracle."

The question about how Jesus could have been raised from the dead may be posed as a question about how the ultimate future of the universe could have any impact on the past. Some speculative ideas of modern physics suggest that such an influence is possible, for the concept of "time machines" has been discussed in serious science as well as in science fiction.[34] I have already noted that the properties implied by the cosmological term in Einstein's equations might allow signals to be sent backward in time, but other ways of doing this, such as the "advanced waves" of electromagnetic theory or the use of black holes, have been envisioned.[35] Such effects have not yet been observed, but they do not violate the presently known laws of physics.

Tipler's ideas then suggest some speculations about the resurrection. An advanced technological civilization in the distant future might be able to gather a tremendous amount of information about some individual who died in the past, information that would allow it to produce a genetic replica of that person through cloning technology and combine it with computer simulation of his or her life experience in order to bring about a sort of resurrection. If this civilization also had the capability of faster than light signaling, it would be possible for the revivified person to be projected back in time to a period just following his or her death. The resurrection would then in a sense burst upon people of that time from the future.[36]

Such a scenario would not *explain* the resurrection of Jesus in any theologically adequate sense, for it would say nothing about the *particularity* of the one who is raised as a prolepsis of the eschaton. A resuscitation of some arbitrary person through science-based technology would fall far short of the gospel, which proclaims the resurrection of the specific Jesus who "was crucified under Pontius Pilate." If resurrection really shows us God's final future, then the one who is raised shows the kind of future God intends. It would be bad news to hear that Nero had risen and that the type of life that he represents is the goal of cosmic history.[37] The message that Jesus is risen is good news because it means that his life of total obedience to and trust in the Father and love for others is the ultimate future of the universe.

The possibility that we have sketched may, however, be a helpful *analogy* in thinking about the resurrection. Such analogies go back to the New Testament itself.[38] In 1 Cor 15 Paul insists that Christ was raised from the dead and that there will be a general resurrection of which he is the "first fruits." But then he has to respond to the question, "How are the dead raised? With what kind of body do they come?" His answer is not an attempt to *prove* the resurrection but some analogies that may help to make it plausible. Different living things have different kinds of flesh, and there are different types of bodies, terrestrial and celestial. Perhaps Paul's best analogy is that of a seed and the plant into which it grows: There is both transformation and continuity, for the plant that grows is not identical to the seed that is buried. Examples from the present world help us to think about ways in which the new creation may be possible. Clement of Rome used not only Paul's example of the seed but also the story of the phoenix, which he and his contemporaries could read of in Pliny's *Natural History*, to argue for the resurrection.[39]

The resurrection body is to the body that dies as the full-grown plant is to the seed, but Paul does not mean that a dead body sprouts and grows into a spiritual body as a wheat stalk sprouts and grows from a grain of wheat. Scientific developments such as cloning, virtual reality, and time travel provide stronger analogies. If God acts through natural processes, these aspects of science and technology *might* be the kinds of things that God will use to bring about the resurrection and the eschatological fulfillment of creation.

THE PRESENCE OF THE CRUCIFIED

The fundamental image in all our considerations has been that of God "placed crosswise in the universe." It is a common belief that God is omnipresent: "Do I not fill heaven and earth? says the LORD" (Jer 23:24). Chiasmic cosmology, however, speaks not only of a ubiquity of the divine nature but of the crucified as present to the entire universe. Pressed to say how Christ's body and blood could be present in the sacrament if he is seated at the right hand of the Father in heaven, Luther replied, "The right hand of God is everywhere."[40] His point was that in Scripture, "the right hand of God" means God's effectual power rather than a localized presence. Jesus' session at the right hand of God thus denotes his endowment with God's almighty power. The union of the human and divine in Christ is so intimate that divine omnipresence is truly shared with Jesus' humanity.[41]

With the same type of caution that we tried to observe in the previous section, we may note that the possibility of faster than light signaling or "quantum nonlocality" could provide a way to speak about omnipresence. One result of relativity is that if something could travel faster than light, we could find coordinate systems in which it would travel with *infinite* speed and would be seen as existing everywhere along a line in space at one instant. This could be seen as an analogy for the way in which the Letter to the Ephesians speaks of Christ having "ascended far above all the heavens, so that he might fill all things" (Eph 4:10).

A complementary way of speaking about Christ's presence is with the image of the body of Christ. This body bears the marks of the cross in its martyrs and in all who have borne the cross. The sufferings of the members of the body proclaim and even make present the sufferings of Christ to the universe. That is what Luther meant by speaking of "the sacred cross" as one of the marks of the church,[42] and perhaps is what Col 1:24 refers to.

The body of Christ is rooted in the people of Israel, in the specific Israelite Jesus of Nazareth, and most vividly in his fellowship with sinners in the early years of the first century. It is a historical phenomenon, as the church continues to be a community in the world. But the continuing unity of the body of Christ is made possible in the resurrection of Jesus, in which the end of the world has begun and God's ultimate future has begun to break upon the universe. The body of Christ lives from the future, where the promise that the creation is to be freed from "futility" and "decay" is to be fulfilled according to Rom 8:18–25.

The "law of increasing disorder" is a consequence of very fundamental aspects of the physical universe, and it is not obvious how it can be overcome in "new heavens and a new earth." I have noted, however, that the second law of thermodynamics does not rule out the emergence of order in the material world. A flow of energy through a system can give rise to dissipative structures and the emergence of life itself might be understood in terms of that kind of order. The existence of dissipative structures could be seen as a sign pointing to God's eschatological order, and to the body of Christ as the ultimate dissipative structure. Out of the turmoil of mortal life God creates a structure in which eternal life is present. The body of Christ continues to suffer while it is the means through which God works to bring the world to the fulfillment that has already been seen in the resurrection.[43] The head of the body bears the marks of crucifixion and its members "are always being given up to death for Jesus' sake, so that the life of Jesus may be made visible in our mortal flesh" (2 Cor 4:11). Though it is continually being broken down, its unity and coherence are maintained in the Holy Spirit.

I have insisted throughout these discussions on the implication of the theology of the cross, that we can understand the world "from the inside," though God were not given. We are able to comprehend the origin of the universe and of life in terms of knowable processes and laws, and no reference need be made to God as the creator. But this is possible because we inhabit the contingent world, which is governed in accord with these laws. We are on the "downstream" side of God's original creative acts, and are free to sample their consequences and learn their patterns. We are in a different situation with regard to the eschaton. Though we have genuine hints and prolepses of it, especially in the resurrection of Jesus, God's final future *is* future. We cannot know its patterns with anything approaching the completeness embodied in our present laws of physics. Thus it should come as no surprise that we have a great deal of difficulty in understanding how death and decay can be done away with in God's new heavens and new earth. Both science and theology can give us hints about the future but, as St. Paul reminds us, "Now we see through a glass, darkly" (1 Cor 13:12 KJV).

NOTES

1. John D. Barrow and Frank J. Tipler, *The Anthropic Cosmological Principle* (New York: Oxford, 1986), 65–68.

2. Cf. Paul Tillich's sermon "Holy Waste," in *The New Being* (New York: Charles Scribner's Sons, 1955), 46.

3. The case for APs is presented in Barrow and Tipler, *The Anthropic Cosmological Principle*. For scientific criticism see Heinz R. Pagels, "A Cozy Cosmology," *The Sciences*

25 (April 1985): 34. A religious view is W. Jim Neidhardt, "The Anthropic Principle: A Religious Response," *Journal of the American Scientific Affiliation* 36 (1984): 201.

4. Barrow and Tipler, *The Anthropic Cosmological Principle,* 21.

5. Ibid., 22.

6. Ibid., 23.

7. Frank J. Tipler, *The Physics of Immortality* (New York: Doubleday, 1994).

8. John D. Barrow, *The World within the World* (Oxford: Clarendon, 1988), 368–73, provides a convenient summary of arguments against AP in the course of defending it.

9. Tony Rothman, "A 'What You See Is What You Beget' Theory," *Discover* 8, no. 5 (May 1987): 90.

10. See, for example, Richard H. Bube's review of Barrow and Tipler, "The Anthropic Cosmological Principle," *Perspectives on Science and Christian Faith* 40 (1988): 110.

11. For example, Hugh Ross, *The Fingerprint of God* (Orange, Calif.: Promise, 1989), chapter 12.

12. Max Jammer, *The Philosophy of Quantum Mechanics* (New York: Wiley, 1974), chapter 11.

13. Willem B. Drees, *Beyond the Big Bang: Quantum Cosmologies and God* (La Salle, Ill: Open Court, 1990), 48–51.

14. George L. Murphy, "The Incarnation as a Theanthropic Principle," *Word & World* 13 (1993): 256.

15. Karl Barth, *Dogmatics in Outline* (New York: Harper & Row, 1959), 58.

16. For example, F. J. Belinfante, *Measurements and Time Reversal in Objective Quantum Theory* (Oxford: Pergamon, 1975), 98–99.

17. See, for example, the discussion in *The "Summa Theologica" of Saint Thomas Aquinas* (Chicago: Encyclopedia Britannica, 1952), part 3, Q.1, Art.3, vol. 2, pp. 704–6, and accompanying notes.

18. Frank M. Robinson, *The Power* (Philadelphia: J. B. Lippincott, 1956), is a good example.

19. Pierre Teilhard de Chardin, *Christianity and Evolution* (trans. Réne Hague; New York: Harcourt Brace Jovanovich, 1971), 16, 66–72.

20. Pierre Teilhard de Chardin, *Activation of Energy* (New York: Harcourt Brace Jovanovich, 1970), 116. He also says that union "creates" and "personalizes" (115–16).

21. H. Wheeler Robinson, *Corporate Personality in Ancient Israel* (Philadelphia: Fortress, 1980).

22. John A. T. Robinson, *The Body* (Philadelphia: Westminster, 1977), 58.

23. Michael J. Crowe, *The Extraterrestrial Life Debate, 1750–1900* (Mineola, N.Y.: Dover, 1999).

24. See, for example, William Speed Weed, "Star Trek," *Discover* 24, no. 8 (August 2003): 34.

25. Tipler, *The Physics of Immortality.* Not just high temperatures but large temperature *differences* are required. Tipler argues (55–65 and 461–65) that the advanced intelligences of the far future will produce temperature gradients by altering cosmic evolution so that the rate of contraction near the big crunch is not the same in all directions.

26. Ibid., 11.

27. A good critique is W. R. Stoeger and G. F. R. Ellis, "A Response to Tipler's Omega-Point Theory," *Science & Christian Belief* 7 (1995): 163.

28. Several articles in *Scientific American* 280, no. 1 (January 1999) deal with this issue.

29. Donald Goldsmith, *Einstein's Greatest Blunder?* (Cambridge, Mass.: Harvard University Press, 1995).

30. George L. Murphy, "A Model of Cosmological Matter," to appear in *Physics Essays* 5, no. 2 (forthcoming).

31. Wolfhart Pannenberg, *Jesus: God and Man* (2d ed.; Philadelphia: Westminster, 1977), 67.

32. Ted Peters, *God: The World's Future* (2d ed.; Minneapolis: Fortress, 2000). For the following quotations, see 320–21.

33. John Polkinghorne, *The Faith of a Physicist: Reflections of a Bottom-Up Thinker* (Princeton, N.J.: Princeton University Press, 1994), 167.

34. Paul J. Nahin, *Time Machines* (2d ed.; New York: Springer-Verlag, 1998); Kip S. Thorne, *Black Holes and Time Warps* (New York: W. W. Norton & Co., 1994).

35. Nahin, *Time Machines,* 217–31 and 341–52.

36. George L. Murphy, "The End of History in the Middle: Speculation on the Resurrection," *Works* 5, no. 2 (1995): 1.

37. Popular fear of a return of Nero *redividus* may lie behind some of the imagery of the Book of Revelation. C.f. N. T. Wright, *The Resurrection of the Son of God* (Minneapolis: Fortress, 2003), 68.

38. George L. Murphy, "What Can Physics Contribute to Eschatology?" *dialog* 38 (1999): 35.

39. "The First Epistle of Clement to the Corinthians," *ANF* 1: 11–12.

40. "Confession Concerning Christ's Supper," *LW* 37:214.

41. Martin Chemnitz, *The Two Natures in Christ* (St. Louis: Concordia, 1971).

42. "On the Councils and the Church," *LW* 41:164–65.

43. George L. Murphy, "Time, Thermodynamics, and Theology," *Zygon* 26 (1991): 359; Robert John Russell, "Entropy and Evil," *Zygon* 19 (1984): 449.

· 13 ·

THE WORSHIP OF THE UNIVERSE

ᔕ

GOD'S GIFT AND THE WORLD'S RESPONSE

We have considered a way of understanding God's relationship with the world of scientific and technological realities. But an important dimension has largely been omitted, that of creation's response to the creator. Our discussion would be defective if we did not include the element of worship—the reception of, and response to, God's gifts. Evelyn Underhill begins her treatment of this subject by saying: "Worship, in all its grades and kinds, is the response of the creature to the Eternal: nor need we limit this definition to the human sphere. There is a sense in which we may think of the whole life of the Universe, seen and unseen, conscious and unconscious, as an act of worship, glorifying its Origin, Sustainer, and End."[1]

This final chapter is not meant merely as a pious benediction on an academic discussion, for in an important sense worship precedes theological reflection. "Thus, *lex adorandi est lex credendi:* we believe according as we worship."[2] Theology must be consistent with the liturgical language and actions of the Christian community. We need to study liturgies and devotional practices, as well as theological essays, in order to understand the faith.

Elements of Christian worship that might have contributed to a better understanding of our relationship with the natural world have not always gotten adequate attention. The approval of icons by the Second Council of Nicaea has implications for our valuation of the material world.[3] The physical, and even technological, aspect of the Eucharist is important.[4] (The sacramental elements are not grain and grapes but bread, "which earth has given and human hands have made" and wine, "fruit of the vine and work of human hands."[5]) And the annual practice in many congregations of blessing animals should serve as a corrective to purely utilitarian notions of the nonhuman creation.

Chiasmic cosmology has a doxological aspect with cosmic dimensions. We encountered this praise of God by creation in chapter 2, when we saw how Ps 148 calls upon all creatures—angels, celestial bodies, physical elements, plants and animals, and humans—to praise the God of Israel. The planets and hills and cattle can't literally praise God, but human beings can. In our species the universe has become conscious and articulate and can sense that there is a reality transcending itself. *Homo sapiens* is *Homo adorans,* the one who worships, the part of creation that can think and speak and sing the praise of God on behalf of all the world.

But the capacity for worship is not by itself sufficient. Paul makes the point in Rom 1 that human beings, left to themselves, set up idols instead of worshiping the true God. It is through God's revelation that we know who to worship. The first commandment is to trust and worship only the God who has made himself known in the exodus (Exod 20:2–3). And it is the crucified one who has been exalted "so that at the name of Jesus every knee should bend, in heaven and on earth and under the earth, and every tongue should confess that Jesus Christ is Lord, to the glory of God the Father" (Phil 2:10–11). The worship of the universe begins with worship by the people of God, the community that acknowledges the God revealed in the cross and resurrection of Christ. Nature is not to be worshiped (Job 31:26–28), but itself participates in the adoration of its creator.

The writings of Teilhard de Chardin provide a good example of this relationship in the science-theology dialogue. His thought involved not only scientific and doctrinal themes but also strong devotional elements, such as "The Mass on the World."[6] Here the world takes its meaning as Eucharist and has its centering in the church's "ordinary" mass at the altar of every village church. The direction of Teilhard de Chardin's thought is made clear in something he wrote a year after this essay:

> To interpret adequately the fundamental position of the Eucharist in the economy of the world . . . it is, I think, necessary that christian thought and christian prayer should give great importance to the real and physical extensions of the eucharistic Presence. . . . As we properly use the term "our bodies" to signify the localized centre of our spiritual radiations . . . , so it must be said that in its initial and primary meaning the term "Body of Christ" is limited, in this context, to the consecrated

species of Bread and Wine. But . . . the host is comparable to a blazing fire whose flames spread out like rays all round it.[7]

The universe can be seen as sacramental when it is viewed in the proper light. We know nature as creation in the light of God's revelation as creator, and we know it as sacrament in connection with the loaf and cup and the body and blood given and shed on Golgotha. We are not to start with a pantheistic theology of glory and worship by finding Christ in flowers and stars. If that were the case, any special emphasis on receiving Christ under the forms of bread and wine and with remembrance of the night on which he was betrayed would be superfluous. We know Christ to be present throughout the universe as the crucified and risen one because this is proclaimed by the words and actions of the Eucharist, not the other way around.

If the worship of the universe is to be centered on that of the church, the worship of the church should take into account the scientific under-standing of the universe. The God to be worshiped is the creator, redeemer, and hallower of the real world, not of some obsolete cosmo-logical model. Sermons are not to be lectures on science or technology, but the biblical texts upon which preaching is to be based offer many opportunities to address God's word to the problems and promises that people encounter in a scientific and technological world.[8] Hymns, prayers, and other liturgical elements can be developed in ways that bring out the relevance of the Christian message for a scientific age while main-taining continuity with the traditions of the church.[9] Prayer C of Holy Eucharist II in *The Book of Common Prayer* is one example of how this can be done.[10] In brief, "today's churches have no other place to fulfill their mission than a world whose basic assumptions are pervaded more and more by science."[11]

The essential features of Christian worship, Word and sacraments, are focused on the cross and resurrection of Christ. Proclamation is, in one way or another, the message of "Christ crucified" (1 Cor 1:23), baptism is "into his death" (Rom 6:3), and the Eucharist recalls "the night when he was betrayed" (1 Cor 11:23). It is hardly surprising then that the sign of the cross became quite early an important part of corporate worship and individual devotion among Christians. It is used in orders of blessing for all kinds of things—people, animals, water, foods, bells, vehicles, scientific and industrial equipment, and so forth.[12] Like other religious practices it is always in danger of becoming a superstition. But there is a profoundly right way of thinking about the placing of this sign upon things, for God has placed it upon the world. God is, as I have continually underscored, the one "placed crosswise in the universe." Making the sign of the cross on someone or something can be a way of recognizing the presence and lordship of the crucified one to all the universe.

Doxological Impact Statements

People who are planning development or construction projects that might have a significant effect on the environment are required to file environmental impact statements with appropriate government agencies so that ecological advantages and disadvantages of the activity can be assessed, and so that the project can be stopped if its harm to the environment would outweigh its benefits. If creation is to proclaim God's praise and worship the creator, we can make corresponding theological assessments. We can ask concerning anything that we are going to do that will affect the environment, "Will this enhance or diminish the praise of God?" A thoughtful response to that question might be called a "doxological impact statement."

It is not possible to give quantitative answers to such a question. The point of asking it is to remind ourselves of a dimension of our relationship with the world that is too easily forgotten in the midst of scientific and economic considerations. The doxological criterion has something to do with aesthetics, but is not identical with a question about beauty in obvious senses of the word. The picture of the ostrich in Job 39:13–18 is not terribly attractive, but the very wildness of the creature proclaims the greatness of the God who cares for it.

These considerations become more pointed when we recall that we are the ones who are called to put the praise of creation into words. Can we praise God in hymns that speak of nature as it has been changed by our science and technology? Or would we prefer to keep silent about those aspects of our lives when we worship?

Easter

There are opportunities to see the universe in the light of the cross at any time of year in liturgy and preaching, but in the observances of Holy Week and Easter this theme demands our full attention. Images of darkness and light are prominent at this time. Congregations often observe Good Friday with the Office of Tenebrae, in which the gradual darkening of the church during the service corresponds to the darkening of the world at the crucifixion (Mark 15:33). A hymn of Pope Gregory the Great sings,

All trembling nature quaked to see
Its dying king upon the tree;
And when you drew your final breath
The dark'ning skies confessed your death.[13]

The Easter vigil on Saturday evening or early Sunday morning is part of the three days that begin with the night of Jesus' betrayal and conclude with his resurrection.[14] These days are to be seen as a unity, for passion and resurrection are not to be separated. The vigil itself begins with the congregation gathered in the same darkness as Good Friday, the absence of light and life before creation, the umbra of the grave. The contrasting image is the paschal fire and candle, acclaimed as the light of resurrection and new creation: "May the light of Christ, rising in glory, dispel the darkness of our hearts and minds."[15]

There are a number of readings for the vigil and some of them are lengthy. It is not a time for haste but for telling and remembrance of the whole story of God's acts, beginning with creation. The readings vary from one communion to another, but all begin with Gen 1.[16] We have already considered different aspects of these creation accounts in connection with scientific views of the origins of the universe and of life. Here the story is simply read without further commentary: The entire series of lessons, by and for those gathered in the light of the risen Christ, is commentary enough. But if issues of cosmology and evolution have been discussed previously in the congregation, they too will be illumined. The hiddenness of God in the origin of the universe and the development of life through privation and extinction are seen in this light as the work of the God "who gives life to the dead and calls into existence the things that do not exist" (Rom 4:17).

The story of Israel's salvation through the sea in the face of Pharaoh's army in Exod 13–15 is the central text for this service, for this is the event in Israel's history that was seen by early Christians as most clearly foreshadowing the passion and resurrection of Christ. The passage through the sea to safety is a journey from death to life. The symbolism of the exodus is especially significant in view of the ancient practice of baptizing catechumens at the Easter vigil. The new life in which they begin to share is the life of the resurrection and existence as part of the people of God, the people that God created in the exodus. When this is described as new birth through "water and Spirit" (John 3:5), we are reminded not only of the waters of the sea but of "the blast of [God's] nostrils" and God's "wind" (Exod 15:8 and 10).

The final reading in some traditions is the story of the three Jews thrown into the fiery furnace by the king of Babylon because of their refusal to worship the idol that he has set up in the third chapter of Daniel. Written in the time of the Maccabean persecutions, it encourages to steadfastness those who are faced with suffering and death because of their allegiance to the God of Israel. It is another story of life out of death. In one of the Additions to the Book of Daniel in the Apocrypha, "The Song of the Three Jews," the young men, walking amid the flames, sing out the praises of God on behalf of the entire universe! The canticle *Benedicite, omnia opera*, adapted from this addition, is sung in the Lutheran rite for the vigil as the paschal candle is brought to the font in preparation for baptism.

> All you works of the Lord, bless the Lord—
>   praise him and magnify him forever.
> You angels of the Lord, bless the Lord;
>   you heavens, bless the Lord;
> all you powers of the Lord, bless the Lord—
>   praise him and magnify him forever.
> You sun and moon, bless the Lord;
>   you stars of heaven, bless the Lord. . . .[17]

As this ancient song is taken up in the church's worship today, it is not simply archaic pictures of the heavens and the earth that are evoked. The stars and winds, plants and animals whose praise is expressed in the canticle are the objects that are studied by astronomers, meteorologists, and biologists. And it culminates with a call for humankind to praise the Lord, to give voice to the worship of creation.

The universe, which is subjected to the scrutiny of scientists, in whose processes the working of God is concealed, whose energies human technology applies, is the universe that lauds the crucified. As another of the vigil readings in the Byzantine tradition says, "The king of Israel, the LORD, is in your midst" (Zeph 3:15).

NOTES

1. Evelyn Underhill, *Worship* (New York: Harper & Row, 1936), 3.

2. Alan Richardson, "Worship," *WDCT*, 606.

3. George L. Murphy, "Cosmology as an Agenda Item for the Eighth Council," *dialog* 30 (1991): 290.

4. A. R. Peacocke, *Science and the Christian Experiment* (New York: Oxford University Press, 1971), chapter 7.

5. *The Sacramentary* (New York: Catholic Book Publishing Co., 1985), 370–71.

6. Pierre Teilhard de Chardin, "The Mass on the World," in *Hymn of the Universe* (trans. Gerald Vann; New York: Harper & Row, 1965), 19–37.

7. Ibid., 15.

8. George L. Murphy, LaVonne Althouse, and Russell Willis, *Cosmic Witness* (Lima, Ohio: CSS, 1996).

9. George L. Murphy, "The Impact of Science on Christian Worship," *Seminary Ridge Review* 1, no. 2 (winter 1999): 63.

10. *The Book of Common Prayer* (New York: Seabury, 1977), 369–72.

11. John M. Mangum, ed., *The New Faith-Science Debate* (Minneapolis: Fortress, 1989), vi.

12. *Rituale Romanum* (Rome: Desclée & Cie, 1952), 415–763.

13. *Lutheran Book of Worship* (Minneapolis: Augsburg, 1978), Hymn 101, verse 4.

14. Gabe Huck and Mary Ann Simcoe, eds., *A Triduum Sourcebook* (Chicago: Liturgy Training Publications, 1983), has many texts from different traditions relating to the triduum.

15. Ibid., 71.

16. Ibid., 80–81 gives a table of the readings in different traditions.

17. *Lutheran Book of Worship,* Canticle 18.

Selected Bibliography

Most of the following works were helpful in the development of this book. A few appeared too recently to be used, but should also be helpful for those who wish to pursue the themes dealt with here.

Barbour, Ian G. *Religion and Science: Historical and Contemporary Issues.* San Francisco: HarperCollins, 1997.

Barrow, John D., and Frank J. Tipler. *The Anthropic Cosmological Principle.* New York: Oxford University Press, 1986.

Benz, Ernst. *Evolution and Christian Hope: Man's Concept of the Future, from the Early Fathers to Teilhard de Chardin.* Translated by Heinz G. Frank. Garden City, N.Y.: Doubleday, 1968.

Bonhoeffer, Dietrich. *Creation and Fall.* Vol. 3 of *Dietrich Bonhoeffer Works.* Translated by Douglas Stephen Bax. Minneapolis: Fortress, 1997.

Brooke, John Hedley. *Science and Religion: Some Historical Perspectives.* New York: Cambridge University Press, 1991.

Brown, Raymond E. *The Death of the Messiah: From Gethsemane to the Grave.* 2 vols. New York: Doubleday, 1994.

Cole-Turner, Ronald, and Brent Waters. *Pastoral Genetics: Theology and Care at the Beginning of Life.* Cleveland, Ohio: Pilgrim, 1996.

Cousar, Charles B. *A Theology of the Cross: The Death of Jesus in the Pauline Letters.* Minneapolis: Fortress, 1990.

Davies, Paul. *God and the New Physics.* New York: Simon & Schuster, 1983.

Drees, Willem B. *Beyond the Big Bang: Quantum Cosmologies and God.* LaSalle, Ill.: Open Court, 1990.

Edwards, Denis. *Jesus the Wisdom of God: An Ecological Theology.* Maryknoll, N.Y.: Orbis, 1995.

———. *The God of Evolution: A Trinitarian Theology.* New York: Paulist, 1999.

Eiseley, Loren. *The Firmament of Time.* New York: Atheneum, 1962.

Farley, Benjamin Wirt. *The Providence of God.* Grand Rapids, Mich.: Baker, 1988.

Forde, Gerhard O. *On Being a Theologian of the Cross: Reflections on Luther's Heidelberg Disputation, 1518.* Grand Rapids, Mich.: Eerdmans, 1997.

Gould, Stephen Jay. *Wonderful Life: The Burgess Shale and the Nature of History.* New York: W. W. Norton, 1989.

Gunton, Colin E., ed. *The Doctrine of Creation.* Edinburgh: T & T Clark, 1997.

Hall, John Douglas. *Lighten Our Darkness: Toward an Indigenous Theology of the Cross.* Philadelphia: Westminster, 1976.

———. *God and Human Suffering: An Exercise in the Theology of the Cross.* Minneapolis: Augsburg, 1986.

Hefner, Philip. *The Human Factor: Evolution, Culture, and Religion.* Minneapolis: Fortress, 1993.

Hengel, Martin. *Crucifixion in the Ancient World and the Folly of the Cross.* Translated by John Bowden. Philadelphia: Fortress, 1977.

Jaki, Stanley L. *The Road of Science and the Ways to God.* Chicago: University of Chicago Press, 1978.

———. *Cosmos and Creator.* Edinburgh: Scottish Academic, 1980.

Jüngel, Eberhard. *God as the Mystery of the World: On the Foundation of the Theology of the Crucified One in the Dispute between Theism and Atheism.* Translated by Darrell L. Guder. Grand Rapids, Mich.: Eerdmans, 1983.

Kaiser, Christopher. *Creation and the History of Science.* Grand Rapids, Mich.: Eerdmans, 1991.

Kitamori, Kazoh. *Theology of the Pain of God.* Richmond, Va.: John Knox, 1965.

von Loewenich, Walter. *Luther's Theology of the Cross.* Translated by Herbert J. A. Bouman. Minneapolis: Augsburg, 1976.

McGrath, Alister E. *Luther's Theology of the Cross: Martin Luther's Theological Break-through.* Cambridge, Mass.: Basil Blackwell, 1985.

Messenger, Ernest C. *Evolution and Theology: The Problem of Man's Origin.* New York: Macmillan, 1932.

Miller, Keith B., ed. *Perspectives on an Evolving Creation.* Grand Rapids, Mich.: Eerdmans, 2003.

Moltmann, Jürgen. *The Crucified God: The Cross of Christ as the Foundation and Criticism of Christian Theology.* Translated by R. A. Wilson and John Bowden. New York: Harper & Row, 1974.

Murphy, George L. *The Trademark of God: A Christian Course in Creation, Evolution, and Salvation.* Wilton, Conn.: Morehouse-Barlow, 1986.

———. *Toward a Christian View of a Scientific World: Fifteen Topics for Study.* Lima, Ohio: CSS Publishing Co., 2001.

Murphy, Nancey. *Theology in the Age of Scientific Reasoning.* Ithaca, N.Y.: Cornell University Press, 1990.

Murphy, Nancey, and George F. R. Ellis. *On the Moral Nature of the Universe: Theology, Cosmology, and Ethics.* Minneapolis: Fortress, 1996.

O'Collins, Gerald. *Jesus Risen: An Historical, Fundamental, and Systematic Examination of Christ's Resurrection.* New York: Paulist, 1987.

Pannenberg, Wolfhart. *Toward a Theology of Nature: Essays on Science and Faith.* Edited by Ted Peters. Louisville, Ky.: Westminster/John Knox, 1993.

Pascal, Blaise. *The Pensées.* Translated by J. M. Cohen. Baltimore: Penguin, 1961.

Peters, Ted. *God as Trinity: Relationality and Temporality in the Divine Life.* Louisville, Ky.: Westminster/John Knox, 1993.

———. *Playing God?: Genetic Determinism and Human Freedom.* New York: Routledge, 1997.

Peters, Ted, Robert John Russell, and Michael Welker, eds. *Resurrection: Theological and Scientific Assessments.* Grand Rapids, Mich.: Eerdmans, 2002.

Polkinghorne, J. C. *The Quantum World.* Princeton, N.J.: Princeton University Press, 1989.

Polkinghorne, John. *Science and Providence: God's Interaction with the World.* London: SPCK, 1989.

———. *The Faith of a Physicist: Reflections of a Bottom-Up Thinker.* Princeton, N.J.: Princeton University Press, 1994.

———, ed. *The Work of Love: Creation as Kenosis.* Grand Rapids, Mich.: Eerdmans, 2001.

von Rad, Gerhard. *Wisdom in Israel.* Translated by James D. Martin. Nashville,: Abingdon, 1972.

Rasmussen, Larry, with Renate Bethge. *Dietrich Bonhoeffer: His Significance for North Americans.* Minneapolis: Fortress, 1990.

Santmire, H. Paul. *The Travail of Nature: The Ambiguous Ecological Promise of Christian Theology.* Philadelphia: Fortress, 1985.

———. *Nature Reborn: The Ecological and Cosmic Promise of Christian Theology.* Minneapolis: Fortress, 2000.

Silk, Joseph. *The Big Bang.* 3d ed. New York: W. H. Freeman, 2001.

Teilhard de Chardin, Pierre. *Hymn of the Universe.* Translated by Gerald Vann. New York: Harper & Row, 1965.

———. *Christianity and Evolution.* Translated by Réne Hague. New York: Harcourt Brace Jovanovich, 1971.

Torrance, Thomas F. *Transformation and Convergence in the Frame of Knowledge: Explorations in the Interrelations of the Scientific and Theological Enterprise.* Grand Rapids, Mich.: Eerdmans, 1984.

———. *Reality and Scientific Theology.* Edinburgh: Scottish Academic, 1985.

Weinberg, Steven. *The First Three Minutes.* Rev. ed. New York: Basic Books, 1988.

Worthing, Mark William. *God, Creation, and Contemporary Physics.* Minneapolis: Fortress, 1996.

Wright, N. T. *The Resurrection of the Son of God.* Minneapolis: Fortress, 2003.

Index

abortion, 153–54
Abraham, 20–21, 29
adoption, 150
agriculture, 134, 135
Anfechtung, 37, 42
anthropic principles (AP's), 178–82
Aquinas, Thomas, 11, 37, 74
Aristotelian philosophy, 38, 61, 76–77, 83
atheism, 52, 116
atomic theory, 52–53
Augustine, Saint, 74

Babylonians, 31, 94, 97, 167, 200
Barbour, I., 77–78
Barr, J., 19
Barth, K., 13, 129, 141, 183
Barthian view of knowledge of God, 10,
    13, 16, 17, 21
Bernard, C., 61
Bible
    conception assistance, 149
    creation, 17–19, 68–69, 94–98, 111–14
    the cross, 28–34
    genetic engineering, 150
    human care for other species, 175
    human evolution, 185
    living things, 111–12
    mathematical order, 69–72
    medicine/healing, 146–48
    nature, place of humans in, 166–67
    randomness of nature, 119–20
    technology, 134–35, 138
    warfare, 142–43
    wisdom, 69–72
    as witness to revelation, 17–21

big bang theory, 97, 99–100
biotechnology, 135
    bioethics, 148, 151–52
    brain death, 157–58
    cloning, 148, 152, 160n. 6
    conception assistance, 148–49
    genetic engineering, 150–51
    human embryos, 152
    organ/tissue transplants, 154–56
    preserving life, 156–59
Bonhoeffer, D., 4–5, 32–33, 81, 96,
    122, 139
breath/air, 111–12
    in defining death, 157
Brunner, E., 13, 19, 104

cell metabolism, 53, 54, 55
Chalcedonian doctrine, 80–81
chaos, God's battle with, 94
chaos theory, 49
chemical evolution, 116–18, 119
chiasmic cosmology. *See* theology of
    the cross
Christ
    early Christian view of, 38–39
    as form of God, 30, 129
    as God crucified, 4, 38–43
    healing, model for, 147–48
    historic crucifixion of, 26–28
    humanity of, 39–40, 128–29
    as model for humanity, 139–41, 168,
        170, 175
    and nature, 168, 170, 175
    as purpose of creation, 125,
        183–84